Who are
Really
Maybe someone
you have
Never met

Dav

DON'T READ THIS...
YOUR EGO WON'T LIKE IT!

Written by Dōv Baron

Printed in Canada

ISBN: 978-0-9810313-1-6

For information, please contact:

Baron Mastery Institute
141-6200 McKay Ave #327
Burnaby, British Columbia
V5H 4M9
Canada

www.BaronMastery.com
604 436 2063

List of Contents

Preface

Some of the oldest philosophical questions are questions that have both frustrated and inspired every great thinker of our time and of time immemorial. Questions such as: Where do we come from before birth, and where do we go to after death, have brought about the kind of debates that have created verbal sparks not just between evolutionists and creationists but also between the different factions within those groups. Moreover, while we could all sit and debate these questions until the cows come home the fact is, the only way to find out is to no longer be here. I do not know about you but for me that seems like a rather drastic way to get an answer.

I have spent a large part of my life asking those same questions over and over and although I may have with time and much self debate, come to an answer or two that works for me, in all honesty there seems to be a more pressing set of questions. Questions that come up are directly related to how we live and how we feel about ourselves as we operate in the world while going about our daily lives. These seem to me to be the questions we should look at first if we want to not only live a better life, but a more meaningful one.

To be honest it seems to me these are the kind of questions that even the least philosophical people find themselves asking at one time or another in their lives. Who hasn't at some point ended up asking a version of: How did my life get this way? Am I somehow creating this, and if I am, how am I doing it?

There was a time when the idea that our thoughts, our emotions and our feelings might influence our reality seemed completely outrageous. But then again it was not that long ago that the idea of receiving information across the world instantaneously was equally outrageous.

Yet here we are getting instantaneous information delivered in any number of ways from a person or persons living in Canada while you are in places like Brazil, Turkey, the U.K., Africa, Israel, China, India, France, Russia, Australia, or anywhere else in the world.

As outrageous as it once seemed to get the information that comes from e-mails, cell phones and any number of other devices, we now understand it's entirely possible to receive information instantly and, as you will discover, we can and do achieve the same with our thoughts, emotions and feelings. More and more scientific evidence is showing how thoughts, emotions and feelings have a direct affect on our reality. For those who learn the techniques and who practice them, developing mastery over their ego-mind becomes as real as receiving an e-mail. I believe mastering your ego-mind and therefore your thoughts, emotions and feelings is one of the great lessons of living in the physical reality.

We live in what science is now calling the quantum hologram; a universe that contains everything in a state of both fulfilled and unfulfilled potential, waiting to burst into a three dimensional reality. According to the greatest minds of our day, in the quantum hologram, everything exists in abundance. Nothing is missing. It is just waiting to manifest into what you and I call 'reality'.

Whether you are new to the idea of manifestation, are an old hand at it, or even if you've been really practicing your manifestation techniques, you are likely very aware that not every thought you have is actually going to manifest. That's probably a good thing! Imagine living in a world where every thought you have instantly manifests into reality. Sure, you could solve your financial problems in about five seconds by manifesting a big wad of cash, and then you could say byebye to those dinner time calls from the credit card company.

But think about it another way… If your thoughts became manifest instantaneously after the last time you got mad at your mom, your dad, your kids, your husband, or your wife, they might be dead or at least performing carnal acts upon themselves in that same five seconds of instant manifestation. So, maybe instant manifestation wouldn't be such a good thing after all. Sure, it's a bit inconvenient for clearing up your debt but it's also a great way of stopping you from doing things that you might regret.

It seems that through ancient stories and myths we have been taught lessons about how important it is to pay attention to what it is that we say we want, because when we think about it, what we want may not be exactly what we are truly looking for when it shows up. As a child do you remember being told the story of King Midas? Here's a very short version of that story that really shows how brilliant the ancients were at teaching us in story form.

> Dionysus was a Greek god who came to King Midas and decided to reward him for the hospitality he had shown to Dionysus's surrogate father Silenus. Dionysus granted Midas one wish. Midas's wish was simple; he wished that everything he touched would be turned to gold. Dionysus warned him about the dangers of such a wish, but Midas was too distracted with the prospect of being surrounded by gold to listen.

> Dionysus gave him the gift. Initially, King Midas was thrilled with his new gift and turned everything he could to gold, (he had instant manifestation of wealth). However, his attitude changed when he was unable to eat or drink since his food and wine were

also changed to unappetizing gold. He even accidentally killed his own daughter when he touched her, and
only then did he truly realize the depth of his mistake.

When it comes to solving an acute problem, instant manifestation
may seem like a good idea; however, instant solutions often have other
long terms problems of their own. What's important to remember, as
you will see throughout this book, is that you are never actually separate from all the abundance of the universe.
A few years ago I read that approximately thirty trillion dollars cir-
culates this planet everyday, (and that's just the legal stuff), some say
there's three times that amount in the black market. It's obvious there's
plenty for everyone. It's natural for us all to live our lives in the full
spectrum of abundance and that's much more than cash.

So what gets in our way?

The short answer is the ego or conditioned mind. The ego/condi-
tioned mind runs the 'software' that is our thoughts, beliefs, emotions
and feelings, all of which determine our re-actions and in turn, our
behaviors. These ideas and beliefs held in the mind are for the most
part old and have gone on doing what they do under the instruction of
the ego-mind without question. This becomes the obstacle in the flow
of life and in the flow of abundance that is available to us.

In spite of what you may currently believe, take a moment and think
about what might happen if you began asking yourself every day: Why
am I so abundant? Now, depending on whom you are and how you see
life unfolding, your answer could be, nothing would happen. If you
think that's true, I'd like to offer this thought experiment up for you
to try. Spend one whole day constantly telling yourself how tired you
are and see if that doesn't affect not only your energy levels but also

your attitude towards everything you encounter that day. In short, you would very quickly discover even running that simple thought would affect your reality, and not for the better. So is the affect of thought limited to our bodies? (And remember that at one time we wouldn't have seen that as possible either). Or are we somehow affecting other aspects of our reality?

As I will outline throughout this book, my thesis is that the mind, its conditioning and the re-actions that conditioning generates is having a direct affect on every aspect of our reality. Begin to master your ego-mind and your reality changes. In my work since the mid eighties I have seen the powerful and positive effects, hundreds if not thousands of times with students who begin to master their ego-mind.

Without trying to over simplify things, I would like to remind you that the first step to living in abundance is recognizing that it's all around you.

Remember, you are unique in the universe. There is no other exactly like you, therefore you are more valuable and more precious than any jewel. Begin the journey that is Mastering Your ego-mind and you will recognize and embrace not only the abundance of the universe but also your own true value.

Introduction

For many of you, these pages are our first meeting… "Hello, I'm Dōv Baron, nice to meet you. This is the beginning of what I trust will be an expanding relationship. Even though before you picked up this book you may never have even heard of me, don't let that fool you into the notion that I'm some Johnny-come-lately, jump on the latest band-wagon kind of guy. I've been teaching workshops and seminars around the world since the mid eighties to a very wide range of folks, many of whom I'm sure are just like you. Having said that I don't claim to have all the answers, (no one does) what I do have is a proven track record for making very complex psychological, metaphysical and even quantum principles easy to both understand and apply. According to those who work with me I have a very specific style of delivery, it's one that cuts through the crap to give you the meat. (Yes, I've even been known to use the occasional expletive).

I decided, at a very early age, to set out on an adventure that would lead me around the world to sit, speak and study with those who would share their great minds, their enormous hearts and their vast spirits. This journey was not of my design at the outset, but I became formed by it, nevertheless. The journey inadvertently became about creating a life for me, the ones I love, and those whose lives I would touch. It was to be a life which—at the time of its conception—I could barely even imagine.

Having said that, I want to thank you for investing in this book, it is my greatest wish that it serves you in the way you want and need. I also want to recognize you for your commitment to your growth. You see, I understand you have many options for where to put your focus when it comes to your development, and I appreciate your trust in me in purchasing this book. Too many people give up on themselves; you can be proud of yourself for being an active part of your growth and development. I would like to say I believe you have chosen wisely.

Throughout this book I'm going to share with you to the best of my ability in the fullest detail, the knowledge, skills and tools that I have shared with people just like you. People who have used these skills and tools to bring them, as they will bring you, the fastest and most sustainable results.

As you go through this book, easily applying these proven methods and powerful knowledge, you will realize that everything you learn can be applied to making you more money, giving you more freedom of choice in your life, gains you respect of colleagues friends and family. In short, wherever you are in life right now, the knowledge contained within these pages lifts you to a whole new level. We hear from our students that; it's a level they had only previously thought possible in their wildest dreams.

However, before we go any further, let me share a simple truth with you… I don't have all the answers or claim to have all the answers.

Yes, I've traveled the world to study with masters and I've shared my knowledge with thousands of people in many different parts of the world. And it is also true that I've been part of the massive transformation of so many personal and professional lives.

However, the one thing I've come to learn about the truly successful (you and I both know it too), we just have to keep on learning more. Each of the highly successful individuals I've worked with would tell you that they are life-long learners.

The truly successful train themselves to be curious, to stay up to date, and remain committed to finding out what they don't know and making sure that they do know. They understand that the truly successful never graduate.

And you know what's great...?
When you now begin taking this material in you will immediately avoid those costly, time consuming and energy draining mistakes that so many people are unwittingly making.

One more thing: Much of this book is dedicated to assisting you in the process of mastering your ego-mind. As I will clearly explain the ego-mind is going to be looking for reasons to not take in anything that challenges what 'it' has held as 'true' (note small 't'). One of the ways it does this is by distracting and confusing you, pulling you off into some kind of mind wondering. Sometimes that means focusing on 'stuff' rather than taking in what's right in front of you. If at any time you find yourself becoming spontaneously confused, tired or thinking about 'stuff' that just doesn't matter, be warned; that's your ego-mind trying to pull you away from a part of the material that could have profound meaning for you. In order to assist you with this, you will find that most of what I write is in a very conversational style. You will be able to hear my voice in your head rather than text on a page. Something else that will help is throughout the book you will likely notice the occasional spelling mistake or what you could consider a grammatical error; they might be there on purpose. The ego-mind loves doing the perfectionist thing in order to delay or just avoid. Your job is to notice that your ego-mind is noticing these things and then quickly move on.

Throughout this book there are many case studies of individuals, some of whom may seem to be 'you' there's a good chance that the person being referred to is not you. However, please be aware that for obvious reasons the names and sometimes the gender of the person being referred to has been changed. As you continue reading you will discover with all certainty that your life is with or without you knowing, on purpose. But first, in order to get things on the right track and for the purpose of opening the mind, let me start by asking you a few friendly questions:

How Did You Get Here?
How did you get to this place in your life, at this time in your life?

Chances are you have had a sneaking suspicion that something or someone has been messing with your life... And it might not be you.

However, despite that, there are certain quiet moments, moments when you get a glimpse of the true you, and how amazing you really are...

Stop for a moment and let yourself really remember that.

You have sensed that you have a purpose to fulfill, that your life is supposed to have positive impact, that your life is entitled to be filled with joy, love, vibrant health, and abundance. Haven't you?

In fact, despite the self doubt that can sometimes be overwhelming, as you read this you can begin to imagine yourself living the kind of life you want.

Let yourself get a sense of what it looks like to live a life filled with purpose and meaning, a life filled with joy, love, vibrant health, and the full spectrum of abundance.

As you see your view expanding, what does it sound like?
Get a sense of how it smells? How does it feel to be there now?

Whether you know it or not, your life is run by your ego-mind.

However, with the right skills, tools, and knowledge, you can run your mind. This is the beginning of you mastering your ego-mind and determining your own destiny!

Secret or no secret... I should caution you, your ego-mind probably won't like where this is going...

Welcome To:
DON'T READ THIS...
Your Ego Won't Like It!

In 2006 'The Secret™' exploded on to the market. It told the world about a 'secret' that supposedly every successful person throughout history had known... The Law of Attraction.

'The Secret™' brought with it excitement about manifestation. People were staring in shop windows and taking expensive cars for drives all with the intent of engaging the Law of Attraction. Sadly, most of those people ended up, to say the least... disappointed.

In truth the teachings about *the Law of Attraction* have been around for a very long time. Certainly the term 'Law of Attraction' has been around for over a hundred years and became popular through the 'New Thought Movement'. The New Thought movement was a spiritual movement which developed in the United States during the late 19th century and emphasizes metaphysical beliefs rather than strictly religious ones. The leading edge teachers of the day who started this movement were people like Charles and Myrtle Fillmore, Dr. Emily Cady and Dr. Ernest Holmes, Florence Shinn and later Neville. These were teachers who shared a certain set of metaphysical beliefs concerning the effects of positive thinking, creative visualization, healing, personal power, and, of course, the Law of Attraction. In all likelihood these principles may go back way further than the late 19th century for millennia to ancient Egypt, ancient India, Babylon and Samaria. 'The Secret™' didn't share any particularly hidden secret, what it did do a great job of was awakening the everyday guy and gal to the idea that they could in fact begin to manifest the reality they wanted.

Chances are that if you are reading this book, you have at least been introduced to the Law of Attraction, and 'The Secret™'. It has made this idea of manifestation nearly common knowledge. However, despite being an international hit, few people are really changing their lives in a measurable way as a result of it. Even after viewing the movie dozens of times, highlighting the book until every word glows yellow, most people are still having a great deal of difficulty mastering this 'secret'.

The Less than Secret Science Beyond the Law of Attraction

O kay get ready! You will find that as you easily glide through this book from one page to the next, I'm about to share with you some real world proven ideas, methods and techniques that will really work for you. Not only will the wisdom within these pages begin the inner process of manifesting whatever it is that you want, but also you will begin to gain control over your sabotaging ego-mind as well... These are ideas, methods and techniques that are going to change your life for the better the moment you get them.

Some of the information contained within these pages may ruffle your feathers, because much of what you are about to learn goes against traditional thinking and may even seem a little counter intuitive. However, as you use these methods you will be able to immediately maximize the results you have from all the hard earned cash you've ever spent and as a result turn all those sunken costs into the best investment you've ever made in yourself.

You will discover how the Equation for Manifestation™ puts you on a straight as an arrow path to your every desire. It's a well-known fact that great achievers set goals. It's a little known fact that they use a system that keeps them on track regardless of the obstacles that jump in their way. Unfortunately, that system is often unconscious even for those who have so much success with it. And so sadly this system has remained at best illusive. Those who fail to use this system dramatically reduce their chances of reaching their potential. You don't want to miss out on this!

Have you ever noticed that highly successful people seem to be in control in every encounter? Life throws them curve balls and they know which way to swing. Even if they get knocked down they seem to get up faster than everyone else. Here's the explanation… They know the insider rules. Yes, you can now discover the number one rule they use and enjoy that sensation of personal power. You are not only going to find out about a technique that is just going to blow your mind, you are going to have all the solid science you need to keep it and put it into action. Along the way you will be undermining the unconscious sabotaging processes that are your ego-mind. This is how you will inspire yourself into action. As we go through this book together, I'll give you some questions to ponder; questions that will awaken the greatness that has slept within you. Your answers to these simple yet profoundly focused questions will instantly reveal what you need to do to get to the top and beat off the competition.

Have you ever wondered why so much training never has a long term effect? Well, after 25 years of research, I've uncovered the reason why.

There is, in fact, a 'Secret Science Beyond The Law of Attraction'; however, it's not a secret because some covert force is secretly plotting to keep it hidden from you, unless that force has been your own ego-mind. It's a secret purely because you probably don't know about it yet. Let's face it; we tend to make things mystical and mysterious until we understand them. Remember the uncle who could magically and mysteriously make a coin appear from behind your ear? Once we understand something we can begin to master the application of it and it can become an everyday part of our lives.

This 'Science Beyond The Law of Attraction' is connected to quantum theory; however, I'm aware that you have already likely been told the Law of Attraction is all about quantum physics too, right? Well, what most people do not realize is when it comes to manifestation, applying these quantum theories is a delicate art, for a couple of reasons. For starters, in the quantum realm it's not as simple as 2+2=4. In fact, in the quantum realm, 2+2 may equal 4 but depending on the circumstances in which we are measuring the 2+2, it also equals 47, 96, 239, or any other possibility as the result is dependent on much more than the numbers themselves. Secondly, this quantum phenomenon is only slightly affected by your thoughts. There are many pieces to this puzzle and my commitment is to lay them all out for you so that you can see exactly what piece you need to pick up in order to construct your reality in the way you want it.

The art and science of manifestation is something that must be honed and practiced. Because, as I just pointed out, when it comes to manifestation; quantum theory alone won't get you what you want any more than positive thinking will. Manifesting what you want, be it: Health, wealth, loving relationships, confidence, weight loss or anything else can never consistently work until you become the master of your own ego-mind. Simply knowing about the Law of Attraction does not fully explain what needs to occur, scientifically, for manifestation to take place. What needs to be understood – or at least what you need to be aware of – is that there is an even deeper scientific law at play. Mastering your ego-mind is the real secret to success in any area of life including manifestation.

A word of caution here: The fundamental law for manifestation is not the Law of Attraction. In fact, the Law of Attraction is really only an observation of what is happening. It is like commenting that 'toasters turn bread golden brown'. Saying so does not mean you have any idea what made the toast golden brown. Nor does it provide any indication that the toaster must be plugged into an outlet. You are simply observing the result; placing bread in a toaster may turn it golden brown. Imagine giving a small infant a piece of bread, and telling him to make toast by putting it in the toaster. He won't even know to check whether the toaster is plugged in because he thinks putting bread in the toaster is all there is to it!

For the bread to become toasted, what it really needs is a toaster that is plugged into electricity – the real source of its color transformation. Indeed, just like a toaster, you need to be plugged into a source – something that will give life to your manifestations. While like certainly does attract like, as stated by the Law of Attraction, something as scientific as electricity is causing it. Bread cannot arbitrarily turn golden-brown on its own. Without the power of electricity it will remain bread, not toast. Nor can you transform your life simply by thinking about it because that would be like standing at the unplugged toaster and having positive thoughts about the bread becoming toast... It could be a long wait!

At this point I would like to introduce you to something that may be fairly new to you, it's called *the Law of Resonance*. To manifest what you want in life, you must have the right resonance. You need to apply *the Law of Resonance* and that is best achieved by learning how to master your own ego-mind. I'll explain resonance in the fullest detail as we move on. Throughout this book my mission is to deliver to you in the fullest detail everything you need to begin mastering your ego-mind. Having said that, what you need to know is your ego-mind won't like it! Many of the things I'll share with you throughout these pages will contradict some of the basic conditions of your ego-mind. But know this with all certainty, I have no loyalty to the ego-mind, my loyalty is to giving you everything you need in order for you to have mastery over your ego-mind. To do what you want to do, get to where you want to go, and be where you want to be. Mastering your ego-mind is ultimately about taking back your power so that you come off automatic and begin to once again take charge of the choices you are making. And ultimately isn't there only one real choice – the choice to be fully, passionately and authentically alive.

This book is the result of many years of research and the conscious observation of thousands of people from many different walks of life, cultures, religious backgrounds and belief systems. What I discovered was, that despite all the obvious differences there was one commonality: The sense that something was missing. I had spent many years nursing that same pain and when I'd distilled a formula for finding what was missing I made a commitment to share it with my students.

That formula has its foundation in mastering your own ego-mind. Because once you even begin to master your ego-mind you can begin consciously using the Law of Resonance to bring you more of whatever it is that you truly desire.

If you are more than a bit uncertain about this new word I have just introduced, 'resonance', then let me reassure you. You will want to know about it. It is big. Huge, actually. the *Law of Resonance* is the real science behind manifesting! Throughout this book, I'll be sure to explain its science well enough that you can set it in motion using the language of manifestation! It is actually quite a simple law. And, don't worry, all you really need to remember is the art of effectively applying it.

Part I

Chapter 1

Don't Read This...
Your Ego Won't Like It

Goooooooooood MORNING!

Maybe you are reading this book first thing in the morning, maybe it's
your lunch break, and maybe you are on holidays with the book in one
hand and a Margarita in the other. Good for you! Or maybe you are
in bed reading the book before you lay down for the night. If you are
reading this at any other time than first thing in the morning there's
a good chance you are wondering why the heck I began this book by
saying, "Good morning!"

As I'm sure you've noticed, good morning is what we tend to say to
people when they first wake up. And that's exactly what I'm committed to do; to wake you up to how powerful you really are! In fact, I
guarantee you that if you are reading this with an open mind you will
find that there are going to be many times where a statement or a
concept will **stick right out** like a sore thumb, slapping you across the
back of the head, waking you like a splash of cold water. Take my word
for it, that is what you want, because if I can show you there is another
way—an easier way—then you will be one step closer to regaining
mastery of your ego-mind.

Let's go back a bit to the end of 2004, when I wrote the book 'What the Bleep Does it Mean'. The book explained in simple language what the movie 'What the Bleep Do We Know'?! was all about. (In fact you can still get it on-line as my gift to you by going to www.WhatTheBleepDoesItMean.com) Thousands of people from all over the world read this book, and many of them wrote to me with questions about different areas of the book. One of the most common questions was, "If we are actually creating our reality, including what we don't want, how are we doing it, and what can we do to consciously create the life we really want?"

It would have been easy for me to email those people back saying, "Attend one of my live programs and begin to understand everything"; however, I realized that people need to do what they can from wherever they are. So I decided to write a book that will walk you through how you have already been **unconsciously creating your reality** and how you can **begin to consciously create** the reality of your dreams.

You will want to know that the contents of this book are very rich. It's going to take you into the depths of **your** ego-mind and **the** mind (that will make more sense as you read on) in a way that will allow you to recognize that you may not have actually mastered your ego-mind ... yet. I have also packed this book full of powerful techniques and real life examples which clearly show how you can now go ahead and master your ego-mind. It is extremely important to me that you get the maximum benefit from this book, so that you can easily and effortlessly begin creating the life of your dreams NOW!

As you study each page of this book, you will be amazed at what you will learn about the ego-mind, and how it - and you – are in fact very different entities.

For those of you who don't yet know me personally, I'd like you to know my commitment to you, as always, is to provide you with the highest quality of powerful, transformational information and tools.

As I look at what is actually in front of me, I realize that I have given myself an enormous task. My wife Renuka watched me as I wrote my outline notes for this book and planned what I was going to share with you, and she said to me, "How are you going to deliver all that in one book?" My answer was: "I'm going to split the book into three separate parts, and make each section easy to comprehend. I'm going to commit my time, energy, and effort and I'm going to get out of my own way."

I would like to suggest that you value yourself enough to do the same (not the split yourself into three parts bit). Commit yourself, and set aside the time and energy necessary for you to really take in and begin feeling the full value of what you are about to learn.

Right *here* within these pages are many of the answers you've been looking for. I have an abundance of exciting transformational knowledge to share with you, and you will want to get it all. So as you read, have your pen ready, take many notes, participate actively in getting all this information, and be willing to challenge your ego-mind in order to master it.

One Last Thing before We Begin

I would like to ask you a very important question. Are you a reluctant optimist? Why would I ask that? Honestly, it's because most of you reading this book probably are reluctanct optimists.

What does that mean?

In a nutshell, it means that you want something better for your life,

9

for your loved ones, and maybe for the people in this world you don't yet know, but still want to help anyway. Another thing, reluctant optimists usually have an inkling that the 'Law of Attraction' is just marketing hype for a small handfull of clever business people.

So what should you do? Should you ignore the intimate accounts given by people featured by credible sources in books and movies like *The Secret*™? Should you run from possibility because it's cosmic underpinnings will not reveal themselves to you?

Absolutely not!

However, there is a need to look deeper because as much as some teachers would want you to believe that the Law of Attraction is a law just like any other law, for instance the Law of Gravity, by opening your perceptions you'll find that this is not entirely true.

Chapter 2

Ladies and Gentlemen, Introducing the Law of Resonance

If you look closely you will see, there is a law in operation behind the Law of Attraction, there is a secret beyond the secret. There is a quantum physics law that is beyond the hype; this is *the Law of Resonance*. And a little later in this book, I'll explain to you not only the science of this law, I'll clarify what sets *the Law of Resonance* in motion so that you can begin to use it to attract what it is that you want.

I believe that in order to help people find abundance, it's important to first reveal the facts—the science behind the magic, if you will. The fact is that most of us are already far too overwhelmed by information and ideas in our lives to absorb much more of that which makes very little sense or might require 'a leap of faith'. So what do we do? If that was true, then we would be ignoring what's going on all around us and move on to what we already understand: *Scarcity*. We would fight tooth and nail to support that concept of scarcity, if deep down, we choose to believe it. As crazy as it may seem to be fighting for scarcity, it is what most people are doing every single day. I'll explain why a little later in the book.

I am here to explain to you why scarcity tends to envelop most of us and how it is that understanding *the Law of Resonance* can break the doors down and change your life, if you let it.

Before we go any further I want to set something straight. We are at a crossroads, and as such must choose a direction. If you are the type of person who isn't interested in learning *why... why* am I feeling the way I do about money or how my finances are never quite enough (or JUST barely enough to 'get by'), *why* am I struggling throughout my relationships or with my spirituality or health, and most importantly, *why* do things in my life always turn out this way—*why why why*? Like I just said, if you are **not** interested in answering those questions then I recommend closing this book and putting it up on a shelf in the back corner of your closet because this book answers those very questions.

Seriously, stop for just one full minute and just ask yourself if you have what you really want in your life.

If, on the other hand, you do want the answer to those questions... If you are the type of person who's tired of hearing all the same old negative speeches such as the ones that start by someone telling you "Life just isn't that way." Perhaps your brain has screamed (or whined) "I'm just not that lucky" (from somewhere in your head), or even if you are simply one of those people finally tired of looking off into your future and seeing more bleak mediocrity. On the other hand, maybe you are someone who's getting this hopeful feeling swelling up deep inside, just waiting to bust out and vivaciously scream, **"I WANT AND WILL GET MORE FROM LIFE!"** If this describes you, *then take a deep breath and get ready to be blown away*, because when you are done reading this book you will take a look at your future through a new pair of glasses. You will easily be seeing the new you getting what you've always dreamed, and if you set aside the time to use the techniques I have spread out before you here, you may very well be at a loss for words because these techniques really work; the techniques within these pages allow you to search within yourself to find out the *whys*.

That's why I suggest you read this book with an open mind. As you dig into these pages be prepared to see things from another frame of mind. Put what you know to the side for safe keeping and you may just find yourself looking through a window of new opportunity at a world full of abundance.

Now, as we find our bearings, let's take a look at the overview.

Overview of this Series
This book is split into three parts. We're going to look at the second part first, the third part second, and then come back to what we're actually going to be covering in the first part. Confusing? Good! It's a great place to start when you are dealing with the ego-mind and you are going to have a lot of fun doing it.

I understand that there are some people out there who want to get 'right to the good stuff—i.e. skipping right to the end to learn how right away—but I'd like to warn you against doing that. Any one of these three parts can be taken out of context and still be of substantial value; however, reading this book in the order it's presented will be of greater benefit to you because, naturally, Part II builds upon everything we will cover in Part I; and Part III will be built on the foundations Part I and II create in you as you read them.

So without Further Ado, the Overview
Part II is called **Coping For Something Better.** One of the most important concepts in Part II you will be understanding is how your ego-mind is actually programmed for addiction, and don't worry, you

will also learn how to break those addictions because the techniques in this book challenge your unconscious beliefs which set in motion a chain of events that result in you re-claiming mastery of your ego-mind.

In Part II we will also discuss how your thinking and your feelings are having a direct effect on your body, even as you are reading this book.

I'll talk about the **missing ingredient of manifestation**, which I believe is rarely taught anywhere with any real level of depth.

Finally, in Part II you will easily understand the biochemistry of why it can be so difficult to truly change without 'snapping back' to your old ways of thoughts and actions.

Part III covers **the physics of manifestation**, where I actually teach you the **Equation for Manifestation**™.

If you just thought, "*Oh crap, I hated physics when I was in school,*" that's all right—I'll explain it in such a way that everyone will understand it easily, including you.

Believe me, as you read this book you will later notice how time seemed to fly by because it's designed so every paragraph and every new section elevates you to another level of understanding that allows you to absorb the most complex information easily and effortlessly, becoming part of your thinking.

For those of you who were a little hesitant or intimidated when you found out that Part III covers a bit of quantum physics, I'd like you to set aside those ideas because I will personally take you by the hand and walk you through the physics that teaches you exactly how manifestation works, the easy way.

What's more, in Part III we will be building a bridge that connects spirituality and science. You will learn how to use that bridge to move between metaphysical concepts, spiritual ideas and the hard science, so that the physics of manifestation can be applied in your life, daily.

So, let's get on top of what you are going to discover in Part I, **Mastering Your Ego-mind**.

One remarkable idea you will come across is that within you, and within us all, there's a force that works like a genie who's been granting any and all wishs you've been desiring—even the ones you wouldn't make if you had known the genie was there all along. Just so we're absoloutly clear, I'm not saying that if you were to rub yourself in just the right way a genie would arrive in a puff of smoke out of your... well, nevermind. That's just a metaphor; however, manifestation of your desires really works in exactly the same way.

Part I also contains a map you can follow in order to find and access your 'genie' right here, right now. You will find that applying the knowledge contained in this book, you will plainly see why you no longer have to feel like a victim of the circumstances that surround you, even if that has been your belief up until now.

You will learn how you have a natural ability to create anything you want ... let me repeat that so it sinks in: **Anything you want!** Not only that, you will learn how to use that natural manifesting ability, starting NOW!

There's also the gravely important matter of the **Six Foundations to Success**; these are the six foundations of what I call the full spectrum of success. We will go through each one of those foundations to help you understand how mastering your ego-mind—or lack there-of—directly affects your future successes.

You will discover how your beliefs may not actually be your own, and how many of the ideas that we hold so dear might not in fact be ours at all.

You will precisely see how your beliefs create something called a **Quantum Resonance Field**™. I'll show you how that field is affecting your life every moment of every day.

You will learn how to change that field, so that you can begin attracting exactly what you want in your life starting today (that is, if you decide to read that far today).

Finally, I'll hand you some simple-to-apply yet stunningly powerful exercises that, when taken, will help you turn on this inner genie to bring you what you want even when you are not asking.

This is just a glimpse of what we're going to cover. There is going to be plenty more! So let's dive in...

I truly hope you, like me, are as excited about reading and applying the knowledge, skills, and tools within this book as I am sharing them with you!

"In order to get the life you want, take lots of notes, keep your eyes and perceptions wide open, let yourself feel this knowledge, so that it can move through you as you move through it!"

~ Dóv Baron

Chapter 3

The Six Foundations of Full Spectrum Abundance

We have all met people who in their own way appeared successful to us. On the outside, these people seem to have it all: Big houses, fancy cars, expensive clothes, and stunning jewelry. Sometimes they appear to have wonderful relationships with a partner they've been with for twenty, thirty, or even forty years.

While others appear *so* intelligent with their office walls decorated with *soooo* many degrees, awards, and certifications that just being around them can actually intimidate us.

Yet *rarely*, and I do ever mean rarely, do we come across someone who, literally, *has it all* ... someone who is experiencing the *full spectrum of success* I'm talking about.

What I'm about to share with you is something very powerful. It's something you have probably never really thought about directly, something you haven't quite put into words, yet might sense from time to time.

What I'm about talking here is what I call **The Six Foundations of Full Spectrum Success.**

As you look through these **Six Foundations of Success**, I'd like you to pay close attention to how your 'gut' *feels* while you read each one and its example. In doing so you will realize why they are so important, you will understand why they are so important you will also start recognizing how mastering these six foundations allows you to turn your inner genie *on* so you can *have it all*. You will naturally begin filling in the blanks one by one, seeing how these six foundations relate to the ego-mind, and why it is so important for you to now *master your ego-mind*.

Here's the bottom line: **Either you master your ego-mind or it masters you!**

Mastering your ego-mind enables you to make empowered choices based on present-time information because you are operating within this moment, or as you might have heard before, 'in the now'.

Mastering your ego-mind frees you of your past, and puts you in the driver's seat on the expressway to your best future. Not only that, your intuition will be riding shotgun holding a map giving you clear direction through your feelings, avoiding any of life's emotional, financial, health, or relational traffic jams.

When you are the **master of your ego-mind**, you will know what you want in each of the five areas of your life that I am going to outline. You will also find it easy to go for what you want in each of those five areas in order to create the sixth pivotal foundation.

In contrast, **when someone is not in control of their ego-mind** they tend to live in the past, often haunted by past mistakes or regret. That person might seem to feel too much—overwhelmed by emotions—or the polar opposite; they may be feeling a certain numbness inside. It can be hard to get excited, or for that matter, become upset about *anything* ... . It can feel like your spirit's broken.

When you don't 'master your ego-mind' you won't know, beyond some vague idea, what you want in most areas of your life. Even if you did, there would either be this dreadful voice in the back of your head telling you 'get it' or a or a rotten feeling of nervousness and discomfort that like a magnet turned upside down would repel you from even the possibility of achieving and receiving what you want.

Once again, it's important you allow yourself to *feel* what happens as I describe each of these six foundations of success. Doing so is one of the master tools I'll describe for mastering your ego-mind.

Now, as you read through these insights, *it's okay to give yourself permission to be honest*, to see whether or not these statements might apply to you. (Remember, no one else will know. All of this will be between you and this book, and as you sift through these next few pages, notice which areas of your life you want to improve. After all, you might as well, you have taken the first step to change it by buying this book).

Foundation 1: Your Physical Foundation
Let's get physical ... physical ... Let's get... .

You may have guessed that your first foundation is your **physical foundation**. For over a hundred years, science had dismissed any connection between mind and body—*even though this connection has been pointed to many times in our past by history's most influential teachers.* Sages such as Socrates, Plato, Aristotle, Descartes, Buddha, Jesus... and even Yoda, have all been pointing out this connection for ages, and that list of teachers can go on and on.

There is an overwhelming cascade of current evidence showing us that the mind and body are, in fact, in direct cause and effect with each other. In the easiest terms: What's going on in your mind is going to have a direct affect on your body.

So, let me ask you this: Why focus on gaining mastery of this thing called your ego-mind? Well, when you master your ego-mind physically you are in outstanding health and you feel connected to your body and its vital health. Your body functions properly, free of most *dis*ease and it carries you through your life *with* ease.

Mastering your ego-mind clearly affects your body in powerfully positive ways because many of the limits your body clutches are set in your ego-mind. Releasing those limited beliefs regarding the bodies ability and health are just two of the major keys to mastering your body.

If you haven't mastered your ego-mind physically, every day you seem to have found another 'real' reason to put off proper eating, or that exercise program you keep saying you're going to start (or stick to!). Here's an example: How about your hair colour? Have you ever felt that if you changed your hair colour from light to dark that people would find you more attractive or smarter? What about its opposite: This notion that if you change your hair color from dark to light guys might take you less seriously intellectually, or find you 'more attractive' or 'more fun'. How about your height? Weight? Are you getting aggravated with me picking on all these stereotypes? Are any of these shaking your tree, making you feel some level of agitation or self-consciousness? If so, that's an indication that you are not yet the master of your ego-mind physically.

In fact, those who haven't mastered their ego-mind, find that physically getting in touch with their bodies seems challenging because as strange as this might sound, you find it hard to be in your body.

This can, and often does, result in a variety of sicknesses, eating disorders (like anorexia, bulimia, and obesity), sexual addictions and frigidity. The list of *dis*ease is endless and these disorders come because it's hard, as I just mentioned, to *be in* the body. Sometimes, when mastery is lacking, there might have been times you wished you had a different body altogether.

Master the Physical Foundation of Success and you can learn to live healthier, which in turn lets you live happier, because understanding where your beliefs about health come from begins breaking your *limited beliefs*. And every time you break a limited belief you launch yourself one step closer to reclaiming mastery of your body and mind.

Foundation 2: Your Financial Foundation
Show me the moneeeeeeeeeeey!

Next in line is your financial foundation. One of the first questions I hear in my seminars when I bring up the financial foundation is this, "What has my mind got to do with my bank account, outside of the fact that I can use my mind to get an education in hopes of getting a better job?"

Well, this is partially correct. Using your mind to make the decision to get an education *might* land you a better job. Then again, if your ego-mind is filled with negative beliefs that, for instance, block you from believing in yourself and what you are truly capable of and deserve, that will **absolutely** affect your financial situation in a negative way. Because if you don't honestly believe in yourself, **all the education in the world won't do you a lick of good**.

A word of caution: If you don't believe in yourself and realize you're capable of amazing things, then you will either not be able to use that education, or you will never feel like you've got enough of the 'right stuff'.

Here are a few short examples of some internal dialogue statements and/or beliefs that **people who do not fully believe in themselves and/or are not the master of their financial ego-mind have**. And once again, pay close attention to any feelings of familiarity while reading these examples because, in this case, those feelings of familiarity are big fat red flags waving around in front of you.

- Any general unending *sense of anxiety* about money
- Sometimes, when the subject of money is brought up, you become *tense or frustrated*
- "Money doesn't grow on trees"

- "Rich people are selfish"
- "Rich people aren't any happier than anyone else"
- Or, maybe there's this fear that *there's just not enough of it*.

And then, even when *there is enough*, you get that sneaking suspicion that 'it's never going to last'.

That last example really hits so many people deep in the pit of their stomach because it's such a common misplaced belief that so many people share.

One point I can't stress enough is that understanding where your beliefs about finances come from allows you to *let go* of any anxiety and frustration you may have had about money.

What truly causes excitement in me—and should always cause shivers of excitement to tingle up and down your spine—is that mastering your ego-mind gets rid of that feeling of 'not enough'.

Mastering the foundation of financial success grants you the freedom to live with a natural sense of abundance. This is because you will have a sense that you have the money to do the things in your life that seemed just out of reach a little while ago, because you believe in yourself and what you are capable of— even if no one else does.

Face it, money is so much more than official notes printed on paper with pictures and numbers. Money, or for that matter financial wealth, is a set of beliefs and these beliefs are a state of mind, or as you will come to understand, a *resonance* (the Law of Resonance will make more sense to you further on in this book when it's fully explained). This book will teach you how to deconstruct the limiting beliefs you had about financial abundance, as well as construct a set of new, empowering beliefs that are necessary so you can tap into abundance.

Foundation 3: Your Relational Foundation
Come a little closer baby and sit by the fire.

Together, let's examine the **relational foundation**. Listen, you know as well as I do that almost everyone who has ever been through a relationship will have quite naturally gone through a break-up and, honestly, it's in your best interest to consider what part you played in the relationship's end.

Now, I'm not saying that the other person didn't have a hand in mucking things up, although in truth, there were two of you in it and frankly, that's what we're here to uncover, 'your truth.'

If you were to now once again, put all your hesitations and doubts to the side, assuming you had one or two, you will discover that you might have had some ideas in your mind about relationships that were more than a little detrimental to it.

So, let's briefly go hunting and pecking inside heads and into minds of the people around us for some real life examples of some limiting beliefs and behaviors.

You may know a handful of people who feel that the people they are surrounded with are not really *there for them*. You know what I mean. You get the impression that they hear what you are saying, but aren't really listening—*that they don't get you*. Maybe sometimes you might feel that you can't be honest with the people around you because you're afraid that if you spoke your truth you may hurt their feelings, or end up getting hurt yourself.

I'm curious, *do you know how many people are afraid of being honest with themselves because they are scared stiff about getting hurt themselves?*

One sure-fire way to tell that you have not mastered your **relational foundation** is if you've ever felt a certain 'disconnection' from the people who surround you. Moreover, a funny feeling that many of your relationships are actually based on obligation—a sense that you must participate 'or else'—rather than a conscious choice, is a massive sign that your **relational foundation** is out of whack.

You see, one of the liberating benefits of mastering your **relational foundation** is that you happen to find yourself constantly surrounded by loving people who love you, people you respect deeply, and in turn, people who deeply respect you. By mastering your **relational foundation** you will establish healthy boundaries with everyone around you. You will also have the kind of honest relationships you've always wanted with both yourself and with others.

Here's the deal: Once you master your ego-mind, *you are not willing to put up with any crap!*

You don't put up with being pushed around, and you don't put up with people trampling all over your boundaries! Not only do you confidently speak *your truth*, you speak it while being open and compassionately able to hear someone else's truth **without the fear of hurting anyone and without the fear of being personally rejected!**

Now come on, how does that sound? Tell me, how bad do you want to be able to do that and be that way?

One final staggering comment on this foundation. By mastering your **relational foundation**, *you learn to eliminate all fear in relationships* so that you can experience love in its fullest form. Need I say more?

Foundation 4: Your Intellectual Foundation
Smarten up, laddy!

The fourth foundation you will want to own is your **intellectual foundation**. With a strong intellectual foundation you are stimulated *and* stimulating because you have a wealth of knowledge, life experiences, and skills at your disposal. As if that's not enough, you are naturally committed to learning more, and you are *excited* by new knowledge.

When you haven't mastered your ego-mind intellectually, you might have found yourself feeling bored much of the time. You will have carried a feeling of *not knowing*, as if everybody else on the planet has this vital piece of information that, somehow, you missed out on along the way.

A famous example of how mastery in this foundation, or lack of, can lift you up or bring you down is best explained by a study that was done with a group of 'pain-in-the-butt' grade sevens in the 1980's.

These were the lowest scoring kids on the bell curve. Many teachers looked over the students' records and tried their best to help them out, but the bottom line was those kids were believed to be write-offs.

In this experimental study, the kids were rounded up and taken to completely new schools where no one knew them or their reputation for being little hell-raisers.

They secretly took all the kids records and altered them to show that *these children were in the top five percent of intelligence*, yet because they had not been getting the level of education necessary for their intelligence they had become rowdy.

What do you think happened? ... I'll tell you. Within two terms, each and every one of these children were in the *top five percent* of their bell curve and *no longer rowdy*. Can you believe it? The top five percent!

How did that happen? Was it the change in the minds of the teachers, the students, or both?

I'm not going to tell you because when you understand more about how beliefs and perceptions interact, you will remember this story and then be able to figure out how and why those students improved for yourself.

Foundation 5: Your Spiritual Foundation
Homo spiritus.

Next is the **spiritual foundation**. If there's one area of your life that's not ruled by the ego-mind, surely it is the spiritual ... while that is somewhat true, the ego-mind fiercely guards the doorway to the spiritual. Without mastery over the spiritual foundation of your ego-mind, you will find that your spirituality is based on other people's ideas of what you 'should' believe in, rather than on what you might *consciously choose on your own.*

Understanding the spiritual will, in so many ways, melt your fears just as surely as the sun melts the ice after a long, dark winter.

Now stop for a moment and understand that this book is not about converting you to or from your religious or non-religious beliefs. It is, however, about looking at the beliefs you have and mastering them. Because as you will soon realize, many of the beliefs you have carried as your own are simply in place because you adopted them. Mastering your spiritual foundation means you believe what you believe about spirituality because you chose to believe because those beliefs are right for you.

First, you will be relieved to know that mastering your spiritual foundation is easy because all of us have a guidance system in place—it's just that most of us forgot how to follow it. I like to call that guidance system 'intuition'. You've probably also heard it referred to as a 'gut feeling'. See, your intuition is like a laser beam, that tells you with pin point accuracy information about yourself and others.

When you haven't mastered your ego-mind spiritually, you could be somewhat disconnected from Source (your spiritual center) or feel lost in life. Another thing, understanding your spiritual beliefs, and why you have/haven't any gets rid of any feelings of guilt or nagging voices jeering at you in the back of your mind because you know your path and why you are on it—you follow it freely, *without feelings of judgment towards yourself or others.*

By regaining mastery of your spiritual foundation you learn to trust your intuition again, because your thorough and open-minded inquiry will help you properly choose your own spiritual path and remain connected with source.

Foundation 6: Your Foundation of Wisdom
Luke: Let the force guide your actions!

Get ready, because I'm going to show how mastering the sixth foundation puts all the foundations together. This is the foundation that will have you living the life you came here to live.

When you master your ego-mind you have the **foundation of wisdom**, and with this foundation mastered you know where you are going in life because you are in the driver's seat racing down easy street, heading to where? Yup, you guessed it: The life of your dreams.

We've all met the smart ass with all the answers, right?
Well, we don't measure the sixth foundation, the foundation of wisdom, by what we know, we measure it by what we do with what we know. I'm going to be straight with you. Knowledge in any of the previous five foundations is not mastery; *Mastery is having the wisdom to use this knowledge in ALL aspects of your life.*

There are many people in this world who have mastered one or two of the foundations I have listed. Yet like I said before, rarely do we meet someone who has it all. We've all seen the financially poor yet spritualy connected. And we all know of the financially wealthy yet devastatingly lonely.

People living with mastery in only a few areas do not have *Full Spectrum Success* and mastery of wisdom. They only have a few foundations.

In the seminars I teach I often hear something along the lines of, "Hey, this is the generation of knowing!" It's a fact; we've never known more than what we know today. Most people are utterly overwhelmed by the amount of knowledge that we already have. We are the most educated and informed generation in all of history, and I realize this may offend a few people but my research shows that in many ways, we are also the most ignorant.

It is true that from the information stand-point we have come a long way. Though, isn't it interesting that with all the information we have, there are so many people living in first-world countries who are still struggling on a day-to-day basis just to make ends meet? The challenge we face as humanity is that we have volumes of information, *yet very little wisdom.*

The **Foundation of Wisdom** comes from *action*, from applying the knowledge that we have to make ends meet, *so you no longer have to struggle.*

Before we go any further, I want to set something straight…You might be "Dear Abby" for everybody you know. You might have all the information and all the right answers. Hell, you may even be the neighborhood sage. But, if you don't have **mastery of wisdom**, it's all nothing more than intellectual 'stuff', and without applying this knowledge in your life, the information will lack substance—masquerading as wisdom. When you can't apply what you know because you don't have the 'cojones' to do what it takes—to walk your talk—then I'm sorry to say, you are lacking mastery of wisdom.

> *"When we move information into application,*
> *the result is transformation – and that*
> *is the basis of all true wisdom!"*
>
> ~ *Dõv Baron*

In the last section I was saying that we've all met the smart ass with all the answers; however, at one time or another we've all been that smart ass. Have you ever noticed how we're all very aware of the solutions to other peoples' problems, while at the same time being more than a little blind to our own?

For that reason, and for the purpose of illustrating what happens when you don't master your ego-mind, I'm going to give you a glimpse inside the life of a client I had. By taking a peek into her life you will gain a real-life understanding about where I'm going and what all this means to you and your level of success.

Obviously for confidentiality, I've changed the name of the person.

By the way, I want to also point out that Suzanne's life is a phenomenal example of the third foundation, **Mastery of The Relational Foundation**, or lack there-of.

Suzanne: *How can I ignore thee*, let me count the ways.

> Suzanne came to see me because she realized that, when things were going great, she didn't really know how to deal with her life. As odd as it sounds, she found herself uncomfortable when things were going right because, to her, there just seemed to be something weird about things going well.
>
> As we sat comfortably facing each other it was clear that Suzanne was more than a little confused and frustrated. Her eyebrows seemed to constantly be pulled together as if she was trying to solve the problems of the world when, in fact, she was trying to solve the problems of her world. She had given me the broad view of what was going on in her life and now I needed to go under the surface. I asked Suzanne to think back to the beginning of her most recent relationship. She began talking about a guy who she called the man of her dreams. As she spoke of him her brow softened as did her eyes. She spoke about how wonderful dating was in the beginning. How they would laugh together and talk for hours. How he would treat her well and all the kind and loving things he said—he was, without a doubt in her mind, everything she had ever dreamed of.

We both smiled and I asked her to go on. Her smile faded back into an anxious look as she told me that she was becoming very distressed about their relationship. She felt very uneasy when things were going right and at one point she had actually told him, "There is something you have to know about me before we go any further."

She said he nervously replied, "Well, what's that?" Suzanne could see the apprehension forming on his face as she said, "I have to tell you, I have really, really bad luck; something always goes wrong when I'm involved ... ."

Well, as I'm sure you can guess... Within a few weeks her prophecy was fulfilled!

When talking about herself, Suzanne would never have openly used the word 'victim', yet as she sat in my office describing her life, it was apparent that Suzanne was holding onto a 'victim-mentality'—the belief that things in her life would generally go from bad to worse because 'that's how it is and she had believed she had no power to change it'.

Suzanne's mind sifted through memories of past partners that she had before the 'man of her dreams'. And as her mind drifted she noticed a pattern; they had all started out being real nice guys and then, as she put it, 'when they got her hooked', they would start treating her badly. They would expect her to pay for things, as well as emotionally and sexually manipulate her; they would become verbally abusive; and when the money ran out, so would they.

Suzanne met the guy that she called 'the man of her dreams' two months after the last of those abusive relationships. He treated her like she had always wanted to be treated; extremely generous, loving, and always kind. She found that even though things were finally going right, she felt stressed-out and didn't understand why. "Maybe I'm anticipating him ending up like the rest of them, great at first and then…"

I'd like to point out that Suzanne, like most people, had a number of stressers in her life, except for him, her relationship was the one thing that had actually been working.

Life was a bit of a balancing act for Suzanne, she had been working two jobs for the last two years. She said she needed the second job to keep the roof over her alcoholic mother's head because her mother had found a lump in her breast and couldn't work.

There was no doubt that Suzanne was clearly struggling to keep up, both mentally and physically, and to top it all off, her mother's latest abusive boyfriend had gone on some kind of tirade. Suzanne felt as though she had to book a flight to her mom's house to 'help out'.

After further digging, I discovered that with all the drama with her mom's situation Suzanne had become completely unavailable to the loving relationship she was in. Up until this point, her boyfriend had been very understanding of her situation, unfortunately, the combination of the two jobs and the total lack of connection he was feeling from Suzanne was becoming too much for him. The man of her dreams, who cared for her deeply, was ready to leave.

The thought of him leaving was unbelievably painful. Strangely, it wasn't painful enough to bring her to my office even though he had suggested that she needed some professional help.

Then, one day Suzanne's boyfriend said something to her that was like a jolt of electricity...this really woke her up. It was one of those moments when someone says something that may not be anything big to the person saying it, just a casual observation. Except when *you* hear it, it's like a bomb goes off in your head, shattering the glass you called reality, leaving you to realize that there is no way to put back together what had once seemed so solid. You know what I mean, right?

One night over dinner, while things were quite calm and they were reflecting on all the stress going on in Suzanne's life, her boyfriend innocently delivered the bomb that shattered her reality when he told her, "I think there's a part of you that likes all this drama, or —as you call it—bad luck."

What she heard right there stopped her in her tracks.

She knew that he was not a malicious or mean man and that he wouldn't say anything to hurt her on purpose. She *also* knew that he wasn't the type of guy to say anything that he didn't feel was true.

Even though she deeply trusted him, at first, Suzanne adamantly tried to reject his comment. Still, after realizing that the comment came from someone who really cared for her, she decided to start examining her life, and this is how she came to be in my office.

Don't get me wrong, I'm sure we both know that most people don't sit around thinking about how they can have *more* crap show up in their lives. Though before we move on to the next section, I'd like to give you something very important to think about: Is it possible that there was a part of Suzanne that actually created all this drama in her life?

Take a moment and sincerely think about that.

If there is a part of her that had created all that drama in her life, then it would have to be the unconscious part of her, right?—A part of her that she has no conscious mastery over, because, as I said, not too many people *consciously* sit around thinking about how they can have more crap show up.

And if that's true, wouldn't that mean that Suzanne is creator of all the crap in her own life, at least at an unconscious level? And wouldn't it also mean that our unconscious minds do the same thing?

The answer is YES!

As you read on you will get all the proof you need. Nonetheless, before I jump into the details, let me say this: The unconscious part of each of us is that 'genie' I talked about in the beginning of the book—and that genie will grant any wish! That's right. **ANY** wish, *including* the wishes we have at an unconscious level, the ones we would **not** make if we re-claimed mastery over our ego-mind.

Imagine what it would be like if that genie could just as willingly grant any of your conscious wishes, giving you whatever you *really wanted*? Is that too far-fetched?

Let's find out…

Chapter 4

Who is the Manifester of Your Life?

As a result of reading this book, you will begin to notice many different patterns of thoughts, emotions and behaviors you have habitually repeated. Those thoughts, emotions and behaviors have held you hostage keeping you exactly where you are today—or more in line with this chapter title, *how you are the manifester of your own life, by virtue of your* habitually repeated thoughts, emotions and behaviors.

You will begin to really notice this because when a truth is pointed out you have no choice other than discovering more and more examples of that truth, (kind of like buying a new car and then driving it off the lot and seeing that model of car EVERYWHERE).

Again, I encourage you to take notes as you go through this book, to help you integrate it— go ahead, write in the margins, a scrap of paper, whatever you feel comfortable using. Allow it to ring your bells and turn on your lights. This material moves along very, very quickly from here on out so you can begin changing your life today rather than spending weeks reading a book, and for that reason I'm reminding you to keep your eyes, your ears, and your perceptions wide open to what you are receiving.

Now, I'd like you to pause for a second, take a deep breath, and consider this question:

What Explanation Have You Had for Your Life Being the Way It Is?
I'm not only referring to the difficulties in your life, I'm also referring to where your life is fantastic. Let me clarify. I'm talking about all of it; *your life as a package.* Maybe you feel you are where you are due to fate. Maybe as you ask that question you hear a voice in your head that tells you, you are lucky; or unlucky. Do either of those statements truly serve as satisfactory explanations as to why your life is the way it is?

I saw a movie a while ago, and heard a description that I think demonstrates how many people see their lives. The lead character asks, "Do you see life this way—with the idea that there's a God that is determining your life? Because, if you do, and your life is the way it is because God is a kid with an ant farm, you are just one of the ants, and the kid is just mucking around with you."

Maybe the way you see it is that you got to where you are in life through something called Karma; that God is some kind of mega-accountant in the sky who does yearly, monthly, weekly, and daily tallies of all your good and bad deeds (or was that Santa?). Then, this magnificent accounting God dishes out the luck, both good and bad, in accordance with what's in your good/bad account. Does this sound ludicrous to you? Great, now we're on the same page.

If those reasons are *not* how you get what shows up in your life, then maybe this concept (which I'm sure you've heard before) is the correct one: "***Let us create mankind in our own image.**"

Over the last twenty plus years of teaching workshops, seminars and working with people one-on-one it has become very obvious that the outer circumstances of your life are a direct result of the inner state of your being. One of the most important things you will ever learn about success, whatever that means to you, is that what's going on inside ends up showing up outside.

We are not victims of circumstance we are both the ones who manufacturer and experience these circumstances. No one magically finds themselves in a divorce court, a prison cell or having a bullet removed. These events are a direct result of all the thoughts, emotions and behaviors you have had up to that point. That doesn't make you wrong or right, what it makes you is either paying attention or being ignorant, either way, it's your choice.

This is not rocket science, and at one level or another you must accept responsibility for your life because that's the only way to change it, if that's what you want to do.

What I believe this teaching actually conveys is that you and I are the result of a creative force. Call it whatever you like, God, Allah, Brahman, the Universe, Source – personally, I like Fred, then again Gladys is just as good. Anyway, this creative force created us and *we, too*, are creators.

Let's suppose for a moment that this is true and you truly are the creator of your world. Imagine yourself as the creator of your own destiny. Now, pretend every thought that swirls through your mind takes form and materializes instantly right in front of you—see yourself fully animated interacting with those thoughts.

Step into this fantasy we just created for a moment and realize if this *is* true, even for a heartbeat, in *this* moment you have all the power that you will ever need to create your life in any way you desire. Do you follow me so far? That means right now in your own life, you are already the manifester of your entire reality!

How could this be true? Is it a pipe dream or some gimmick? Well, keep reading—because what you will discover in this book may very well surprise you.

I'm taking you by the hand to a place where you can realize just how powerful you really are—a place where your body is the bottle and your mind can be the genie (and like I said before, not literally, so don't start rubbing yourself hoping to explode into a dream).

If you are willing to follow me to this place, then I have some fantastic news for you. When you begin to master your ego-mind if there's something in your life that you don't like, as the manifester of your own reality you can use your wish-granting-power to redefine reality around you to create something else, something better. Don't celebrate just yet. Before we jump too far ahead, you must first discover what this manifesting power *is* and how to get back in touch with it. So— right now—allow yourself to cast any doubts aside for a minute and pretend to believe that somehow you've actually created the life you now have, and that you can also actively create the life you crave.

Remember, your doubts are cast aside!

Now, imagining that this is true, that we are the manifesters of our own lives, why would any of us create a life that has so many unnecessary challenges; a life that for some people is so full of fear and pain? I ask this question because if you have this 'genie' in you, surely you'd make your life magnificent, right?
Let me share with you my belief of why we create our lives the way we do. Although you need to understand that *this is something I believe.*

It's not *the* truth, it's *my* truth. If you don't like what I believe, it's not mandatory to take it on because you are always free to chuck it in the nearest garbage can and go back to what you have believed in the past—that is, of course, if what you are now believing is truly bringing you everything you want in your life.

How do you want to learn?

Before I share with you my belief about why people create the life they live (full of 'lack of ...'), I need you to understand one of the reasons I believe we come here (to this planet, to this life); and it's to learn.

I'm guessing as you read 'we came here to learn' you naturally asked, "To learn what?"—and that's actually not the right question to ask. The question you need to be asking is *'how' do you want to learn it?*

Here's a hint. There are only two possible right answers.

1. Do you want to learn through joy?
2. Or do you want to learn through pain?

I'll leave the choice up to you.

The problem is that if you didn't know which question to ask, you also didn't realize you have a choice in how you learn what life has to offer. Up until now, you might not have even considered that all your life you've had the ability to choose *how* you would like to learn.

By the way, up until this point how *were* you choosing to learn: Through joy or pain?

Here's something very interesting: The question of how people choose to learn connects directly to the relationship they have with their life lessons.

I know we're still not that deep into the material; however, I'd like to warn you: I'm not going to hold back here and as a result what comes next may offend some readers.

There are two types of people in this world. The first type wouldn't know a life lesson if it sauntered up to them with a flashing neon sign and did an Irish Jig on their carpet. While the others have a knack of noticing that there are life lessons sitting in the palm of their hands and are eager to learn them. Now if you were to open your eyes and see that you have the power to *choose* how you want to learn life's lessons, then you could choose to learn through joy or pain.

So tell me, if you had to choose right this second, which would it be? Joy, or pain?

"Joy, of course." I can practically hear you say it, "Joy, of course." Well, maybe not the 'of course' part, and maybe I can't really hear you, but I do know you are thinking, "Joy!"

Thinking about it right now, and you will know simply by being honest about the way your life has been so far, most of you up until today may have been choosing to learn life lessons through pain. Like I said earlier, it's not likely that you sat down and consciously chose to learn through pain. However, if that is the case, then you were also unconsciously making choices that lead to you learning your life's lesson based on fear. And the only reason you would learn through pain is because your unconscious was programmed with fear.

Because we are dealing with the stuff that has gone on at an unconscious level, I'm going to summarize this section of the book early because, in truth, it's very important.

I'll do this because I want to give your unconscious mind a head start on soaking it in: **You are here to learn, and the only reason that you are learning the lessons you are learning through any form of pain is because you have been programmed with fear.**

You could just as easily learn those same life lessons through joy. The fear you have been programmed with activates what I call that *inner genie*, and that genie has been bringing you your fears. Fear is a powerful force in the manifestation process.

> *"If you fear it, it will come."*
>
> ~ *Dōv Baron*

Unconscious Beliefs and the Illusions They Create

Let me ask you a question: Are all dogs naturally vicious? Of course not. Even the most dog-fearing of people have met at least one calm and affectionate canine.

So here's another question: What happens when a dog is trained to see everyone but its master as a threat? Obviously, the result can easily be a vicious dog.

Ask yourself this: Because the dog was trained to see most things in the world as a threat, does that make the threat real? Will that dog be able to discern between benevolent and threatening individuals? Or will this particular animal live out its entire life constantly fearing a vague sense of threat? The dog has been trained to believe the world is a dangerous place, and as a result, it believes the world is a dangerous place. Once the program becomes embedded, it is not looked at as a belief; it is simply seen as fact.

Like I said, your outer circumstances are nothing more than your inner circumstances made manifest in the outside world. To say it another way: *Every aspect of your life is a manifestation of the beliefs you unconsciously or consciously accepted.*

You are not a dog, and I don't intend to compare you to one. You are a conscious and evolving individual who has the power to do what it takes to change your own training. However, we're all trained from a very early age to be fearful and the majority of these fears have no basis in truth.

Let's take a look at just a few of the concepts that were presented to us when we were young that inadvertently trained us to feel fearful in our adulthood.

Warnings like:
- Be careful
- Don't screw up
- Put on your coat or you will catch a cold

... and oh yes, let's not forget this one:
- **Don't talk to strangers**

Many of these messages can appear innocent, even helpful at first glance; however, when approached from the perspective of mastering your ego-mind, or not, it doesn't take long to see that many of these messages place both our minds and the direction of our lives in the hands of fear. And that is just the beginning of this mess.

WHO IS THE MANIFESTER OF YOUR LIFE?

We have received these fearful messages for years, and years, and years!

Without our knowing it, these fears have buried themselves in our unconscious and from there they have inadvertently programmed us to be fearful. Because, whether we know it or not, when we are living in fear, we are not the masters of our ego-mind, and we are no better than the dog trained to see everyone and everything as a threat.

Don't just take my word for it, consider this message: *"Don't talk to strangers."*

In a world that we are told is full of freaks and weirdos, 'don't talk to strangers' has never been a stronger message than it is today. Every day in popular culture we're getting messages about why strangers are dangerous.

Before we even go one step further, *chew on this*: If you can't talk to strangers, then you can't talk to anyone outside of your immediate family because at some point *everyone* is a stranger. Seriously! Think about it: How are you ever going to work? Even if you are the world's biggest techno-geek, at some point you will have to talk to a stranger, if only on-line.

It's no wonder so many people are miserable. Many of us are avoiding one of our most basic needs; human contact. If you can only talk to immediate family and not strangers, what's going to become of your love life? Taking it one step further, any scene from the Burt Reynolds movie *'Deliverance'* is going to seem pretty normal. If we can't talk to strangers, is it any wonder that internet porn is such a huge industry. After all, finding a date is pretty hard if you are afraid to walk up and talk to strangers, right?

Using *'don't talk to strangers'* is an outstanding example of the subtle programming that gets into our unconscious mind leaving us totally untrusting of others without even knowing why. By now I'm sure you can already appreciate how this one simple message inserted deep into your unconscious can have a devastating effect on every area of your life. The big question I would ask is: If that ONE message can have such an impact on your life, what other ones are affecting you that you haven't yet noticed?

That's just one small piece, how about this humdinger of a message: **"Be careful what you say, you don't want to look stupid."**

Growing up, almost *all* of us heard some version of that one.

"Keep your mouth shut, that way you can't put your foot in it."

Is it any wonder that so many people are walking around filled with self-doubt, constantly second guessing themselves? Carrying beliefs like that around are as useful as packing a broken umbrella for an up-coming rainstorm. That's the kind of unconscious programing driving you to 'fit in' at all costs, telling you that 'fitting in' is more important than being *you*—your wonderful, authentic self. Sadly, anyone growing up afraid to express themselves, sluggishly walking through life and second-guessing the choices they make, strips them of their ability to make empowered decisions.

You see, the message your unconscious heard every time you ran that program, 'be careful what you say' was this: You should trade your authenticity for approval. **Don't do it, I beg you, don't do it!**

Often times, well-intentioned elders and the powers that be (such as the media) are tattooing fear on our brains with these kinds of negative messages, messages that are unknowingly—or, in some cases, know-ingly—squeezing the brilliant, authentic life out of us.

Chapter 5

It Must Be True, I Saw It on the News

There is a grand illusion out there, one that never ceases to amaze me when I consider how many people buy into it. The grand illusion is this: Older people (as in people of the generations before you and older), the government, and the media (you know, CNN, Fox News, whatever it is) **always tell the truth**!

Come on, you are bright! Think about all the times when what 'they' were calling the truth turned out to be a lie! (Does the term 'weapons of mass destruction' ring any bells?) We can all easily think of examples of this. Think back to the last time someone told you a story they heard on the news and stating "It *must* be the truth, it was on the news."

Well, I think we're all too intelligent to not at least *consider* that the 'truth' we are being spoon fed by every newspaper and news anchor might be an illusion.

Over time the lies that we have been told repeatedly— from whatever source —became disempowering messages that, in turn, became our own deep-seated unconscious beliefs (our programs), ones that you took on when you were very young, without ever considering that they could be questioned.

I don't know if you've noticed, but all lies can be justified by the one telling those lies. Here's one powerful example that goes on from the highest level of government to the pillow talk in your bedroom: **Protective lies**.

Here's the scary part: Many of the beliefs that we absorbed when we were young were given to us with the best of intentions... in order to protect us from some *perceived* threat.

I call these *'protective lies'*, lies such as, *"Don't get any big ideas; you will only end up disappointed."* Although that nonsense may have been given with the best of intentions, that is pure fear programming in action!

We all know children believe what adults say—lock, stock, and barrel—at least long enough for it to become programming. Many parents and adults have inadvertently been teaching their children that thinking big ONLY ends up in disappointment, so the message actually becomes that the child shouldn't even try. Is it any wonder why so many people have a hard time picturing themselves as successful doctors, business owners, lawyers, or even college /university grads? (ok, maybe not lawyers...) Heck, we were even taught that ourselves.

I'll admit that those kinds of messages were designed to protect you from things like disappointment. *In spite of that, what they actually did was program you to believe that you are not worthy or able to fulfill your own dreams, after all, if you get any big ideas you will only end up disappointed, right?*

Well, is it right?

Here's another common example that gives me chills whenever I hear it, and imagine the unconscious power that comes with programming a child with this belief: **"Money doesn't grow on trees."**

I guess we've all heard that one about a million times. It's designed to protect you from, I would guess, blowing all your cash on comic books and candy. What it actually taught you is that there is not enough of money, so you better scrimp and save every penny. Although saving is a smart money management strategy over time, **"Money doesn't grow on trees"** message often became a belief that you are not worthy of living and enjoying full financial abundance. I have seen this so many times with the person who has abundant finances living like a pauper.

I need to say it again because this statement is immensely important:

Every aspect of your life is a manifestation of your beliefs.

I want you to take a quick second and write that statement down. Write it down and tape it to your mirror, so you really get it: *Every aspect of my life is a manifestation of my beliefs*, beliefs that I may have taken on, accepting them without ever consciously choosing them.

Please do it, because it's *that* important. Not to me, heck my life won't change course if you do it or if you don't. However, doing this alone will change the way you see your reality and your ability to shift limiting, unconscious beliefs in your favour. Come on, go ahead, write it down. I'll wait; the book will still be here when you get back.

Done? *I hope so!* Because after reading and writing down that last statement you may feel a little lost and not yet able to see the connection between beliefs and perception. Just relax, because in Part II, I go into full detail about the link between the beliefs and perceptions under the section titled 'Lenses'. After reading that, everything you have learned here in Part I will make perfect sense.

So, where were we? Oh, yes...

Chapter 6

Perception is Personal Reality, and Perception is Trained

Take another moment and ponder just what this means: Perception is reality, and you were trained how to perceive things. Just the way that dog I mentioned earlier was trained to 'perceive' everyone other than its master as a threat, you and I were trained to perceive certain people, things, and situations in a particular way that's in line with that training.

Far fetched? Not at all. Here's a current example of how perception becomes reality, and this one holds especially true for North Americans—although, no matter where you live in the world—I'm sure you are very familiar with this perception.

What we are being told in the early part of the twenty-first century is that dark-skinned individuals with turbans (specifically Muslims, although as you will see, anyone with a middle eastern name or a turban will do) are people we should be afraid of.

Think about it and you will see how absolutely ludicrous that is! First of all, generalizations are just that—generalizations. They generalize, which means they exclude everyone who doesn't fit the generalization.

Moreover, this generalization says everyone in a turban is a fundamentalist Muslim.

Once again, this is an illusion, because, first of all, most Muslims don't wear turbans. Sikh people are the people you are most likely to see wearing turbans, and you should also know that there are people from more than one faith who wear turbans. Secondly, most of the Muslim people you are likely to meet are extraordinarily peaceful people who would no more think of blowing up a building than you would think of sawing your own leg off with a rusty bread knife.

When your mind is open you can begin to see that the generalized perceptions we are fed are absolutely ridiculous and potentially very dangerous. If we're fed the perception that every time something 'terrifying' happens it is because of people who look like the people I've just described, then that becomes what psychologists call conditioning. That conditioning shapes our perceptions about who and what we're supposed to be afraid of. The result: *Perception is reality, and perception is trained.*

Furthermore, our personal beliefs follow our perceptions and our perceptions follow our personal beliefs, it's a vicious cycle. Whether it's about people in turbans, what people in 'our family' can and cannot achieve, how smart or how gifted you are, or whether this is a safe world, all depends on how you perceive yourself, others and the world at large.

Listen, we all like to think we are free thinking, "I make up my own mind," type of individuals. However, the question is; who is really in control? One of the biggest awakenings anyone can have is to realize that their lives have been determined not by outside forces, but by the perception of those outside forces. Because from these programmed automatic perceptions we generate knee jerk responses that have us thinking and feeling in ways that bring us more pain and less joy. In my twenty plus years of experience, you'd be stunned if you knew how many people are shocked to discover that their unconscious beliefs have been running their lives all along.

So here's the deal: You will want to get this, because it's really important! ... **It's not your fault!** And I want to say that a few more times because it's essential that you swallow this:

It's not your fault!

It's not your fault!

If you don't have the life you want, it's because you didn't know *then* what you know **now**—it's the sum of your life experiences, the subjective meaning you've given those experiences, and the beliefs you adopted and created to support the way you percieved those experiences that determines the kind of people and quality of events you experience in your life.

Without fully understanding what I've just shared with you it's impossible to change your reality. Without that understanding the Quantum Resonance Field™, (hold on, I'll explain) you generate is going to continue to attract to you whatever fits with what is *'in phase'* with the beliefs and perceptions you hold. Without eliminating all negative/limiting unconscious beliefs you have you will be hard-pressed to live the life you have been dreaming.

Chapter 7

The Genie

I think it's time to share a subtle yet vital piece of your manifesting power. I know you will find this fascinating because, at some level, you may have intuitively suspected it for years.

Rather than jumping headfirst into the details of Quantum Resonance Fields™, (the real secret of manifestation), let me explain a few terms to you so that you can fully comprehend what a Quantum Resonance Field™ is. At first, these terms may seem complicated but they really aren't because understanding the definitions of the individual words allows you to get a clear idea of what I mean. So here goes.

What's a Quantum?

Quantum. It's the new buzz word and it seems to be everywhere lately. Actually, just the other day I saw a truck with the company name 'Quantum Carpet Cleaner'. I don't know what the heck could be quantum about that; it certainly is a word that's getting a lot of current usage. The word Quantum comes from the Latin meaning 'amount'; however, in the context we are referring to, it has two meanings ... .

- The descriptive label for a branch of physics: •
  Quantum Physics
- It also describes an amount or packet of energy known as a
  Quark.

Quarks

One of the easiest ways of describing what a Quark is, is by looking at the objects you see around you. Because a Quark is both energy and matter, it's not so easily seen, although, it can be very easily imagined. So follow me here while we deconstruct an illusionary chair, just to see what it, and for that matter we, are made of ... .

See if you can picture a hammer and a large wooden chair in your mind. Then have the hammer smash the chair down until you see some wooden chunks. By looking at those chunks you might still be able to recognize it as part of the chair, but I want you to take that hammer once more and smash down those pieces to even smaller sizes so that you will end up with tiny pieces of wood; wood so small that you couldn't recognize that it was once a chair.

Now take hold of that illusionary hammer in your minds eye and continue to smash down the tiny pieces of wood again, and again, and again, until you eventually no longer even recognize that it's wood; it's more like a pile of dust.

Let's just take one spec of that dust, give you a massive magnifying glass and a very tiny hammer and get ready to both remember and learn something new and exciting.

If you were to use that very tiny hammer to smash down that tiny spec of wood dust it wouldn't be wood anymore at all, eventually it would be a bunch of molecules (think back to high school). Now if we used that hammer again to smash down the molecules, they would break up into atoms (think BOOM).

What they didn't know when I was in high school is that when you break open atoms, they break apart into two main things; *subatomic* particles (some of you may have already learned that last part, depending on what era we were in high school, of course!) and empty space.

Subatomic Huh?

Stay with me here, we're going down the physics rabbit hole, and I've got your hand. A subatomic particle is what we call an elementary particle; simply put they are the 'stuff' atoms are made of. How this relates to our broken wooden chair is that every subatomic particle consists of three things: Electrons, protons, and neutrons—and all protons and neutrons are made up of *Quarks*. "So what," you say.

Well, here's something to keep in mind: *Quarks* seem to be what everything in the universe, including you, has as a basic building block; the earth, the stars and everything in between—*everything*.

Remember, even if you forgot the entire process of how we broke the chair down into a Quark, as long as you can clearly understand that everything is made up of Quarks, (quantum packets of energy) you will be one step closer to manifesting your reality.

Bet you thought we were done, right? Not quite. One last thing about Quarks is that if we took our hammer and smashed up the Quarks one more time, we would end up with vibrating strings of light. These vibrating strings of light are akin to the strings on a violin, guitar, or even a piano.

On any instrument, when the strings are plucked, they vibrate, they *resonate.* In music it's called *resonation* as well. And that is one reason we call it a Resonance Field. It really is a Quantum Resonance Field™ (QRF). Now, I want you to keep that word in mind, *resonate*. Actually, I want you to let that word resonate with you because in a moment you will learn a little more about what resonance is, and then all this physics stuff will ring clear as a bell around an open field.

As I promised to hold your hand while we travel down the quantum rabbit hole, I will help you rebuild the chair in order to help solidify these outstanding and pivotal concepts in your mind. When the vibrating *strings* of light gather enough energy, they create a Quark. When three Quarks get together, they create subatomic particles. When enough subatomic particles get together, they create atoms, which create molecules, which create STOP ... They do not ONLY create wood particles.

Strings and Quarks are the foundation of everything in this universe, **including you**. If we had a hammer and broke you down far enough, you would be made up of Quarks, and eventually strings as well. We all would be made up of Quarks and vibrating strings of light, and so would the wooden chair.

Look, you may not realize it right this second, but that is a TON of valuable knowledge right there, in fact, when used properly it can become powerful wisdom. Wait till you are seeing how all this ties together when it comes to manifesting the life of your dreams—you will be in awe! Though before we go into how that can change your life, we have to explain the second word, 'resonance'. I promise, you can relax; this word is much less complicated.

Resonance

In a nut shell resonance could be described as a vibration AND energy. Think of your phone on vibrate. If we were to call the phone a quark and the act of it vibrating a *resonance*, you would now have a pretty clear image in your mind of what quantum resonance is. The reference to energy earlier applies to the fact that, when anything vibrates, it is also giving off an energy field. We can't physically see the energy field, although we can feel it as well as measure it because it emits something similar to radio waves.

Chapter 8

The Language of Manifestation

U nderstanding the manifestation side of this book depends a lot on your understanding of this likely new word: 'Resonance'. For that reason, I am going to take a little extra time to make sure resonance makes perfect sense to you.

At the quantum level 'Resonance' is the universal language.

> *"The problem with communication...*
> *is the illusion that it has been accomplished."*
> *~George Bernard Shaw*

Did you know that there are more than 6,000 recorded languages spoken in the world? Think about it. You are reading this book in English and presumably your native language is English, therefore you understand its words. Yet, if this book had been written in another language, would you have understood it? There is a good chance you would not have understood a word of it.

Anyone who's ever had any kind of a serious relationship knows that the quality of your communication is the response it generates. It doesn't really matter that you *didn't mean it that way*. It's the way the information is received that decides the result you get. A message is either transmitted or it is not; it is either received or it is not.

Essentially, this chapter is about *the importance of effective communication* on both a personal and universal level. While it is essential to our life, most of us give language far too little thought. We generally take for granted that what we say will inevitably be understood. (Except for those of us in a serious relationship who have quickly learned that what is said and what is understood can be two very different things).

Most languages serve small pockets of the world's population, being highly specific to an individual nation or region. The point is, if you wanted to communicate with anyone in one of these places, without knowing its unique and specific language, you would definitely have a challenge. Communication is not as simple as it may seem.

Imagine the following scenario ...

You are working for a multinational corporation doing your best to climb the corporate ladder. Suddenly, your boss arbitrarily decides to uproot and transfer you—to the *Japan* office. Oh, and it is not in Tokyo either. It is in some small town, or 'prefecture', as it is referred to over there. Your boss also wants you there yesterday. Time to plan? Forget about it.

When you arrive, exhausted from your flight you are happy to see that at least the basics are set up for you. You have a nice—though smallish—apartment equipped with the essentials: Basic furniture, kitchenware, and a television. The only real problem is lack of food—and the fact that you have no idea where to find it.

For the sake of this example, let's say your boss tends to be a rather negligent one. So, you are due to report to work the next morning, but it's looking like it might have to be on an empty stomach. Unless you can rustle up the ingredients for a breakfast—somewhere—tonight.

You take a deep breath, and venture out into the great unknown, your hunger as your only guide. In the distance, you spot the welcoming neon light of what appears to be a convenience store. As you approach, you discover that indeed it is. You enter, nervously realizing, of course, your own absolute ignorance of the Japanese language's sounds and symbols. What you have instead is a determination to abate your hunger. And what you crave more than anything is eggs, an English muffin, and some peanut butter.

In the tightly-packed shop, you are befuddled by its odd organization. Nothing is familiar, nothing is where it would have been if you were still at home. Thoroughly puzzled, you now need to find a way to communicate your needs to the store clerk. First, you attempt English. It is a gamble, but there is a chance that he may have studied it or at least seen enough American movies to have picked some up. But judging by the look on his face, this is not your day. His bewildered stare is not getting you your muffin.

You are unfazed, and your determination is growing in proportion to your hunger… You decide it's time to step up your game with sign language—of sorts. It doesn't help. This grocery charade game has the clerk—and everyone else in the store too, for that matter—laughing at you. Hysterically. In fact, there's a boy on his phone, and you are sure he is mocking 'the crazy foreigner'.

As it happens, your best efforts at signing or acting are not successfully conjuring up visions of eggs, English muffins or peanut butter in anyone else's head. That much is glaringly clear. The fact is, no matter what you do, you are not speaking their *language* – through words or otherwise. So, effective communication with locals just isn't going to happen. For breakfast, you will have to settle for a packet of noodles with a large side of frustration.

In this scenario, the simple task of buying groceries turned into quite the challenge, didn't it?

It didn't really matter whether or not the store actually carried any of what you wanted, did it? Because you, (the guy in the story) were not able to communicate in an understandable manner.

I should let you know, this story is not entirely made up. Back in my early twenties, I experienced this situation almost exactly. In a little Italian town, I ran around a small grocery store impersonating a chicken laying an egg, in an attempt to communicate my desire for a few breakfast items. Can't you just imagine the hysteria? While I succeeded at providing the locals with a measure of evening entertainment – I had everyone in the store laughing hysterically – I left egg-less and without any of the food I really wanted.

Now, back to the little, Japanese shop. Let's assume you are more committed than I was, and you are determined to leave with the desired food. What should you do now? Is the food going to arrive in your bag if you continue to communicate in an ineffective language?

Of course not.

Maybe you think that your breakfast ingredients are going to appear if you apply enough positive thinking? Sorry! If you want the food, you need to communicate in the language that is relevant to the store clerk. At this point, it's time to go find yourself a dictionary or a local translator, and start communicating your needs again – Japanese style this time.

The real key to effective communication is choosing the most appropriate language. However, language can be much more than words.

Chapter 9

The Need for Specificity

I know you are probably a very healthy eater and it would never cross your mind, but work with me here. Imagine that you are craving a Coke®. You also happen to be standing in front of a coin operated cola vending machine. Unfortunately, as you search your pockets, you realize you do not have enough coins, and instead have mostly bills. Unless you find more coins, you are not going to be sipping that Coke® any time soon. While the bills are indeed a form of money, they are not the appropriate type of money. In a metaphorical sense, a dollar bill is not the right *language* for communicating with that machine. The language it speaks is coins. So, by offering it bills, you cannot possibly receive your beloved Coke®.

The same principle applies to life. Earlier, I told you that this chapter would be about communication. It is. Now comes the really fun part...

This chapter is really about the most important communicating you will ever do. Yes, it's even more important than speaking to your mother in the right tone of voice... This chapter is about communicating with the universe.

Just as you need to speak the right language to the Japanese store clerk and the Coke® machine, you need to speak the right language to the universe too if you want to get what you want from it. After all, when you use the right language, there is a much higher probability that you will be able to receive that which you desire into your life. In fact, just as coins can quickly buy that Coke®, the right *language of manifestation* will enable you to rapidly attract your desired circumstances.

Manifestation has a very specific language. Use it and the universe will deliver. Guaranteed!

> *"What would you attempt to do*
> *if you knew you would not fail?"*
> ~ *Sydney Smith*

Now, you may be thinking that you have heard this before. After all, if you are like me, you have probably been given this 'secret key' to making positive changes in your life so many times you've lost count. You have also likely tried the goal setting, the positive thinking, affirmations and the plethora of other funky stuff that somehow seemed reasonable at the time. In fact, you have probably collected so many of those 'secret keys' that your personal empowerment key-ring is becoming an unmanageable dead weight that's got you walking with a limp.

Chances are that even with all of these keys, if you are like most 'searchers', you are finding that your circumstances are not changing substantially. As a result, you may find yourself asking yourself the following questions: "Is my life going to be any different in 5, 10, or 15 years?" or "Will I ever get the life and recognition I want?" If that's the kind of stuff that floats around in your head, then understanding the *language of manifestation* is essential!

Sadly, for most people, those 'secret keys' are about as much use as a Catholic priest at your Jewish buddies Bar Mitzvah. They mean nothing unless employed effectively, in the right place at the right time.

What is great about using resonance (the *language of manifestation*) is that it goes beyond simple affirmations, visualization and positive thinking and you can use it just about anywhere, at any time. In fact, employing the language of manifestation will help you apply all of those other keys you've learned more effectively. Basically, my years of research have taught me that while most of these other keys can result in limited success, they rarely achieve lasting change because they lack an essential element. For most people, using them is like spending a hot day at the beach and then returning to a cold climate. It is great in the moment, but then, like a tan, the effects always quickly fade afterwards.

To find the missing element to success, I devoured hundreds of books and attended enough workshops and seminars to educate a small nation. I needed to find *the true key to making a lasting, positive change in my life and in the lives of the people I cared about.* I am convinced that I have found the answer—*the most essential element*—to creating lasting change and have been teaching it for many years now. In fact, this topic is at the foundation of my life's work and an exhaustive dissertation.

The missing element in all of these other approaches to success is simply the understanding of how resonance works and the application of it. Applying the Law of Resonance is learning to speak the universal *language of manifestation!*

This *language* goes far beyond anything you have learned before—it supersedes all previous 'secrets'.

After reading this chapter, you will clearly understand how to **effectively communicate with the universe**, and truly **manifest your desired reality**. I should warn you, though. Using *the right language* to communicate with the universe does mean taking responsibility for your life. Claiming ignorance will no longer be an option. You can't just take credit for the good stuff. You also need to accept the stuff you are not so keen on (as you will see, that's the only way to change it). You will need to understand that what you are receiving into your life—good or bad—is *always* based on the *language* you are using to communicate with the universe.

Just as trying to feed bills into a coin operated vending machine can never work, and will only leave you frustrated and without your precious Coke® fix, communicating the wrong things to the universe will leave you at least as frustrated and unfulfilled. Using *the right language*, though, will get you everything you want.

> *"To make an apple pie from scratch,*
> *you must first create the universe."*
>
> ~ *Carl Sagan*

The language of manifestation is as much an art as it is a science. Let's first talk about how it is a very precise science, with a precise formula, that you can and will learn to use with ease. So there's no need to worry that the science side of it is too difficult to clearly understand, let me assure you that you do not need to understand the science in depth, only the application.

After all, do you have to thoroughly understand the laws governing electricity in order to make yourself a slice of toast in the morning?

No. You only need to know that the toaster must be plugged into an electrical outlet, and that electricity is behind this seemingly magical transformation that takes bread to toast.

So, at this point I'm going to briefly explain the science behind the *language of manifestation* so that you know which scientific laws of the universe it plugs into and how it applies to you getting what you want. Okay? So stay with me, because this is not difficult and who knows you may even find the science of it kind of fun, you never know.

> *"All truth passes through three stages.*
> *First, it is ridiculed.*
> *Second, it is violently opposed.*
> *Third, it is accepted as being self-evident."*
> ~ *Arthur Schopenhauer*

The *language of manifestation* has its roots in quantum science. Quantum science has been around since the early part of the last century. However, like all scientific approaches, in its early years it was dismissed as outrageous and unbelievable. Hey, this should be no surprise! There was a time when people laughed at the idea that the world was round! Only in recent decades has quantum physics become more acceptable. In fact, quantum physics is now able to explain so much about the universe's workings that two previously incompatible realms—spiritual and scientific knowledge—are suddenly complementing one another.

During the early part of my career, I was fascinated by different spiritual and cultural philosophies. I traveled the world to study with people I consider to be spiritual masters from various religious backgrounds.

As I studied each of these philosophies, I began to uncover common truths, and became committed to letting as many people as I could know about these common truths.

However, explaining the similarities between such vastly different religions and philosophies was a hard thing to do. Yet, I knew, on the fundamental level, that all of these teachings did have something in common. At their most basic level it seemed to me that they essentially all sought to empower the student to create harmony between him/herself, mankind and a universal power. But this commonality was hardly concrete enough for me to find a way of explaining it, until ...

One day in the early nineteen eighties, I stumbled upon the answer I had been seeking. I found the answer in a very unexpected place—a quantum physics book. Without knowing a thing about the subject previously, I intuitively picked up the book at a used bookstore. I have to tell you, it was like having a flood light shone onto the field that was my life. It made scientific sense of everything I had previously learned from all of these great spiritual teachers.

> "Science without religion is lame,
> religion without science is blind."
>
> - Albert Einstein

Quantum physics is the physics of the incredibly small. Both Newtonian and quantum physics explain how all matter interacts. The difference is that the Newtonian laws of physics begin to diminish as we investigate matter on a smaller scale. Quantum physics explains the behavior of everything smaller than an atom—things like electrons, protons, and neutrons. It explains that the Universe is not as we once thought, made of matter suspended in empty space but instead, as energy vibrating.

Quantum physics describes this energy as constantly vibrating (or resonating) and exchanging frequencies. So, every material structure in the universe, including you, me, the sun, the moon and everything else, broadcast a unique vibration or energy signature.

Pretty cool stuff, wouldn't you agree? When I came across this stuff I was stunned, because it was the science of what I'd always suspected.

Unless you went to a very sophisticated high school, the atomic model you were taught there was likely wrong, or at least incomplete. Quantum physics shows us that the electrons don't orbit like planets; they are instead blurred clouds of probability around the nucleus of the atom. At that point, they are not even particles and, as strange as it sounds, they are more like the ghosts of particles. They are simply waves of probability waiting to come into existence.

At the foundation of quantum physics there is a curious, yet scientifically proven truth and it's this: Simply observing something changes both the thing being observed and the observer. This contradicts conventional knowledge on so many levels. We have been taught that we are inconsequential in the grand scheme of the universe while in truth, we are integral to it.

Scientifically, we choose our path in life, second by second. As will soon become deeply evident, the way we observe, think about, and feel about our life, and what's going on in it, all work together to literally create our reality.

*"Quantum physics has found that there is
no empty space in the human cell, but it is a teeming,
electric-magnetic field of possibility or potential."*

~ Deepak Chopra

A great movie that helps describe the concept of quantum theory is *"What the Bleep Do We Know!?"* In fact, an important section of the movie describes a Japanese researcher's water experiments. Using water, the researcher, Dr. Emoto has actually been able to prove that feelings and thoughts do have a physical reality at the subatomic level.

His book, *The Hidden Messages in Water*, displays microscopic pictures of water crystals; his work demonstrated that water actually re-acts to thoughts, feelings, and sounds. To demonstrate his point, after the same water droplets had been treated with certain written or spoken words, or musical sounds, they were flash frozen and photographed using something called a dark field microscope. The results of his experiment were astounding, to say the least.

After water had been blessed, with words such as 'love' or 'angel', its crystals appeared as a beautifully formed crystalline structure. Meanwhile, water that had been 'cursed' with words such as 'you make me sick' or 'demon', appeared disjointed, sickly and the crystalline structure distorted. In fact, one of the most beautiful crystals resulted when water was exposed to one of Mozart's symphonies!

For more information about *"What the Bleep Do We Know!?"* I've written a book, which is available in a free downloadable ebook format for you and your friends at www.WhatTheBleepDoesItMean.com

Chapter 10

Beyond LOA...
Applying Quantum Understanding

What most people do not realize is that applying these quantum theories is a delicate art as well as a science. It is something that must be honed and practiced. Besides, simply knowing about the Law of Attraction does not fully explain what needs to occur, scientifically, for manifestation to take place. What needs to be understood – or at least what you need to be aware of – is that there is an even deeper scientific law at play. This is the real secret to success. In fact, I call it 'The Secret Beyond The Law of Attraction™' some folks even consider me to be an expert on the subject.

The fact is, as my on-line coaching program, 'The Secret Beyond The Law of Attraction™' explains in greater detail, as I've been saying for awhile, the fundamental law for manifestation is *not* the Law of Attraction. Actually you cannot transform your life simply by thinking about it. To manifest what you want in life, you must have the right resonance. You need to apply the *Law of Resonance*.

Now, I really have your attention, don't I? My guess is you are either wondering "Why?" or "How?" and there's a good chance that it's both. You will want to know all about this new word, 'resonance' because the *Law of Resonance* is *the real science behind manifesting!* Over the next few pages, I'll be sure to explain its science well enough that you can set it in motion! It is actually quite a simple law. Again, all you really need to remember is the art of effectively applying it.

What's Your Vibe? Learning to Play the Universe like a Fiddle.
The Law of Resonance describes the way that everything in the universe is linked and communicating to act as a cohesive whole. And I do mean everything. As I shared a few pages ago, everything, including you, me and what you want to attract—even feelings and emotions, such as love are all connected. And the way that it all connects is through vibrations, or *resonance.*

Things that vibrate at the same frequency create resonance and resonance sets up the attracting force to determine what we either attract or repel.

Remember, Quantum Physics explains that everything is energy. For our purposes, it is important for you to always be conscious of the fact that even your thoughts have this resonance. Everything about you has a vibration. When you are resonating "positive energy" – such as love or gratitude—quantum bound subtle energy travels instantaneously out from you to the entire universe. The energy you have sent out then seeks its match out in the universe, and brings this matching vibration/resonance back to you. Here's what you will find fascinating: The returned vibration/resonance has all of the same positive characteristics as the energy of love and gratitude you originally broadcast.

This exchange of energy between you, the universe and everything in it occurs instantaneously on many different levels—emotional, physical and even metaphysical. And the reverse is also true. 'Negative' vibrations/resonance can just as easily be sent, and often are. This actually helps to explain why sometimes bad days never seem to end. What happens is you are vibrating/resonating negative energy, creating a negative resonance. The universe then keeps responding to your negative energy vibration by matching it for you. All day long!

To help visualize resonance, imagine this experiment. A student is instructed to hold a tuning fork by the stem while another student holds a similar tuning fork just a few feet away. One of the students strikes the tuning fork, while the others are instructed to simply pay attention to what happens. Within a few short moments, the un-struck tuning fork begins to vibrate/resonate. It comes into what is called *sympathetic resonance* with the struck tuning fork. Suddenly, the un-struck tuning fork is emitting the same note as the struck one. Isn't that cool? No effort needed. It just complies. **That's resonance!**

It, being resonance, exists all around you—not just in the science lab. No matter where you are, what you are thinking or what you are doing, you are resonating. Think of yourself as a two legged tuning fork sending out vibes.

Don't just take my word for it: Dr Bruce Lipton outlines that the once 'woo-woo' new age idea that we create our own reality now has scientific evidence to support it. In several interviews and in his books, Dr Lipton outlines how our thoughts and beliefs give off vibrations that effect the entire energy field, and he highlights how *we are like a tuning fork which emanates from our head out into the field*, thus shaping the world we are in. Scientifically confirming what I thought to be true back in the early 80s.

Chapter 11

Give Me Some of those
Good, Good, Good Vibrations

So, now let's talk a bit more about what is required to get you into a preferred state of resonance. It is now time to get excited because this is where we get right into speaking the *language of manifestation*.

To *manifest* what you want, you first need to generate and then maintain the required resonance. You need to send and receive vibratory frequencies that are identical, or at least very similar, to the experience or entity you wish to attract. This is the language the universe understands. Thus, the more you stay in that desired resonance, the more you can attract of what you want.

I'll start by giving you a simple way to get into the resonance you want. We will use money as the example. Let's say you've been having a bit of a financial challenge. You've got the classic too much month at the end of your money. Could you answer me if I asked you, "What does it feel like to have excess cash?"

My guess is that you might have a bit of a hard time getting connected to that feeling. In fact, if you have been struggling with too much month at the end of your money for a while, you are likely now resonating 'lack', 'not enough', 'broke' or something similar. And that resonance is not going to fill your bank account any time soon.

What if I got you to go and stand in a Wall Street bank to just watch the massive cash-flow happening all around you. It won't take you very long for you to understand exactly what it feels to have excess cash. That bank and most of the people going in and out of it carry the resonance of wealth and abundance. Standing there, you begin to pick up that resonance of wealth and abundance. That resonance will inject your field with loads of juicy abundance and, in turn, inject your thoughts, emotions and feelings leading you to resonate at a higher financial frequency.

Every time you repeat this, it is like recharging your battery. The energy ultimately reaches a level where the things you desire also desire you as their match. They will pull you as surely as iron filings are pulled to a magnet.

Ultimately, whatever it is that you desire in life, you must attract it in such a way that *it pulls you as much as you pull it*. Do you want more money? Then you must attract it in such a way that *it pulls you as much as you pull it*. Do you want better health? Then you must attract it in such a way that it pulls you as much as you pull it. It really is that simple... get in the resonance of whatever it is that you want to manifest and it begins to want you as much as you want it.

The point is, you have to be in the same frequency as the things you want to attract into your life. If you are not in the same frequency, it will not matter how hard you work... you could never attract that which you desire. As I'm sure you've experienced, effort + more effort = frustration. Your goal needs to be to mimic the vibration given off by your desired experience.

When you know how to be in resonance with what you want, life becomes fully synchronistic. The most successful people in the world have mastered this method. Despite what you may think, they are not simply luckier than you. They simply know this *language of manifestation*, even if they are not consciously aware of it. They know how to speak to the universe – how to be in resonance with it – so as to easily attract everything that they want. As a result, they not only attract wealth, they are more likely to get the connections they need to stay wealthy.

"Each of us literally chooses,
by his way of attending to things, what sort
of universe he shall appear to himself to inhabit."
~ William James

When you get in resonance with your life, you will be amazed by the speed and clarity of this phenomenon. When my students start manifesting greater success into their lives, in the beginning they often say to me, "Dōv, all these great things just keep happening *for me* and it seems like it's coming out of nowhere."

It's not coming out of nowhere. What has happened in their lives is that their resonance has changed. The vibrations they are broadcasting out into the universe have changed. They have begun to really speak the *language of manifestation*. Using the Law of Resonance creates a synchronicity that brings your desired experiences to you again and again.

Let this truth soak in for a moment. My guess is that when you understand it, you will realize that, on some level, you already intuitively suspected it.

Now, let yourself imagine how resonance can positively affect you and your abilities to create health, wealth, loving relationships or anything else you may desire. What if you could actively choose your life's resonance? What would that be worth to you?

Chapter 12

Resonating Abundance: What is Your Wealth Potential?

If you cannot imagine what consciously applying resonance – the *language of manifestation*—would be worth to you, I'll help you.

Let me put it another way. All too often we learn something new and exciting, swear we are going to use it and then we put the book down, do nothing and guess what? Nothing happens! What if, after everything you've already discovered within the pages of this book you completely ignored your resonance, and kept on behaving the same as you had in the past? What might that behavior cost you? How much energy and effort would you spend trying to accomplish your goals? How frustrated might you be?

Let me be a bit more specific: The past has essentially gotten you to where you are now. So, the obvious question is, "Are you where you want to be?" If you said 'yes', that's great. Congratulations! If not, "How will it feel to be in the same place you are currently in, if you are still in it in five years from now"? What I am referring to is the emotional cost of not applying what you've learned.

That's why I encourage you to read sections over again, take notes, do the exercises, talk about what you are learning with friends. The more ways you allow yourself to get this material the better chance you have of retaining and using it.

You are either In Resonance or You are Not.
If you still doubt resonance's ability to transform your life, let's go back to that classroom with the students and the tuning forks. Suppose one of the tuning forks is set to the C note, and the other tuning fork is set to the D note. Now, just like last time, one of the students strikes his tuning fork. This time, however, no matter how hard he strikes it, the other tuning fork will not come into sympathetic resonance to match the note of the other. The tuning forks are literally not 'tuned in' to one another, or out of synch, and their attracting abilities are disabled. Resonating lack and 'trying' to attract wealth, is no different. There's simply no resonant match for attraction to happen.

Now are you beginning to fully see, feel and believe the importance of resonance? Can you see how resonance truly drives your ability—or lack thereof—to create wealth, health and success in your life?

Basically, you are either speaking the *language of manifestation*, or, as in the Japan grocery shopping example, you are becoming frustrated by speaking English to a non English speaking clerk. You are either resonating what you want to manifest, or you are not.

You cannot resonate a poverty mentality and expect to be attracting wealth and abundance back to you. That's like tuning your radio to the country station and then complaining about country music blasting from it. What you are tuned into is what you will be getting – in life and on the radio!

If you are not in resonance, saying that you want to manifest something is about as effective as asking for your dry cleaning to be delivered from the toy store. It is a waste of energy, you are in the wrong place! The thing that you want to manifest has as much chance of showing up as the D tuning fork has of taking on a C vibration. Of course there is zero chance of that!

Chapter 13

The Missing Link

Resonance is a very pure form of communication. As stated, it's how we communicate with everything around us, both physical and non-physical. Whether we are consciously aware of it or not, it is always occurring.

What I'm about to share with you is the real 'secret', the missing link if you will, in the Law of Attraction hype: *Every emotion and feeling that comes up in you has a corresponding energetic resonance.*

For years the success industry has been telling us that our thoughts create our reality and that's somewhat true. "Think positive," the experts say. It will bring you unlimited joy and success. Sorry to be the bearer of bad news. If you are stuffing your real feelings down in order to think positive...It won't work. I've been a psychologist for more than twenty years, and I have never seen mere thoughts on their own change anyone's life. Thinking it can is both naïve and a form of denial! Because, as you will soon see, it's not about whether a feeling is 'negative/bad' or 'positive/good'.

I know, if you were brought up in any kind of an emotionally repressed society (and who wasn't), you might be a bit skeptical. Right?

Let me show you how this works: Back in the 1980's Lydia Temoshok who at that time was a psychologist at UCSF, did extensive research that showed that cancer patients who kept emotions such as anger under the surface had a much slower recovery rate than those who were more expressive. Another common trait in these slow to heal patients was self-denial which stemmed from their unawareness of their own basic emotional needs.

Meanwhile, the immune systems of those who were in touch with their emotions were consistently stronger and their tumors smaller.

According to Candace Pert PhD in her excellent 1997 book, 'Molecules of Emotion': *"Health is not just a matter of thinking 'happy thoughts'. Sometimes the biggest impetus to healing can come from jump-starting the immune system with a burst of long suppressed anger."*

Obviously, there is a need for discernment about how we express what has been repressed. However, the key is to express it away from the system of your own body so that it doesn't fester, build, escalate out of control or, and maybe most importantly, resonate with the universe to attract more of the same.

Some individuals will tell themselves that they don't want to express these 'negative' emotions because they don't want that to be what they are vibrating into the universe. Well, the hard truth is that the more you 'stuff it' the more you resonate it!

While thinking positive can't hurt, as you can now clearly sense, denial can! Thinking positive is only a small piece of the equation. What you experience in life is the result of much, much more than your thoughts. Resonance is not produced by your thoughts alone, but by your beliefs, emotions, and most importantly your feelings that lay below your thoughts. That is why the Law of Resonance—not the Law of Attraction—makes all the difference. The Law of Resonance addresses the totality of your experience on this planet. Thus, it is crucial that you master it through monitoring not only your thoughts, but also your beliefs, emotions, and feelings. They all carry the resonant information that determines what you do or do not get out of life… Essentially, what you can and cannot *attract*!

Society has conditioned us to believe that emotions are bad and that we must control them by stuffing them down and repressing them until we explode. Don't do it! As you now know, it doesn't help and in all likelihood it can hurt. I'm here to tell you to embrace your emotions!

Emotions are not bad. In fact, they are the fuel for manifestation. It is a misconception that life will be better when you control emotion, because it's not about controlling your emotions … it's about directing them. You *can learn* how to direct your emotions toward a place where life is synchronistic. You *can learn* to emote toward a place where life is effortless. Otherwise, your energy is being wasted and out of synch with all that you desire!

So, no matter what it is that you are looking to manifest, to make it happen you must be very specific and just as importantly, emotionally charge your desire to create the strongest resonance.

Okay, you now have your feet firmly planted in the understanding of what resonance is and that it is intrinsically connected to the feeling you have and the feelings you may have been repressing. One last thing before we move on to how quantum resonance connects everyone and everything together through something known as field effect. Remember you don't need to be a rocket scientist. Keep it basic… you are communicating with the universe. Speak its language if you want to be understood!

Quantum Resonance

Quantum resonance theory is a very exciting part of the whole 'quantum consciousness' movement that has us examining what our part is in the manifestation of 'reality'. It offers some clarification of questions that had remained mysterious within the more conventional paradigms of Newtonian (traditional) physics. I'd love to roll up my sleeves, put on the gun boots, and jump right into the depths of the subject. However, within the parameters of this particular book we are only going to go into the subject as deep as we need to for you to apply it to your own life. If you are really interested, I explore the subject with considerably more depth in some of my live events, especially Attracting Force™ which you can find out more about at AttractingForce.com/bookbonus

What I will share with you now is this: Quantum resonance gives us profound insights into concepts such as consciousness, the origin of life, and the very nature of subjective experience.

The term 'quantum resonance' refers to a collective or unified field of consciousness. Quantum resonances are also referred to as 'self-moments', meaning that these fields organize themselves as a complete part of something bigger.

What this means is your QRF (Quantum Resonance Field) is both complete within itself and held within a larger whole, which is comprised of an infinite number of smaller parts.

Let me make that super easy to understand: Think of watching a small child blow bubbles; every now and then there is a complete bubble within a larger bubble. On the one hand, your QRF (your bubble) exists as a unique individual within a larger collective; on the other hand, your QRF also exists as the larger collective (the larger bubble) within which the individual exists.

If we stay with the 'bubble within a bubble' analogy, it's important to note that the process of describing quantum resonance itself can be a challenge because it implies some separation from the thing we're describing. Here's the way I explain that in my workshops: Ask a fish to describe water and its response would likely be: Water? It wouldn't even know what water is. (Try describing air.) Suppose this fish is of superior intelligence, can speak clearly, and we take it out of the water. Do you think at that point it could better tell us what water is? You bet, it would. Remember, you don't even notice air, although, if it wasn't there you'd have a dynamic understanding of what was missing, right? And I imagine, pretty quickly too!

Quantum resonance theory is a theory of life; in some sense, it is also a theory of everything.

Okay, take a breather, just let that last page or so sink in. In fact, it's perfectly okay to go back and read it over again. (When I came across some of this stuff twenty or more years ago, I would read the same line ten or more times until it sank in. Back then no one was making it this easy). When you now begin to let this knowledge in it becomes easier and easier to understand. After this is where the pace picks up a little, and we cover some cutting edge science very briefly, so allow your perceptions to open up a little more and let your senses guide you through this next part. You are going to love it, and you will impress the heck out of your friends when you tell them about it.

Back in 2002, I wrote a dissertation on Personal Emotional Quantum Resonance Fields™. In this dissertation, I was able to show how our unconscious beliefs hold an emotional energy, and that emotional energy becomes transformed into something called a 'Quantum Wave', which in turn builds a Quantum Field.

Towards the end of the twentieth century, a scientist named Alain Aspect examined a few very intriguing features of quantum physics; **quantum communication and wave particle duality.**

Even if you hated physics in school, you will find this fascinating. When Alain Aspect was researching at the University of Paris in the 1980's, he was able to show that a particle could communicate with another particle instantaneously. *Remember that.* Instantaneously, whether that particle was ten feet away, ten centimeters away, or ten billion miles away. No matter how far apart, these subatomic particles could communicate instantaneously.

So what?

Well, wait till you understand what that means when it comes to manifesting!

Physicists like Aspect and the brilliant David Bohm, who was a student of Albert Einstein, believed that consciousness had similar properties. Bohm believed that consciousness, like the subatomic particle, is both local and non-local, and that it, too, can communicate instantly across a distance, no matter how short or long. This means that at a certain level you are able to communicate with all consciousness—with the whole universe, in fact—instantaneously. In physics, this is called **non-local quantum communication**. Bear with me. You will see how relevant this and wave particle duality is to you in creating your reality in just a moment.

To put all this within the framework of what we're talking about here in this book. Let's look at the difference between local and non-local in very easy terms. local means, 'within the perception of your five senses'; non-local is, therefore, at a distance beyond those five senses.

Here, let's say I blow a whistle; you can hear it, and as you travel further away from it, the sound gets weaker and weaker, diminishing in intensity until it is outside your 'local' hearing range. When something is non-local, using the same example, a person could hear that whistle from anywhere in the universe—beyond the local range. What's more, the sound would not diminish with distance.

Okay, back to why you might have some significant interest in all this. You, me, everyone has beliefs. Those beliefs become translated into quantum energy and that energy collectively bonded becomes a Quantum Field, and that Quantum Field is both local and non-local. These beliefs, as a Quantum Field, broadcast out across the universe, instantaneously communicating with all other consciousness.

This field itself, i.e. your QRF , is actually **an attracting force**. By the way, for those of you now interested, as mentioned earlier I also teach an entire program about how to master the Attracting Force™.

> Psst: I have a gift for you…
> You can find out more by now going to a special page I've had my team set up for readers of this book.
> www.AttractingForce.com/bookbonus
> There, you will not only find out about this outstanding 3 day live event you will discover how you can save more than $1,000 on the tuition for you and a friend.

Okay back at it, this attracting force pulls to you everything that matches (or is in-phase with) whatever is in your programmed personal QRF. In essence, what's contained in that field is your unconscious beliefs and the thoughts and feelings that go with them. Or, to put it another way:

Your Resonance Field is your personal genie for manifestation. The problem is that it can only deliver what is programmed into it.

Chapter 14

Lessons from Aladdin

Did you ever read the story of Aladdin when you were a kid? In my adult life I read the original and it was a fantastic and brilliant tale that excited the imagination. While it apparently depicts this young guy who finds a lamp, rubs it, meets a genie and gets three wishes, more importantly, it illustrates how things show up in our lives. If you haven't read the story in years, I would suggest you give it another look because, after reading this book, Aladdin will have a whole other level of depth. It is a wonderful allegory for how manifestation works. Anything that shows up in our lives that we are less than delighted with is there mostly because we don't actually know what we really want or how to ask for what we want! More about that in a bit...

First off, let me point something out: Most people, at least until they truly understand how manifestation works, will complain about what's showing up in their lives. It's important to recognize that there is one major reason for that: Most of us are not clear about what we want. We tend to be more clear about what we don't want while being 'fuzzy' about what we do. We say things like: "I don't want to be fat anymore. Or, I'm sick of being broke; I don't want to struggle anymore." And although it has great value to get clear about what you don't want, if that's all you are clear about you are going to be in trouble.

The beliefs that we hold in our unconscious communicate out to the universe through this Quantum Field I was just telling you about. That field is asking for what you want—the problem is that we're sending out mixed messages. What we consciously say we want and what we are unconsciously communicating can be quite conflicting.

Here, this will clear up what I mean about mixed messages. Imagine walking into a vegetarian restaurant and you are craving steak. I'm going to guess that you will be rather disappointed when your menu arrives. You see, that's a very mixed message. If you want some steak in life, and continually walk into vegetarian restaurants, you will just end up craving a whole lot of steak and eating a whole lot of tofu (and for those of you who are vegans, switch that analogy around and imagine a big juicy steak on your plate instead of some steamed veggies).

Similarly, you might be consciously saying you want healthy partnerships, loving relationships, wealth, and to live in great health, while at the unconscious level you may have a whole bunch of other mixed messages that are derived from your unconscious beliefs that are being broadcast out into the universe. For instance, you can imagine the result of asking for a healthy partnership while unknowingly believing you don't deserve one. That's a mixed message baby! It ain't gonna happen until you find and then obliterate those negative, limited beliefs.

Earlier, I said that, just like Aladdin, you have your own genie and this genie is your QRF that will manifest anything you want. Here's something to keep in mind: This genie isn't bad or good, it's neutral and—more importantly—it's automatic. It simply delivers whatever it's told to deliver.

The beliefs you hold (whether they are conscious or unconscious) become your QRF, and your QRF determines what you are ordering from the universe, and the universe can *only* deliver what you order. That order you place through your QRF, therefore, establishes what you can and cannot attract, because every time you consciously or unconsciously emotionally connect to a belief, it's like rubbing the lamp that activates your wish-granting genie.

Before we move onto examine the concepts of fate, luck, and other myths, I'd like you to remember the analogy of ordering steak from a vegetarian restaurant because recently I was speaking with one of my students who was working at a restaurant when this happened, and it's just perfect:

It had been two days after he finished attending my Quantum Mind Mastery™ workshop and he was driving to work for the first time since. Now, as he was telling me this he was chuckling because during those five days we talked in-depth about intuition and how it will communicate with you whenever you are willing to listen.

So here he is driving towards work, running parts of the material from Quantum Mind Mastery™ over in his head, doing his best to make sense of it when he realized he drove right past the exit he usually takes to get to work. He admitted to thinking that it *could* have been his intuition, yet instead of taking it seriously he joked about it in his own mind and continued off to work.

When he finally got there he felt sick to his stomach and then started seriously considering that it might be his intuition giving him a huge hint on what to do. A few hours later, his mind had drifted on what he should do about this *gut feeling* and something his boss said snapped him back to reality, just not the reality he thought he knew, "Stop what you are doing and get back to work!"

That feeling he felt as he walked through the door swept up so fast inside of him that before he even knew he was talking, he had already said, "No. I quit." I would like to interject here that even as he told me those words, "No. I quit.", his face lit up like a Christmas tree in the dark.

Now, the story doesn't end there. It's not all roses and potpourri. That was merely one choice in one moment, and his ego-mind wasn't ready to let him get away without some guilt.

He spent the next few days agonizing about whether or not he made the right choice. He joked that it felt like a part of him died and it was as if he was mourning it.

If he could have worried about his new plight, he did.

- *How am I going to pay next months rent?*

- *What if I fail, will they take me back?*

- *My family is going to think I'm nuts!*

- *How am I going to justify quitting over missing a stupid turn-off for work and a feeling in my stomach, after all, everybody hates their job, even a little, right?*

His ego-mind dragged him to the next stage: Anger.

- *It's Dōv's fault. He put these crazy ideas about intuition in my mind!*

- *Why couldn't the world be different? It's not my fault.*

- *If I was just a little luckier I wouldn't be in this mess.*

Thankfully, anger didn't last long because he was warned about that many times during the Quantum Mind Mastery program. Even knowing that didn't mean that he wouldn't transition to the next stage: Bargaining.

- *Maybe I can work part time here, and part time doing something I love, and maybe it'll work out, and if it doesn't, at least I'm safe here, right?*
- *Maybe who I am now is all I'll ever be, maybe this is my path, or what God intended for me.*
- *Maybe I should save up a ton of money and THEN make an attempt at living my dream, after all I'm young. I'm not even 30 yet! I have my whole life ahead of me. I've been doing it this long, what's another year, or two? Three to five at most.*

Then depression set in and with desperation comes panic.

- *Great. Nearly everyone I know thinks I'm nuts, or going through some mid-life crisis.*
- *I just walked away from the one sure thing I had.*
- *I'll probably just end up sitting around at home and wind up failing miserably, ending up as a waiter again in no-time.*
- *Can't wait to hear all the "I-told-you-so's".*

Finally, he moved onto acceptance. In his own words:

"I realized that if I want to live the life I dreamed, I have to go out and get it. I have 29 years of proof that it's not going to get handed to me. In fact, in hindsight, as I look back, life has always given me chances and opportunities to bust free and live it: I've been too scared, too comfortable where I was, and too filled up with stupid useless reasons why I would fail or what other people would think about me if I had succeeded OR failed to really put any effort or commitment into doing it."

I can tell you in all honesty that's what he said and what he went through. How? He wrote it into the book himself.

The point is: When you follow your dream there's a good chance that your ego-mind and its conditioning will go crazy, just the way his did. Why? We will get into that in detail a little later in the book. But for now let me just say the reason the ego-mind freaks out is because of fear and to the ego-mind all change is threatening.

One last thing, once this student made his choice to commit to leaving the job and following his dreams, even though he felt like he was riding a rollercoaster of emotions, he kept noticing that life was giving metaphors to wake him up and see how he'd been living. One in particular sticks out:

In the last few days of his old job, his old life, a customer called him over to the table to complain about what he was bringing her. Now, bear in mind she is a regular at that restaurant.

She called him over and said, rather impolitely, "The water you brought me tastes horrible."

He replied, "Oh, I'm sorry, let me bring you a new one."

She barked, "No, it won't help. It's bad every time I come here".

Stunned he replied, "Err, ok. Can I bring you a bottle of water instead?"

"No. I'll just drink this."

He said that he laughed harder than he had in years (not in front of the customer of course). Right there he could see this was a metaphor of how he'd been living his old life, he'd been complaining, while having no interest of changing what he had been complaining about; it was also the push he needed to fully commit to the decision he had made to do what ever it takes to live the life of his. Or as I like to put it: He stopped ordering steak from the vegetarian restaurants of life.

I wonder what metaphors are showing up in your life? It's worth thinking about isn't it?

Let's put this baby into the next gear...

Chapter 15

Fate, Luck, and Other Myths

At one point or another in our lives I think most of us have wondered about fate or luck, as it does 'appear' that some individuals have more of the good version of those things than the rest of us. But what if fate and luck are not random or external, meaning no one and no 'thing' outside of ourselves is creating it? What if without even knowing it we had been generating our own fate and our own luck? Then wouldn't it make sense that once you had the formula for how you generate your fate and your luck you could generate the kind of luck and fate you would prefer?

Right in this moment I want to ask you to open your mind a little wider, because as you let in this next piece you will now begin to regain some of the personal power you had inadvertently given away. I would like you to realize that whether it's consciously or unconsciously, we are each creating our own 'fate' and our own 'luck', and we're doing this by virtue of our unquestioned beliefs. Recognize this now and you are already on the path to creating the life of your dreams!

You know, most of us don't bother questioning the beliefs that we get. We just take them on and accept them as if they were actually ours by choice, when rarely is that the case. The bottom line is your unquestioned beliefs are a big part of generating the QRF you project out into the universe and that field determines what you can and cannot attract. We ignorantly call this our luck or our fate! We're all creating our own luck, fate and reality by virtue of what it is that we believe and by how we're operating in the world in accordance with those beliefs.

Thoughts and Beliefs Create Reality

If you are from my generation or a little older, you might remember an old movie called *Sybil*, which was based on a true story about a woman who had multiple personalities disorder. It is a powerful movie showing how very different reality was for each of the personalities contained within this one woman.

In that same vein, there was an intriguing study done many years ago that I want to share with you about *Multiple Personality Disorder*. I'm going to share this with you because it so well demonstrates the power that our beliefs have over our reality, and it will take that piece about the body-mind connection to a whole other level for you.

In the study, researchers took a blood serum sample from a person with severe multiple personality disorder and found that this individual was diabetic. The evidence in the blood was very obvious and, some would argue, indisputable.

Hold on to your chair tightly because what's compellingly memorable about this study is that this very same person, ten minutes later, was operating out of another personality—and therefore experiencing their reality and their body from a distinctly separate set of beliefs.

Amazingly, when a blood serum was taken of that same person, who was now operating out of a completely different set of beliefs, there was actually *no* sign of diabetes. Here is what's *truly* intriguing: Medical doctors will tell you that diabetes can be managed with medication, although it cannot be cured. If that's true, then how did the individual in this study *have and not have* diabetes when in different personalities? It really begs the question: *How powerful can the effect of human belief be on reality?* I know, it's absolutely fascinating isn't it? Well, take a gasp of air because there are even documented cases where the eye colour of people with multiple personalities changed as they move from one personality to the next.

If we think for a second that we don't create our own reality, we immensely underestimate what we are capable of, and multiple personality research is a fantastic model for us to see how powerful we are.

We can actually change our own bodies!

So what does this mean?

It means *thoughts and beliefs change matter!*

It means *your* thoughts and beliefs change *your* reality!

I bet that for some of you, your ego-mind just went, *huh? What?*

Let's look at the deeper implications of this: The programming that is in your unconscious mind—the underlying thoughts and beliefs that you're not quite aware of 'yet'—*becomes* your Quantum Resonance Field™. And your QRF has a direct affect on what we know as physical matter. This is why there can be conflict about what we want internally and what we tend to get in our external reality, there is conflicting messages between the conscious and unconscious desires.

The result of having unconscious beliefs that conflict with conscious desires is that things show up in your life that don't match what you say you want. Or said another way, when you consciously say you want 'X' yet unconsciously *believe* (or believe you deserve) 'Y', your order gets jumbled up and you end up getting 'Y' some of the time, 'X' occasionally and nothing at all most of the time because 'X' and 'Y' have cancelled each other out... Boom, reality repeats itself. This is why affirmations and positive thinking don't work for most people— they don't really address what's going on underneath the conscious self, at the level of the subconscious mind where our belief systems are held—a level most of us aren't yet aware of.

It doesn't matter how you attempt to apply some form of 'positive thinking' to manifest your reality; it doesn't work because there is a huge step missing. The important thing to recognise is that when we speak of the mind we are speaking of two parts, not one: The conscious and the subconscious and there are two very essential qualities that distinguish these two parts.

Firstly: The conscious mind is way slower than the subconscious mind; in fact scientific research shows that the subconscious mind is over a million times more powerful than the conscious mind. Secondly: Neuro scientists have shown that the conscious mind, as Einstein suggested only operates at about five percent. That means that ninety five percent or more of the time we run our lives from the automatic knee jerk re-actions of the subconscious mind's conditioning. According to the brilliant Dr. Bruce Lipton in his book 'The Biology of Belief'(2005), the subconscious mind processes 20,000,000 environmental stimuli per second verses 40 environmental stimuli interpreted by the conscious mind in that same second.

Think about this, it makes sense, (and excuse my crassness, but I think it's a really good model); 'positive thinking' (i.e. affirmation) is kind of like *Saran Wrap over dog poop*. The Saran Wrap will cover up, possibly disguise the smell; however, it won't get rid of the 'poop' itself—and that's kind of what affirmations and positive thinking do. They appear to cover 'it' (the unconscious issue) up, but they don't deal with 'it'. That being said, until you deal with what's underneath 'it' doesn't go away and *nothing changes*. The QRF draws to you whatever it draws to you *because of what's underneath*.

That's powerful information, isn't it? Think about whom you need to share that with, I know that someone comes to mind right away, and that's good because sometimes we need to share something in order to really get it ourselves. In fact, in order to assist you staying on track I'm going to ask you that question many times throughout this book.

Chapter 16

Why Drug Dealers Can Win the Lottery

Again, it's what is carried in the QRF that is determining what you attract and what you repel, and that's why good things happen to bad people and bad things happen to good people. I'm sure you've known people in both categories. We've certainly all known the wonderful, intelligent, loving, kind, and generous person who always seems to be with an absolute jerk. You know what I'm saying here, the type of jerk who is openly rude and abusive. Yet, this wonderful, intelligent, loving, kind, and generous person keeps attracting these jerks, one after the other, each seemingly worse than the last! By contrast, another person can be extremely manipulative and yet attracts a whole stream of sensational partners who appear to be just hanging around waiting to have a relationship.

Another example still is somebody who is really honest, lives with integrity, and manages to constantly get ripped off. Meanwhile, a drug dealer wins the lottery. You are catching the drift, right? We've all questioned this kind of situation at one time or another and I suggest to you that you start to *really* question it! Now you are learning why bad things happen to good people and why good things happen to bad people.

Perhaps you are even already beginning to see how it's not about good or bad, right or wrong, anymore than it's about colour, race, or religion. So why do bad things happen to good people and vice versa? All situations come from the *resonance* of something I call: **Unconscious Deserving.**

Unconscious Deserving is held in place by a set of beliefs that you have held without question, up until now. This is a set of beliefs that tell us what it is that we deserve, for the most part this is all unconscious and all too often doesn't make sense to the conscious mind. None-the-less whatever it is that we unconsciously believe we deserve is what is being fed directly into our QRF. When you begin questioning your beliefs, you are inadvertently questioning the level of unconscious deserving and as a result you begin changing your QRF. As you begin questioning those unquestioned beliefs, you are beginning to shake the foundation of your old QRF. In doing that, your inner quantum genie starts to bring you very different things!

Exercises for Mastering Your Ego-mind and Getting What You Want
I'll bet you can relate to this. I struggled for years to understand why some people were 'lucky' and others were not. It's what originally inspired me to write this book. If you've read my biography, you may know that I traveled the world to sit at the feet of masters to find true wisdom and to find the answer to that question.

What I found was not that one religion is right and others wrong, what I found was that they all contained answers if we are willing to look beyond the apparent differences. What I learned (in one form or another) was this:

Resonance is the Only Logical Explanation
Resonance! Not luck! Not karma! Not some cruel God with an account

116

book! Resonance is the only explanation that makes sense. Resonance is a scientific word; and therefore, was not likely to be the word that would flow off of a spiritual teacher's tongue. However, it is the word that describes what many of my teachers were sharing.

As you will discover, tapping into and accessing the full spectrum of wealth and abundance has very little to do with many of the things we think it does, like luck, or for that matter even academic education. The difference between someone who constantly struggles and some-one who lives within the flow of abundance is their resonance. Even though living in the full spectrum of abundance is achieved within a psycho-spiritual context, meaning the way you think and feel about the life you have, the real spiritual laws have their own scientific coun-ter parts that are quite tangible.

Stay with me here, because I'm going to show you how giving up those previously mentioned disempowering ideas (karma etc) about why your life is the way it is changes absolutely everything. Believe it or not, whatever is showing up in your life is there because there's a belief in place (and as I keep reiterating, most times that belief is unconscious—i.e. not in your awareness quite yet).

Chapter 17

The Food Chain of Consciousness

Put on your tanks, we're diving deeper into the matrix of personal reality. We now understand that what is showing up in our reality is a result of whatever we have attracted and what we have attracted is whatever is in-phase with what's in our QRF. We now get it that our QRF is held in place by the mostly unconscious beliefs we have held. Therefore, as we go deeper we must ask: So what's holding those old and all too often crappy beliefs in place?

It all comes down to this: Beliefs held in the unconscious mind are still being fed by reoccurring emotions, or emotional energy. The emotional energy comes from your 'unconscious deserving'. However, the challenge can be that your unconscious deserving is defining the resonance for what you attract.

Look at the following diagram that describes this cycle through a self perpetuating system. However, before we go any further, I want to set something straight...as you will discover until we master the ego-mind it is running the system of how we build reality.

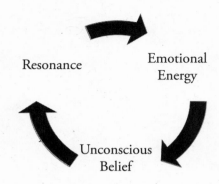

Resonance — Emotional Energy — Unconscious Belief

I'm guessing that some of you are thinking, "Wait a minute! *Fed by emotional energy?* Huh? What is he on about, what does that mean?" Trust that if I elaborate on this term right now it would be premature and confusing and I don't want to get ahead of myself or you. So, bear with me, because I'm going to show you not only how your ego-mind has been running the show but how you can take back the reins and master you're your ego-mind because without being monitored the ego-mind becomes the manifesting mind. In Part III, I cover emotional energy in depth; however, I'm willing to bet that before you even read about it, you will have an intuition as to what it is somewhere in Part II.

The truth is that what you need to know right now is that taking the time to look at your unconscious beliefs is essential when it comes to reclaiming mastery of your ego-mind. After all, you can't fix what you are not aware of... Right?

As we begin to deconstruct how we have created our reality it's easy for your ego-mind to chirp up with some excuse about how it's all too big and you will never be able to do it. Well, let's shoot that one down before it even gets off the ground: You don't necessarily have to start making massive changes to transform your QRF because little changes will reorganize your field, too. Keep that in the forefront of your mind when that nasty little voice in your head wants you to give up.

Chapter 18

Little Changes, Big Effects

In my seminars and workshops, I start the ball rolling by giving participants exercises to help them change very small things. In a moment I'm going to give you an exercise that will demonstrate the power and value of looking at or changing something that is seemingly small.

I'm sure that after all the reading you've done so far you must now be excited to get your hands on one of the exercises I've promised. So, let's start right here with something reasonably small that will get you going in a direction away from what you don't want—and towards what you *do* want.

A few pages back, you read that most of your beliefs have formulated and been held in place because you've never bothered to question or examine them. The first thing that you will need to do is to see a few of your beliefs, because by seeing what had only previously been unconscious you can begin changing your QRF, and in turn attract what you want into your life. Now, I'm going to give you a series of questions to answer and you will want to write down the answer to each question in short, single sentences because I'll ask you to come back later to each of them. You not only want to get this, you need to get this so you can change your life and have what you want! Later, I will also be giving you some other exercises that you can continue with after you have finished reading this book. (Think of it as the book that just keeps on giving).

Okay, let's get started. This is where the integration starts, and remember my purpose here is to have you get the very most you possibly can out of this book. So pick up a pen and some paper and write down five things you believe to be true, (these are your 'true-isms'). No one else need know, so be honest with yourself.

Start now. Just write short single-sentence answers to those five things that you absolutely believe to be true! (On the next page I've left some space for you to write down your answers, or you can get a piece of paper, just make sure before you go on you do the exercise).

To get you started here are some examples, but you don't need to be limited by them.

Now when you've written the question... just let your mind give you the answers. Write down everything that comes to mind, even if there are multiple and contradictory answers, even if the answer that comes doesn't seem to make sense yet.

Money is hard to come by.

It's hard to get in shape.

I'm lucky.

I'm unlucky.

It's hard to find a good man.

It's hard to find a good woman.

God is a man.

Rich people are ruthless.

If I'm poor now, God will make me rich in the afterlife.

Movie stars, musicians, and big corporate CEO's are all over-paid.

Money corrupts good people.

It's spiritual to be poor.

Whatever it is, write it down!

Now that you've finished, stop, take a deep breath, allow yourself to get centered, and ask yourself this question: Why do I believe that?

Go through each of your five answers one-by-one, and allow yourself to answer the question: Why do I believe...(whatever the belief was that you wrote down)?

Don't turn another page; just write down your answers. There is no need to read any further until you have done this exercise.

Belief #1

Belief #2

Belief #3

Belief #4

Belief #5

I asked you to do this exercise before reading on because after you've completed this exercise, everything that follows makes greater sense. It will do so because you will begin feeling the significance of what you've learned by simply allowing yourself to explore your answers.

Okay, I've put my trust in you. You've done the exercise and finished writing your answers, *right?*

Chapter 19

Whose Beliefs Have You Been Believing Anyway?

Now that you've completed the exercise, I have a very simple—yet extraordinarily powerful statement—to share with you.

If you actually take this upcoming statement to heart, you will begin changing any piece of your life about which you are not really happy, because when you truly grab hold of this statement, you will fully understand where I'm coming from here. You will understand how to remove the blocks that are holding you back from living the life you imagine you should be living.

I know you are reading this right now; however, pay close attention, because what you are about to do is very important, so please take a moment and write this down in the first person singular (the personal form is signified by the use of the 'I' statement rather than the generalized 'you' statement).

"I can't honestly claim 'it' as my own if I didn't consciously choose 'it'."

I'm going to repeat that for you again because the implications are mind-blowing.

"I can't honestly claim 'it' as my own if I didn't consciously choose 'it'."

"I can't honestly claim 'it' as my own if I didn't consciously choose 'it'."

Here's the point: It doesn't matter what belief it is— because if you didn't consciously choose it, it's just a belief you took on; therefore, it's not really yours. You don't really own the beliefs you didn't consciously choose as an adult, and as a result, they are a part of your mind that you don't yet own.

I know for some people that can be quite a mind blowing statement, while others just find it hard to believe.

As a thinking person, I challenge you to begin questioning what it is you believe, particularly about yourself. If that little voice in the back of your head is, all too often, whispering that you are not good enough, I want you to understand that it's just a belief because it's not a truth. It's a belief, and not only is it okay, it's *good* to question your beliefs.

Okay seeing as we're in exercise and integration mode, how would you like a totally potent exercise that you can begin applying right here, right now that can dramatically enhance your self-confidence and self-worth? *You would?* Fantastic.

You will be able to do this exercise over the next seven days as part of the process for taking back ownership of your ego-mind. As I promised earlier this is potent!

Another reason you will want to do this exercise is because it helps you turn on that 'inner genie' and have it work for you. Purely as a bonus, you will see that following the exercise for seven days will also raise your self-worth.

126

I'm going to give you two questions that you can ask yourself and the way to get the most out of this exercise is to find multiple answers to each one.

The first question I want you to write down is:
What do the people who love me, love about me?

By the way, if your ego-mind is telling you to do it later, that's a sign that you don't yet have mastery of your ego-mind and this is the time to grab the reins. Feel what I'm saying here: Doing this exercise is another step in taking back ownership of what is rightfully yours, 'YOUR POWER'!

Write the answers down and, if you get stuck, you can always ask someone who loves you what it is about you that's so lovable. Allow yourself to explore all the different aspects of who you are. For example, what do people love about your physicality? Just because you look in the mirror and find all the faults doesn't mean that's what others see.

Think about it. Did one of your previous partners really love your toes, your belly button, your hands, or some other piece of your anatomy that you never really noticed? I know that it never crossed my mind that I had nice ears, yet it's a body part my wife's very complimentary about. You get the idea, right?

Now, do the same with your emotional self, your intellectual self, then go on to your spiritual side. Keep going until you've looked at every aspect of yourself: Your smell, your voice, your laugh, your sense of humour, your faith and that's just a few off the top of my head. I'm sure that you will find some that I haven't even thought of—allow yourself the freedom to explore all the possibly wonderful parts of who you are.

Do this without fail every day for seven days. Write new answers down each day for a full week, and notice how much better you feel about yourself by the end of the week. If you are a real keen learner, do it for a month. Take my word for it, you'll be shocked at the positive and powerful impact of this exercise on your self-confidence, and self-worth, and also on the mastering of your ego-mind away from the old self destructive beliefs. How will you know that you are beginning to master your ego-mind? Well, as you keep practicing these exercises, that voice in your head that so often told you what's wrong with you begins to get quieter and quieter. Just imagine how great that alone would be!

Now, on to the second exercise. This exercise, like the previous one, will boost your self-confidence and begin laying the foundation for you to master your ego-mind. Simply making a commitment and doing these two exercises radically changes your life. How do I know? Well, don't take my word for it, take a look at this...

Steve: He knows the nose.

> Steve is a nice enough looking guy. In fact, many people would make statements about how he was good looking. Steve however, just couldn't see it. When he caught a glimpse of himself in the mirror or in a store window all he could see was his nose. To him his nose was an ugly, crooked mass that took all his attention. Now the fact is, to my eye and everyone I had seen around Steve, there was absolutely nothing wrong with his nose. That, however, didn't stop him obsessing over how ugly it was to him.
>
> Now, at this point, you might be thinking the guy's

obviously just vain and needs to get a grip on reality. However, that statement ignores the fact that we all live in our own subjective reality. You see, I had sat down with Steve on many occasions and he in no way struck me as a vain person and, in some ways, he was anything but vain.

Steve and I worked on this issue for a little while and I had him go through the exercises. When asked to answer something he absolutely believed, you can guess it, he wrote: I have an ugly nose. I then asked him to examine that statement again from the perspective of whether this was, in fact, his own belief. He immediately snapped back: "Of course it's my belief, I'm the one who just said it."

"That doesn't make it yours originally."
Steve look baffled.
"What do you mean?"

Looking him straight in the eye, I could see that despite his snappy response a minute ago, he really wanted to get this.

"Steve, if you didn't consciously choose it, it's just a belief you took on; therefore, it's not really yours, it's just a message that was given to you and you have been repeating it as if it was real. However, repeating it as if it were real doesn't make it real."

Even though Steve is a really good guy he tends to keep his feelings close to his chest. However, when

I'd finished telling him how there's a good chance this is just a belief he took on, his eyes automatically filled up with tears and softly spilled over onto his face in relief.

In that moment the light went on where there had only been darkness for Steve: "I never made the connection before, but my aunt would grab my nose when I was a kid. She would tell me how much I reminded her of my grandfather and, to be honest, I saw it as a compliment. I had seen her with him and she clearly both loved and respected the man."

Steve took a long breath: "But the piece that had never tied in before was that I would hear her and other family members talking about grandfather's 'ugly nose'. How weird is that? Is it possible that I took my aunt's message about me being like my grandfather and made it about my nose?"

I was filled with compassion and I said: "You tell me Steve, you are the one who no matter how many times you've been told the contrary has believed he has an ugly nose."

"Wow, that's nuts."

I shook my head: "No, that's what happens when we take on a belief without questioning whether it's true for us or not. I know you thought this was your own belief, but the fact is you can't honestly claim 'it' as your own if you didn't consciously choose it to start with."

For the next thirty days Steve did the: What do the people who love me, love about me, exercise. Within the first two weeks his previously unmovable belief about his 'ugly nose' was absolutely nowhere to be found. To use Steve's own words: "It just didn't make sense anymore."

Let's get back to your next integration exercise: This exercise is about the success you've had in your life. Before we go any further, I want you to know that I know we have all walked around at one time or another with a set of ideas about where we 'should' be and how that doesn't measure up to where we actually are. I know that at the point of asking people to tell me about their successes, so many people's minds go blank or worse, become dismissive and tell you that they either haven't had any success or none worth mentioning. If that's you... Do yourself a favor and do the integration exercise anyway. You will love yourself for it! Pushing through it will give you a much better sense of who you are, while demonstrating to you that you are in fact capable of much greater things than you could have ever imagined.

Before you start, there are a couple of very important guidelines that go with this exercise:

    1) It doesn't matter what category your success falls in
    2) Your successes are not comparable to anyone else's

Alright, with that in mind, ask yourself this question:
What has been my greatest achievement?

Next to that write:
What were the achievements that led to the big one?
(No success comes without a whole bunch of smaller successes that were the stepping stones to the big one).

Remember even if your ego-mind says that you've never achieved anything worth mentioning find something that's not worth mentioning and start there.

Next to that write: **What else did I achieve?**

And beside this write: What else was my greatest achievement?

Then repeat:
What were the achievements that led to the big one?
(Again, no success comes without a whole bunch of smaller successes that were the stepping stones to the big one).

Write the answers down and again, if you get stuck, you can always ask someone who loves you; because chances are that person sees your successes better than you do yourself. Again, allow yourself to explore all the different aspects of your life; and this is not all just about financial or career success. For example, there's the success of leaving an unhealthy relationship, or even making the decision to leave. There's the success of taking the steps towards doing something you really want to do, even though it scares you half to death. There's the success of putting yourself into therapy, or leaving a job that was draining your soul. For that matter, there's the success of getting your hands on this book, committing to reading it, doing the exercises, and integrating it into your life. The point here is that success is not about doing bigger things than someone else; it's about doing things that are big for YOU.

> *"Success is not about doing bigger things than someone else;*
> *it's about doing things that are big for YOU."*
> *~ Dõv Baron*

I'm going to ask you to commit to doing the above exercises for a minimum of seven days (although longer is better) first thing in the morning! In other words, get your butt out of bed ten minutes earlier, fifteen minutes earlier—whatever it takes—and write those questions and answers down every morning before you start your day. It's life changing!

Imagine what will happen to the beliefs you have about yourself after you do these few simple and potent exercises, even if it's only for seven days. Without doing anything else, focus on just this —*on what people love about you and about what you've achieved*—and you will be blown away because things will change. Do you hear what I'm saying? Do you get the idea? Remember I said you don't have to do a massive thing, that you can shift your field by doing the little things first. And I know you can do these integration exercises I have just given you. You don't have to do momentous acts. It's just as significant to focus on very small features, and the more of those minor aspects we note, the better your life gets.

> *"Life is changed by the little decisions we make*
> *and the little things that we do accumulatively."*
> ~ *Dõv Baron*

Remember, how you got to where you are was not because of one grand decision you made at fourteen, eighteen, or even twenty-five years of age. How you got to be where you are in life is through all the tiny decisions you made along the way. Each little decision is either moving you closer to, or further away from the life you dream of.

Chapter 20

The Common Denominator:
The Case For and Against Adoption

Before picking up this book, was there a part of you that had been living with the idea that it's not okay for you to be, let's say, more successful than your mom or your dad? (or your brother, sister, best friend, or for that matter anyone else?) If you said yes ... . Question it! That's a belief. It's a belief that your ego-mind is running, and as you've already begun to understand that doesn't make it true!

Here's another example: If you are running the idea that you will never find a loving partner ... that's also a belief! Question it! If whatever is running in your mind does not empower you, it's holding you back. Ideas come from beliefs, and here's what I want you to understand: Until we become conscious of the beliefs we have been running ninety-nine percent of them are adopted! *Yes, ninety-nine percent!*

> *"Whatever is running in your mind*
> *that does not empower you,*
> *is holding you back."*
>
> ~ *Dõv Baron*

135

So really let yourself know this, say to yourself, **"I now understand this! Ninety-nine percent of all my beliefs were adopted, without consideration, without question."**

Now, at the risk of sounding like a broken record pointing this out every chance I get, but it really is important that you get this: *Your unconscious beliefs determine everything that you attract and everything you repel.*

Here's the thrilling news about what you've just learned (or the horrific news, depending on how you want to look at it): *The two things we all have in common with our experiences are:*
   1) Ourselves
   2) Our beliefs

I'll say it again; so that you can really let it sink in—it's that important. What you have in common with every experience in your life is 'yourself' and your 'beliefs'. Or as the heading suggested: **You are the common denominator in your experience.**

So, by first questioning the beliefs that you've adopted throughout your life you can begin changing your resonance and in turn your QRF. Because those old beliefs have been supporting the field you were broadcasting out into the universe, *determining everything that you attract and everything you repel* (bet you didn't think I'd sneak that statement in that quickly again, did you).

Once you understand that those beliefs are actually not ones that you have chosen, many of them simply go away. And once they go away, that changes your QRF! When your QRF changes, you change what 'frequency' you are resonating at, which in turn changes what you are attracting, which changes your fate, and your luck, and that is how you begin attracting exactly what you want!

Have you noticed that sometimes you are reading and you are a few pages into reading when you realize you have no clue what you just read? And, it may have been something very important. Well, you don't want that to happen at this juncture, so just stop for a moment and really let that last section seep in. If need be, go back and read it again, highlight it and take some notes as this is powerful stuff and it will change your life if you let it.

Chapter 21

Why Would Anyone Adopt Limiting or Derogatory Beliefs?

So, let me quickly summarize and review; we've taken some quality time to find out about the beliefs you've been carrying around. If you've done the exercise a few pages back where you wrote down 5 (or more) beliefs you had and asked, "Why do I believe that," you've discovered that many of those beliefs were not actually your own, but rather beliefs you had adopted.

That still begs the question: Why would anyone adopt someone else's beliefs, particularly ones that are limiting the amount of joy, love, abundance, or any other terrific thing that we can experience in this life? The answer might surprise you because it's probably not what you think.

The limited beliefs that you adopted, particularly about yourself, were adopted for some very simple, yet enormously important reasons:

1. You wanted (no, let me correct that—you NEEDED) to be loved and accepted. You see at the most basic level your survival as an infant depends on those around you taking care of you.

And...

2. Your survival also depended upon your ability to let in the dominant programs of your community. That means being able to 'download' the 'appropriate' language, behavior etc, as this is a very important part of how we are biologically designed for survival.

To support this integration during the first five to six years of your life your mind is in a state known as a hypnogogic trance. It's at this level of brain wave activity your mind records all experiences of your world, and stores the information for future reference. (The hypnagogic state is still available to us after the age of six, it's just that, at that time, that's from which we are operating on a full time basis. Our EFM (Equation for Manifestation™) Audio Technology™ is specifically designed to put you into this state so that what you want to go directly into your subconscious has a much better chance of doing so).

The answer to why you and the rest of us got stuck with some crappy ideas about who we are and what we are capable of is because we were afraid that if we didn't adopt these often half-baked, limited ideas, someone would or some group would reject us, they wouldn't love us, we'd be all alone and maybe we wouldn't be able to survive.

It's actually this need to be loved, accepted and fitting in that keeps us holding onto many of those crappy beliefs that control everything we're experiencing and how we experience it. Limited beliefs limit us by their control over what we believe we are capable of achieving.

In Part II of this book I'll talk about how our ego-minds twist and shape reality to have us 'fit it'. I'll use the terms *lenses and maps* when we get there. Understanding how our minds use lenses and maps to colour and plot out our experiences answers so many of the questions you might have about why people see things from one perspective or another. You see, we often have filters in place, and they are there for good reasons. One of which is because without them we believe that we would be lost. That may seem a little puzzling right now, but that's a good sign. That means you are really thinking about what you are reading here. Just keep your senses open, and as you read Part II, so much of what we covered here in Part I will start not only falling into place but also become more integrated into the way you empower yourself.

Until then, all you will need to understand is this:

"The outer limits of your experiences will never be greater than the limitations of your adopted beliefs."

~ Dõv Baron

Listen my friend, it may have been all right (and maybe even necessary) to adopt beliefs without question when you were a little kid, because as kids we are so naturally desperate to be loved and need to be taken care of. Back when you were three, or four, or even as old as ten, those beliefs might have been okay. But many childhood adopted beliefs are not very useful, or particularly empowering if you are thirty-five, forty-five, or eighty-five years old!

If the phrases, "That's what I grew up with" or "Those were my family values," or "That's the way it is because that's the way it's always been" bring any sort of comfort or feeling of justification when you look at your beliefs, remember this: If our beliefs remain unquestioned, we can't claim to fully be adults because we may be running our adult lives with a set of beliefs that belong in a child's reality.

Many people are living with a voice in their head that has been there

DON'T READ THIS... YOUR EGO WON'T LIKE IT

since childhood; a voice that's telling them that *they just can't, they are not capable, or they are not good enough!*

One of the big things about adopting these beliefs in order to gain love, or to fit in, is that we get the idea that we must put others first in order to survive. Although the theory is sound (if you are a small child), in practicality, this is self-destructive behavior which leaves us with the feeling that we need to check-in with someone else as to whether or not we're 'okay' or on the right track. I don't know about you, but I don't want to second-guess myself or have to check-in with someone else to know whether or not I'm happy with my decisions. Hence, the necessity to question our beliefs.

Even though this may have been the way your ego-mind has run your life, the important thing is that *you can change this pattern now*!

Where do you start?

Let's get down to business: You have to put YOU first!

Think about it this way: **You can't truly take care of others until you learn how to take care of yourself first.**

Chapter 22

Am I on First?

M any of us grew up with the idea, no, the belief that we must put others first, and although I'm all in favor of us all taking care of each other, if you are not in the mix your life is going south faster than last night's dinner. If you have been carrying the idea/belief that you have to put others ahead of you, then you can look at your own life to see the kind of results that have been achieved. As stated, most of us got this message about putting everyone else first, loud and clear.

What you may want to pay a lot of attention to is that in your hunger to fit in you may have gone a little over the edge on this one. You know how much you have done to win their love. You know how much you have done to win their approval, and as long as you keep running that program in your mind, you will get the same result you always have: Failure! It never works, because the resulting and consequent feelings are an emotional emptiness that can't be filled with even more approval, more money, more toys, more booze, more sex, more drugs, more rock and roll, or more *anything*.

Sharon: *"Of course I'll help, there in a moment, I'm just taking my anxiety meds."*

Sharon was without doubt the reigning champion of; everyone and everything else first. Every day had been a long series of actions planned out within her mind down to the minutest detail about how to please everyone. The problem was that by the time Sharon was in her mid twenties she was a walking anxiety attack. Every act she did to please others was followed by a thousand self doubting thoughts about how it, whatever she had said or done, might be misinterpreted.

Of course, Sharon didn't think of what she was doing as trying to win love or approval. For her she was just a 'giving person' who liked to help. However, it was evident that all that 'help' was completely burning her out and what was just as apparent was how deeply lonely she was.

Sharon like so many of us, had never learned how to take care of herself first and as a result she was unconsciously living in hope that if she took care of enough people enough of the time, someone would take care of her in return. It was becoming obvious even to Sharon that it wasn't working.

This is the manifesting ego-mind in action.

Let's go back to earlier on in the book: A few chapters back, I shared with you a story about a lady named Suzanne. Remember how she struggled when things were going great or when things seemed too easy?

144

What I didn't mention was that Suzanne's mother had always told her, for as long as she could remember, that the women in her family were unlucky. Particularly, they were unlucky in love, especially when it came to finding a decent guy. Her mother, an alcoholic drama queen, had driven every decent guy out of her life—including Suzanne's father—and continually pursued dysfunctional relationships. Maybe you can imagine what it would be like to grow up in that kind of environment and what kind of beliefs it would tattoo into your mind.

The message relayed by Suzanne's mother about the lack of luck experienced by women in her family imprinted a set of beliefs that affected Suzanne's own perceptions. As a result of her mother's training and dysfunctional reality, that set of beliefs was what Suzanne had unconsciously and without question adopted. Without ever realizing it herself she was unconsciously following in her mother's footsteps.

Up to that point, if you would have asked Suzanne if she thought that maybe she was following her mom's path, she would have said, "That's ridiculous!" She would have told you that her own health was good; she had never been unemployed and no one would have ever considered her an alcoholic. On all those counts Suzanne would have been correct, but as is so often the case, the big one, the one that's causing the most damage is the one that we are often most blind to.

You have already begun learning how we've all, at some time or another, adopted the beliefs around us because we wanted to be loved and accepted. Knowing that, is it any wonder that Suzanne had partners who treated her badly? Is it any wonder that she didn't know what to do with 'the man of her dreams'; a man who treated her well?

Of course not!

Is it any wonder that Suzanne became less and less available to the man of her dreams, and more and more available to her alcoholic, drama-queen mother?

No, of course not!

Like everyone else who has never examined their reality, Suzanne was drawn to what she found familiar—even if it was draining her soul—and *unconsciously repelled* from what was not familiar, and—in her case—what was unfamiliar was what's healthy.

The resonance of the beliefs that Suzanne had adopted from her mom (especially that the women in her family didn't have any luck when it came to finding decent guys) had drawn abusive relationships to her. Another thing that you could notice is how the belief Suzanne carried about 'love and men' set up a 'lack of' mentality when it came to Suzanne's unconscious deserving.

This is where it gets juicy, because in a moment you will see how the concepts of unconscious beliefs you adopted and the urge to *fit in* snap together. Beyond the illusory feelings of comfort gained by believing that luck or fate was to blame for her bad relationships, Suzanne also unconsciously adopted limited beliefs in order to bond, *to fit in*, to feel loved by her mom. As a result, she was still unconsciously pursuing her mother's affections—a mother who was actually incapable of healthy love—while actively ignoring someone who would genuinely give her healthy love.

Again, I want to urge you to stop for a moment and think about what you've just discovered and how some version of it may be playing out in your life. Because, with what I have shared with you so far, understand that it is a *belief-action cycle* and it is an example of the manifesting mind in action.

The beliefs you adopted, either out of fear (they might not love me or they could hurt me if I don't accept this belief) or out of love (I love them and they love me so 'it's only right' that I accept this belief) were embraced in order for you to fit in, be loved, or just survive. Do me a favor, and re-read that last paragraph. Honestly the gravity of it is profound.

Each one of those beliefs that were adopted holds an emotional energy that has been setting up your QRF and your QRF has drawn to you situations, circumstances, people, and things that are consistently in line with whatever is held deep in your subconscious mind. Keeping that in mind as you remember that your field is made of the beliefs you adopted: Beliefs you get to change if you don't like the result they are bringing you.

Chapter 23

It's An Elegant,
Non-Judgmental Universe

To the holographic universe, which reads and responds to your QRF, there is no right or wrong—there is just what you are communicating to it and the results you get.

The universe also doesn't look at where or from whom your beliefs came from. A belief, and what that belief attracts, isn't bad or good because the universe doesn't look at it that way. It's just a quantum frequency wave. Let's put it this way: Your belief systems are like orders in a restaurant. The orders are taken unquestioningly and given to the kitchen, the cook cooks them, and the server delivers them to you. You can't blame the server or the cook if it's you who was unclear in your order by sending a mixed message.

Manifestation via your beliefs works in exactly the same way. The universe delivers whatever is in that QRF. You may or may not actually understand how it works. Then again, you may not actually understand how something like electricity works—and it still works! You can be certain of that!

Just like electricity, the quantum field doesn't judge where it goes or what it does. Electricity can cook your food, feed you, and as a result, save your life. OR it can cook you and take your life.

Your QRF, like the universe doesn't judge whether you like or dislike what you are attracting. Until you are consciously directing your quantum field by consciously choosing your beliefs (and consciously removing certain limited beliefs that you've adopted), you are certain to get unwanted results. The universe will always just keep on delivering your order right to you! And if those adopted unconscious beliefs are not checked, if they remain in an unquestioned place, then sorry, the fact is you are going to keep getting more of what you don't want.

Just so you know, all the concepts and terms we've discussed up until now, that for some people (not you, of course) seemed incomplete at times, will be covered in full detail in Parts II and III.

Insights into the Quantum Mind Mastery™ Program

Some of you may have thought, "Where does this Dôv Baron guy come up with this stuff?" I'll tell you. Much of this book is based on the five-day, life-changing, immersive program I teach called Quantum Mind Mastery™. You will be able to find out more details about this program by visiting: www.QuantumMindMastery.com/bookbonus

In this program, I teach you how to uncover and change those unconscious beliefs that are creating your QRF which is determining what you attract and repel. Here's what's wonderful about using the skills, techniques, and tools from the Quantum Mind Mastery™ Program. You will begin resonating with what you want to attract and what you truly deserve, and you will begin doing it right away.

Due to the fact that the Quantum Mind Mastery™ Program is experiential, the changes are suprisingly fast and long-lasting. From the beginning you will see that the program involves a progressive development of consciousness which steadily collapses the limited beliefs that you have, beliefs which are creating the pain and limitation in your life. Now, how is that significant? Cast your thoughts back to the beginning of this book when I shared with you the six foundations of Full Spectrum Success. You heard me say that the sixth foundation for total success is mastery of wisdom, and this wisdom is in evidence when we take the information we have and put it into action. This book is packed full of knowledge; the wisdom, as you know, lies in taking action. The Quantum Mind Mastery™ Program offers you the opportunity to steadily, over a period of five days, watch your old limiting belief systems start to collapse under the realization that what they were built on can no longer stand.

What kind of impact would that have in your life?

Again, we believe in rewarding action.

You can find out more by now going to a special page my team has set up as a reward for readers of this book. Simply go to ... www.QuantumMindMastery.com/bookbonus

There, you will not only find out about this outstanding five-day live event, you will also discover how you can save more than $1,000 on the tuition for you and a friend.

Here's how it works: In this program, we actually shock your belief systems. There is a very deep level of learning that goes on. We use plenty of music, exercises, and even movie clips. My role (in case you haven't guessed), is to be there in your face, to push you and to support you to get past your blocks and to become your absolute very, very best. I believe you are way more than your conditioning, I believe there is greatness within you, and I am committed to you becoming who you were born to be.

Chapter 24

How Do You Know
that You Know?

I want to give you a warning that relates to what you learned in the Six Foundations of Full Spectrum Success: It has taken me more than twenty years of research to develop the Quantum Mind Mastery™ Program. Over that time, I've heard many people tell me how much they know. "Oh, Dōv, I've taken this program, I've taken that program." Or, "I know this, and I know that."

Frankly, many of those who spoke this way were people whose lives were clearly not going in the directions they claimed they wanted their lives to go. So my response is simple and direct: "Are you really doing what you learned in the programs you took? Because **if you are not doing it, you don't know it!**"

Personally I think that's a good guideline for discovering if you really know something. **You only really know it, if it's what you do.**

I promise you this: Throughout this book, and during the Quantum Mind Mastery™ Program, you will be doing what you are learning. That's why I'm giving you the exercises here and in the workshop. You will be using the acquired information, knowledge and tools during the program. You will integrate that information, knowledge and tools to make it second nature after the program is completed so as to take the knowledge and make it into wisdom!

From Poverty to a Manifesting Mind
I know that some of you reading this book are loyal students of my work, and therefore know a little bit of my history. However, even if you know my history, I'd like to go back to one piece of my past because it's relevant to what we're talking about here.

When you were a kid, did you have a bike? I did. It was one of my great salvations. No matter how bad things got, I could always get on my bike and cycle away from the problems. I loved my bike! On my single-gear, home-made-from-scrap-parts bike, I would ride off into a land of freedom, which was anywhere away from my pain.

Pushing down on the peddles, I would suddenly be aware of the pump ... legs filling with blood to such an extent that they felt like over-filled balloons that could burst at any moment. Still ... .

I would keep pedalling until something changed. The screaming in my head that echoed my emotional pain would eventually get quiet, and I no longer noticed anything other than the wind on my face as I sailed down some hill, arms extended out to the sides, legs also out at the sides of the front wheel and, in the words of the great Martin Luther King Jr., I would feel, *"Free at last, free at last, thank God almighty, I am free at last."*

Throughout my childhood, I suffered strange pains in my legs and back, pains that were often so debilitating, many times I would have to drag myself along the floor on my belly.

My mom, in her concern, took me to several doctors, who gave her a range of diagnoses, from growing pains to early onset of rheumatism. I have to say, if those were growing pains I should have been making millions in my twenties as the tallest NBA star. (I'm five feet eight —so that clearly didn't happen!) Time went by, and no one really had an answer for what was causing this often-crippling affliction. At eighteen I'd had enough; I was waking up every day with severe back pain and the torment in my legs just kept getting worse. People would think I was crazy because the only thing that would ease the pain in my knees was for me to punch them as hard as I could.

Filled with equal amounts of physical pain and the emotional frustration of not knowing why I was suffering, I went to my doctor and asked to be sent to a specialist. Along I went, looking for an answer, and even more importantly, *relief*. After a very extensive exam with someone I was told was one of the leading experts in the country, I was diagnosed with the 'incurable' *dis*ease called *ankylosing spondylitis*. I was told that, by the age of twenty-one I would be in a wheelchair, and there was nothing 'they' could do about it.

The diagnosis came at a point in my life when, after leaving school and going out in the world, I was still living on the edge of poverty, looking for a job to pay the rent, and attracting extremely dysfunctional relationships. My dreams of freedom were way beyond getting on my bike to find peace; I now had dreams of travel to exotic places and equally exotic experiences.

As you can well imagine the specialist's diagnosis felt more like a verdict of death delivered to an eighteen-year-old life filled with dreams. Visions of walking along thickly wooded mountain paths filled with the fragrance of exotic flowers leading to hidden temples in far away locations were fading faster than a ten year old's belief in Santa Claus.

It was devastating, and this time my bike could not get me away from that kind of pain.

Fortunately, I already had some mental training from a few teachers and books. I began using what I knew and three years later, at the age of twenty-one, I left the northern industrial city I'd grown up in and seriously began my journey of self discovery. . .wheelchair-free.

I'm not telling you all this to impress you and have you think I'm in any way better than you, quite the contrary actually. I'm telling you all this because by using some of the techniques taught in this book and in the Quantum Mind Mastery™ program, you will develop the mindsets and skills necessary to tackle anything you need to work through to change your life—just as surely as I have mine.

I'll bet that right about here, there are a few of you who are thinking, *it seems rather incredible that with the help of a few books and teachers you made such a vast shift in your life!*

Well, it's true. In fact, in Part II of this book I talk about a caller I had on the radio who said nearly the exact same thing. She said, "It can't be that easy."

It can be.

It really can be.

I know that because I've gone from that young man living in poverty with a diagnosis of a crippling *dis*ease, to living in one of the most beautiful cities in the world, with panoramic views of ocean and mountains.

As I write this, I am looking out of my window at my flowers, and the sun is shining. It's absolutely spectacular! All the colours of nature surround me—there are yellows, reds, and purples.

It's very, very, beautiful and I am very, very grateful.

All the beauty I just referred to is magnificent; however, as so few people realize, it's the quality of your relationships that determines the quality of your life. The greatest blessing of my life is that I am married to the woman of my dreams, and I thank the creative force of the universe and my resonance for having her in my life. I am surrounded by people whom I love and who love me. I'm doing work that deeply fulfills my soul and have been for a very, very long time now.

The work that I do has me spring out of bed with genuine excitement every morning, even when I am up working till three a.m. the night before (as I was many times, writing this book). I get out of bed delighted and grateful to be teaching what I know, even when it's through the words on these pages!

As a result of using the techniques that I'm teaching you, I feel connected to the universe, because I'm actively manifesting my reality the way that I design it. By the way, I'm also in fabulous health and about a million miles away from that wheelchair that I was diagnosed to be in at twenty-one. Of course, this has all become possible by using the techniques and skills I've put together—the same ones that you will be taught throughout this book, and should you decide to attend one of my live events, there too.

I'm telling you this because you, like me, can change your mind, beliefs, resonance, and life, to attract exactly what you want. And you can do it now! Because if I can do it, overcoming absolute poverty (and by that I mean emotional poverty, mental poverty, financial poverty, all the poverties that I was coming from), then you can certainly do it, too!

Chapter 25
Living The Life of Your Dreams

Do you want things to get better? I know that may sound like a silly question, but listen, how many of you answered yes, yet barely put any passion behind it—if any at all. Did you feel any chills up and down your spine as you said yes? It may seem like I'm badgering you or being long-winded but if you don't *feel* the emotion and excitement behind your 'yes', then you are not fully commiting yourself to mastery of your ego-mind. I understand it's harsh to say that, but it's the truth. In order to make change; in order to reclaim mastery of your ego-mind you need to be excited and passionate to do so or, like that exercise bike in your garage collecting dust, *it ain't gonna happen.*

As you read on you will fully understand the importance of using excitement, to propel you in the direction of your dreams.

For those of you reading this wanting to feel some excitement growing inside you, I'm going to run you through a little imagination exercise; I'm going to ask you to come with me for a moment on a little journey.

Now, one way of doing this is to simply read it to yourself, which is okay. An even better way would be to record yourself reading this slowly and clearly then playing it back while you are sitting comfortably with your eyes closed. In fact, I recommend that you listen to the tape of yourself reading this every day for a month. Then you can write to me how wonderful you feel having done it and the impact it has had on your life.

For those of you who are couples, I deeply hope that you will take the time to read this small two paragraph section to each other! The effect it would have on your life would be so immense... So here goes ...

Imagine You Are Now Living the Life of Your Dreams
What would be all around you? Picture the details...see the house you are living in, what kind of furniture do you own, what colour is it, reach out and touch it, is it soft and fuzzy or leathery? Make the picture in your mind brighter and bigger and see how beautiful it is. Now slow down for a moment and look down, are you wearing socks and if you are how do your socks feel on your feet? As you begin looking up notice what color are your walls and the floors and how does it feel to be there? Now, notice the sounds around you, is there any music playing in the background, if so turn up the volume of what it would sound like to be living in the life of your dreams! Just listen to what it sounds like to be there, and then dive deeper into the experience, take a sniff... and smell success!

Taste your success; notice that the life of your dreams has a flavour and... taste it...and then run your hands across the images you made in your mind of living the life of your dreams, and feel what it feels like...dive even deeper and feel what it feels like inside...**feel the wonderful emotion of living the life of your dreams**. This can all be yours! You can live the life of your dreams. Take control of your beliefs as your mind begins developing Quantum Mind Mastery™. Do it now because... it's your life, and you get to decide how it goes from here on in.

Now take a deep breath and let it all sink in.

It is your divine right to have the life you want.

I want to remind you of something that you may have forgotten. *It is your divine right to have the life you want! It's your divine right to be inspired!*

The word 'inspired' comes from the Latin 'inspiritus', which is to be in spirit. *It is your divine right to desire,* and 'desire' means 'of the Father'. It is your divine right to desire, and it is your spiritual nature to do so. Do you remember the teaching that says "Let us create mankind in our own image?" Well, what if you were created to be/with the purpose of being a creator of your own reality? Let me tell you a secret: You are already unconsciously a very powerful manifester.

Please remember this because it's time to use your powers to manifest consciously—to bring to yourself the life of your dreams—because you, like me, deserve to live in the full spectrum of abundance as it applies to all six of the Foundations of Success.

Think back, a few chapters ago, I shared with you that your life's direction is not determined by the massive changes you make, it's by all the gradual shifts you consistently make adding up to huge results in your resonance field.

Each of those little changes are the result of a decision, and you will need to make the decision to do what it takes. You need to do that now! Pay attention here, because as I've shared, much of this book's content is based on the Quantum Mind Mastery™ program. There will be times reading this book where you wish I would have dove a little deeper with some of the explanations and I wish I could, except there's no way I can cram five-days of information into every corner of this book.

I'm not saying, "Be at my program, you have to be there!" That's not what it's about. There's nothing I'd love more than having you come and experience one of our life-changing programs and for us to meet in person. However, what I am saying is, "Use this information, please!" Take this information that I've given you here, within these pages, and use it: Really, really use it! Apply all that you've learned even if in the beginning you felt a little hesitant because within these pages is enough knowledge to completely change your life—so use it!

Remember, you can learn through joy or you can learn through pain and in the words of one of my favorite, and widely-known teachers, Master Yoda, "Fear leads to anger. Anger leads to hate. Hate leads to suffering."

Fear Keeps You Stuck, Fear Keeps You IN Pain
Pay attention to what's going on around you. If the governmental machine wants to keep you believing that this world is a scary place, and that they are your only hope—or if your family, friends, spouse, and those around you want to keep you down, even if they think they are doing it out of love—you will need to stand up and fight for what it is that *you* want. You need to claim your divine right to live the life that you desire. Remember, in order to help others you are required to help yourself first!

Now, I've already given you a ton of powerful information to remember and apply and I hope you've been taking notes as you read. There's still a little more before I finish up this section. I'll warn you, this next section is short, yet straight forward. The next thing you read in bold may sound a bit ruthless, but I promised to be honest with you. Here goes.

Chapter 26

Misery Loves Company

Okay, I know you've heard that before. You maybe even asked what's so bad about that, right?

Take a moment and underline it and before you read on, consider what that saying means to you: *Misery loves company.*

Underlined? Good.

Here's what it means to me: If you are inspired and you want to live the life of your dreams, though you've been struggling, then your *resonance* has attracted to you other people who are *also* inspired but struggling.

Remember, misery loves company. So **don't expect those who have given up and lost sight of their dreams and aspirations to support you in yours.**

There it is. I said it and I meant it. Get yourself around people who want to be successful; people who are successful; and people who are aspiring to be *more* in every aspect of their lives; people who are living the way you want to live.

A Further Quick Review of What We've Learned So Far.

Here's where I would like to take a moment and review what we've covered up to this point. It may not seem like it, but we've covered so much in such a short time.

I've gone ahead and recorded in very brief form what we've discussed to help you absorb all of this. If any of it seems fuzzy, or you don't recall some sections, then I encourage you to go back and re-read those areas because it's very important you understand all of this in order to reclaim mastery of your ego-mind. As we delve deeper into the material, I promise you that you will be amazed at how the statements and quotes in this book have meaning that run on many different levels.

So, let's go back now, not only to where we left off, but to where we began.

In Part I we talked about the six foundations of the Full Spectrum of Success and described what each of these foundations are:

- Physical Mastery

- Financial Mastery

- Relational Mastery

- Intellectual Mastery

- Spiritual Mastery

- Mastery of Wisdom

If reading those foundations didn't spark a clear understanding of what they were and how to master them, don't worry. You can always flip back and re-read the areas of mastery you feel unfamiliar with.

Meanwhile, to quickly recap, most of us have grown up with a singular vision of what success is: Money.

What people eventually discover is that success through the singular vision of financial mastery leaves them lacking fulfillment in the other areas of their lives. Most of us come to realize the need to master all six foundations for what I call 'Full Spectrum of Success'.

Remember, if you don't own your ego-mind, the ego-mind will own you, and it will not allow you to master those foundations.

Back to the review ...

I asked: How do you know if the beliefs you carry are your own; where or whom did they come from, did they form when you were a child, a teen or in adulthood? By the way, if they are not your beliefs, then whose are they?

I asked you to imagine how your life would have been different if you began to question your beliefs.

When I started questioning my beliefs I know what I imagined: A world of abundance on so many levels, instead of a world of 'not enough'.

Remember: Anyone or anything that tries to set a limit on what you can achieve in life is lying to you and holding you back.

I'll ask you again, why would you ever adopt a belief that's not your own and disempowering you? The answer to that question hasn't and will not change: To fit in and to be loved.

That is why we accept crappy beliefs and pessimistic outlooks on life. That is the same reason why some of us can feel trapped. Don't worry, the keys to unlock the box you feel trapped in will literally pop off the page as you read on.

I spoke about how your Quantum Resonance Field™ is an attracting and repelling force of energy that acts as your own personal genie (like Aladdin). I explained how it brings you anything you want—although it can only bring you what it's programmed with. Since we program our QRF through our conscious and unconscious beliefs, if we change our beliefs, we can change what we create in our lives. This, right here, is another reason why you should be practicing those exercises I gave you, daily—so you start attracting the things you want.

We went over how some people mistakenly confuse resonance with fate or luck.

More specifically, you learned how your unconscious deserving influences what you can and cannot attract in life. In fact, it doesn't matter how hard you work towards something—you may even be pushing it further away—because the resonance of old beliefs held within unconscious deserving can trump your conscious efforts in the long run.

What you have mistakenly labeled as luck is really your QRF in action, drawing the people and situations in your life towards you. Notice now, that if you feel unlucky it's because you have certain beliefs in place which draw 'unlucky' events towards you. In a bit, I'll also show you some of the science behind your QRF which proves beyond a shadow of a doubt that what we draw into our lives is more than a product of positive affirmations and wishful thinking.

I also included the short story of Aladdin because I wanted you to notice this message has been right in front of you all your life. I mean, if you think about it, it's as if the universe has been conspiring to find a way to deliver this very message right into the palm of your hands.

Like the genie in Aladdin, your QRF can only bring you what you ask for. In Aladdin's case, he was able to ask the genie directly for what he wanted in life. Your QRF works a little differently. It can only attract what it is programmed to deliver, and that program is comprised of your beliefs. This book teaches you how to learn that language.

Once again, I'm going to step up and be bold; if you are not loving what you are getting in life, there's no way around it; you will have to look at and most likely change some of the beliefs you've been holding onto that have been preventing you from attaining the success and happiness you want in your life.

Next you learned the three common denominators in every area of your life:

- Your beliefs

- Your perceptions

- You

Though it's always easier to point the finger and blame others for your circumstances (and *of course*, who hasn't done that before), this is the bottom line:

If you take any one of the experiences in your life, you will discover that **you are the common denominator in everything you are doing.**

As a wonderful Buddhist teaching puts it:
"Wherever you go, there you are."

In order to change any area of your reality, you must change the beliefs you hold in that area of your reality.

By learning to change your beliefs, you begin learning how to change your QRF .

Chapter 27

Learning Is Mandatory:
How We Learn is
a Matter of Free Will

In case you didn't realize it before, realize this now: You have the choice to learn through fear, or joy. So choose.

Growing up, most of us learned through fear. This was because our parents were fear-based and frequently used fear as a motivator in our upbringing. I'm not only speaking of obvious threats such as, "Do your homework or you are grounded!" Most people were also brought up with fear-based ideas such as, 'there's not enough' (be that not enough money, time, etc.). You would be surprised how the ego-mind can take a simple presupposition like there is 'not enough', absorb it, then justify that belief's existence by 'convincing' itself that there is indeed, 'not enough'.

Not only that, the ego-mind must convince itself that there mustn't be enough because if there is and you don't have it, then you can't *deserve* 'it' ('it' being more money, time, and in the worst cases, love, happiness or respect). Once again, you can see it's a vicious cycle.

Those deep-seeded beliefs can be rooted out and changed for the better, and know this: By doing something as simple as learning how they are formed you begin changing any limited negative beliefs you might have had.

At some point, while reading this book, you probably felt motivated to put some of this knowledge into action because you realized that knowing something and doing something are two entirely different things. That's because on some level you've always known that having the knowledge to master your ego-mind is only the beginning of change, while *doing* something with knowledge represents the wisdom of change.

> *"Having the knowledge is only the beginning of change.*
> *Doing something with knowledge represents*
> *the wisdom of change."*
>
> ~ *Dōv Baron*

I laid out some exercises in Part I that began teaching you how to start changing the beliefs you held, you know the ones that did nothing other than hold you back. By doing this you could then begin attracting the things you want in life, and do it today.

Now, if you did the exercises you should be very proud of yourself because it's not easy to look at yourself in the bright light of honesty. Being able to honestly question your beliefs is a major step in learning to reclaim control of your life. It allows you to see that beliefs are not set in stone which means that if a belief you have is holding you back then you can simply look at it head on, and sweep it to the side getting rid of it (and by the way, you can question the same belief more than once in your life. After all, beliefs that 'last forever' are rare; very rare...)

You did run through those exercises, right?

I know in some cases there were a few of you who chose not to do those exercises (not you, of course, I know you have your notes). For those of you who did, I'd like to quickly review your notes with you. Somewhere, you wrote down five beliefs and for each one asked yourself:

"Why do I believe that?"

Little did you know that by recording those beliefs, you started a chain of events. One of those key events was acknowledgment. By acknowledging you own a belief, you took hold of it. Holding a belief gives you the opportunity to really take a look and decide if it's empowering you or not. Once you've made your choice, you can either put it back in its place, or crush the life out of it. When you are the master of your ego-mind, you have choice.

In a bit I'll show you some of the wonderful results of those exercises, as well as how to remove the more stubborn beliefs that stand in the way of you thriving.

First…I want to make sure that you took action and started using the seven-day exercise that helps you turn on your inner genie because that exercise begins to change your QRF, which in turns attracts more delectable things into your life.

The first part of that exercise was to ask yourself why the people who love you, *love you*. By asking yourself that question, as well as by looking at the accomplishments in your life, I'm positive you found many things that made you feel better, right now.

Keep your eye on those accomplishments. Focus on the joy, and continue to focus on it for seven days (and if you like feeling good about yourself I'm sure you will take me up on the challenge and focus on it for twenty-eight days).

Again, people all around the world have been using these exercises, challenging their limited negative beliefs, and reporting astonishing results. I've had tons of amazing feedback from people who have told me how they've changed their lives using the very techniques in this book. It's pretty wonderful. In fact, I look forward to hearing how this book changed *your* life!

We both know that we've covered a lot of material just getting to this point. And I've just provided a quick summary of two of the exercises we undertook. So there's something I'd like to say:

Congratulations! You've made it this far. I commend your commitment and I promise it will pay off, big time!

How Hard Do You Need to Make It?

I'm sure that as you keep reading this you will begin to noticing ways in which your life is changing because you are taking the necessary steps and practicing the exercises you are learning here.

As I write this, I remember a caller I spoke to during one of my radio seminars. Let me share that memory with you because I believe it has a strong message to which I'm sure you will relate.

We had just completed a fun, high energy program, and as we opened up the lines to take questions there was one lady who said something very quietly in the background. She spoke so faintly that I didn't quite pick it up. Luckily, Damian, my co-host, did.

I had just finished describing how to bust open and obliterate a disempowering belief by using one of the techniques you have read in this book, when in the background this lady softly said, "It can't be that easy."

Damian caught her comment and asked her to repeat her statement for everyone to hear so that I could help her, knowing that others were potentially thinking the same thing.

She told me it couldn't possibly be *that* easy.

In response I said, "Well, maybe the belief that it can't be that easy might be true for you, but that doesn't make it true for everyone."

I told her to take a chance and look at any belief she felt she couldn't sweep aside, now, *and using the exercises you've been given in this book* I had her explore where it came from and if it was helping her or holding her back.

I was happily surprised when a few weeks after the show she contacted me excitedly and explained how my comment had encouraged her to cast her doubts aside for a moment. She told me that after hesitatingly applying the exercises to that one belief and getting such quick and staggering results, she immediately recorded a number of life-long limiting beliefs surrounding money and relationships and successfully deconstructed them.

Another person contacted me revealing that after listening to one of my radio shows she was able to let go of a belief she was holding onto about her health that just wasn't true, and this was a belief she had held for **twenty-five years!** Can you imagine how free these people must have been feeling after destroying beliefs that were holding them back that long?

I bet that if you were to concentrate for a moment, take a peek at one of those limited beliefs that you wrote down and imagine what your life would be like if it was gone, just like that, gone... right now, you would grab a bookmark, or dog-ear this page, and begin using these techniques on the rest of your list.

That ends the review of Part I, which naturally leads us into Part II. So let me give you a very short overview of what we're going to discuss in Part II.

Soon you are going to discover how your mind has been programmed for addiction and why change can seem so difficult. I am going to give you a technique that will reveal to you more of your unconscious beliefs and the behaviors those beliefs demonstrate.

I'll tell you why your very survival depends upon your ability to change and why reclaiming mastery of your ego-mind is so vital to your capacity to thrive.

This section also outlines why the ego-mind believes that change equals death. That may sound a little dramatic, but I promise you will understand how, and why, when I give you some examples shortly.

I'm going to share with you how both thoughts and feelings have a direct effect on the body. In one example, I demonstrate how thoughts and feelings rob the body of nutrition. We will also go deeper into why some people keep getting what they don't want in their lives and how you can break that cycle.

Doesn't that sound exciting? Great, let's get into it!

Part II

Chapter 28

Coping for Something Better

Now just stop for a moment, because this is important. You will have to realize I'm serious here and (you will not be able to read another word) unless you are REALLY excited about learning how to attract the things *you* want in life.

Maybe you are wondering how someone could become excited reading a book... Imagine the expression on a child's face who's waiting to open up a huge present that's sitting right in front of them. Hear them laughing and giggling in anticipation. Chances are if you can do that, you can easily begin feeling some joy.

Do yourself a favor and remember some of what you have already learned. Here's the simplest reminder: Your reality is manifest most dominantly from the feelings you generate in any given moment. So with that, just to feel better as this powerful information flows into your conscious and subconscious mind, sit up straight, take a deep sigh out, stretch your neck and sit on the edge of your seat as if you were totally excited about what's coming next, because it is exciting!

Now that's a good start, so ...

Let's get started!

The techniques I'll be introducing in Part II are both simple to do and powerful in their results.

To prove how easy this is, let me share an example of how powerful your manifesting mind can become when you take charge and focus it.

Chances are you have driven a car before. Have you ever eaten a burger while driving ... while talking on a cell phone ... while changing lanes ... (not that I condone that, it's just an example!). Anyway, have you ever considered how hard doing all that would have been on the first day you ever drove? Having to pay attention to the road, the pedals, and not drop the burger on your lap would be difficult.

When your mind has a purpose and when your mind is focused as you read this, it becomes open to all sorts of new ideas and understandings. So, since your mind's already open, let's keep it open and see what else is inside.

John

> John came to me with a lot on his mind. He often mentioned how he could pinpoint that exact moment when his life took that turn for the worse. John felt tired of living a life masking his pain. He finally noticed the masks he wore to cover his pain were only doing just that—covering his pain; he no longer wanted temporary escape; he wanted true relief.

At first glance, from the outside looking within, it seemed that he came from a pretty stable family, yet when speaking of his past the pain in his voice mirrored his true feelings within.

In high school he began using pot, meth and alcohol, his drugs of choice, to ease his suffering because up until now, avoiding pain was easier than facing it.

According to John, his mother had always been a controlling woman. She justified her behavior by reminding John it was for his own good, after all, she cared for him.

John had spent a large portion of his life unaware that in resisting the fear he held of being controlled by his mother and using drugs to escape the reality of his situation, he would be trading short term gain, for a bus-load of long-term pain. The result of living life avoiding pain created a newer, far more devastating reality: He was addicted to a drug that no longer masked the pain while deeply fearing the pain that the drug was supposed to mask.

John began realizing that no amount of drugs could fill the emptiness he felt inside; life had come full circle and he thought it was too late.

As long as he could remember, he had always felt neither of his parents were really there for *him*. His relationship with his father wasn't much better than the one he had with his mother. Although his father hadn't physically left, he seemed to be working all the time, not paying much attention to John or anything else on the rare occasions that he was around.

John could remember his dad constantly telling him that he worked so much for the *good of the family*.

When I first met John, I immediately sensed a void inside him. Later, I learned I was right on target. I even discovered he had a nickname for that emptiness; he called it his *lonely hole*.

One morning John woke up and saw himself standing at a crossroads. Looking at the path behind him he realized pain had led him from fear to anger, and now into deep resentment. As he turned his head and looked towards his potential future, he saw himself living as his mother lived—angry, both controlling and controlled. The path to his right would lead him to his fathers life; filled with emptiness, absent of passion, and with no true purpose beyond getting out of bed every morning and going to work at a job he wouldn't even like. John had seen enough of that brand of pain for two lifetimes.

There was one good thing about his loneliness; it offered him opportunity to question himself; to question why; he began to question who he was. You see, he couldn't identify with his mother because she constantly tried to control him and he hated that. On the other hand, he couldn't identify with his father because he saw his father as a robot whose life seemed hollow outside of work.

Imagine if you had met John back then. You would have probably described him as a smart kid who had the capability, brains, and potential to go anywhere, to be *anything*. Unfortunately, he was still lacking the tools and the wisdom to make good choices.

John's life goes on.

John realized that his drug-use became a drug addiction when his life became about one thing and one thing only—the next fix. The now newly-realized addiction had taken such a strong hold over him that he became involved in greater and greater levels of criminal activity in order to have enough money to buy himself another fix.

At one point, a couple of his family members confronted John about his addiction and said, "Come on! You are a smart kid! How could you not know that getting hooked on drugs would lead you down this path?"

As I said, John was a smart kid. He quickly responded by saying, "I've been out on the streets, I've slept in dumpsters and I've got to tell you drug addicts aren't stupid, at least not when they start out. There are so many people out there who have all kinds of education and degrees that are just as hooked as the guys who dropped out of school at fourteen. Being hooked isn't about being smart or dumb, it's a about trying to cope, with a pain you don't believe anyone can ever understand!"

> Little did he know, what John had said cut to the
> heart of the matter. *"It's a result of how you cope."*

If John had known that using something to ease pain rather than dealing with pain would lead him down that path, he would have taken a different route I'm sure. Then again, we can't blame John outright for making the wrong decision because at that point in his life, he didn't have the tools or resources required to truly deal with his pain or much of anything, really. Without the right map to guide us, we all run the risk of getting lost.

Think about it for a moment. Have you ever met a drug addict? Do you really think that they start their day by asking , "Umm, gee, I wonder what new way I can find to screw up my life today?"

No. Of course not.

What happens is this person has been living with some kind of pain. It could be physical; more often than not it's emotional or mental. Nevertheless, when it comes down to it, we all desperately want to ease our pain.

Most pain is the result of some type of fear and by hiding from our fear, by masking our pain, we run the risk of losing control of our lives because anything we use to mask the pain eventually creates the opportunity to become an addiction. Once we rely on our drug of choice to suppress pain, *addiction takes control of us.*

As John so wisely put it: **"Losing control isn't a plan, *it's a result!*"**

Results like that indicate that we either lack knowledge of the steps it would take to regain control of our lives or the courage and wisdom it takes to do something about it. As a consequence, rather than dealing with the pain, rather than dealing with your pain, you keep using whatever suppresses and numbs the pain.

You know as well as I that everyone has some kind of pain about *something* in their lives. That's the result of being alive; the key is to make sure you have way more joy in your joy-to-pain ratio. We've all used something to ease our pain or to try to ignore it, and every time we do so we gamble with the possibility of creating an addiction.

I know for a fact that anyone reading this is tired of simply numbing or suppressing the pain. They are looking for a way to truly deal with and remove the pain.

If you are not yet living the life of your dreams, then do the exercises. Question your beliefs because when you begin to question where they come from, you shake the foundations of the limiting ones. Once you find out what's been holding you back, you can free yourself and push forward.

In Part I, I told you that it's my belief that we're all here to learn. The question I asked you was, "How do you want to learn, through joy, or pain?" (And for the record, I hope we all chose joy). In that section I also suggested that if we're learning lessons from a place of fear, using fear as a motivator, the lessons we learn are gained through experiencing pain.

There's an important lesson from one of my favorite mentors, and someone who is considered to be an almost mystical teacher, to paraphrase Master Yoda, *fear leads to ... pain.*

You may laugh, but that's not just true in Star Wars. It's real—it's our reality. ***Facing our pain is as simple as questioning our beliefs.*** *And if you are not the master of your ego-mind, questioning your beliefs can* *seem like a terrifying idea.*

Later on in the book, I explain why questioning our beliefs can seem fearful. First, let's look at how the mind gets directly programmed for addiction and how that has an impact even on those of us who would never consider ourselves addicts.

Chapter 29

Addictive Minds

For the average person this might seem like a crazy question, but do you think you are the master of your mind? As someone who has read this far into the book maybe your answer isn't so clearly a yes or a no, yet. However, if you answered yes, how do you know for sure? Are you consciously aware of each and every thought your mind is processing every second, every minute, every hour, every day, every month, every year?

Come on, think about that for a moment. I'm willing to bet a couple people reading this didn't even notice that they could hear these words in their minds while they read this very sentence! A number of years ago, the National Science Foundation estimated that we produce as many as twelve to fifty thousand thoughts per day (depending on how 'deep' of a thinker you are); other more recent estimates run as high as sixty thousand a day. So, if you are not always aware of that voice you hear while you read, how can you be sure you are aware of ALL the thoughts your mind is processing all the time?

You see, of those twelve to sixty thousand thoughts you are running, *eighty percent of them are repetitive, negative, and limiting.* *Yes, eighty percent.* Do you really think that you are always aware of all those thoughts?

Before we dive too deep into how you can be aware of your thoughts, you will need to become familiar with how thoughts, beliefs, perceptions, and addictions work together to influence our lives.

Thoughts, Beliefs, Perceptions, and Addictions
The who, what, where, and how of your mind, and why we lie.
In order to fully understand why you attract certain situations into your life, you will need to first comprehend how your thoughts, beliefs, perceptions, and addictions shape reality. And while we're on the subject, I'm also going to demonstrate how we were all trained to lie, particularly to ourselves.

Let's take a peek.

I Think, therefore I Attract
Let's start by looking at our thoughts and how they, to say the least, can cause some confusion.

Have you ever tried doing one of those tongue twisters? Peter piper picked a peck of pickled peppers, etc. Well, here's one for the ego-mind or as I like to call them: Mind twisters: Do you think your mind has a mind of its own?

Who or what is that voice in your head that often times gives you an opinion on what you just read or saw, or provides unsolicited advice whenever you try to make a decision? Where are those thoughts coming from? Is it *you*?

Listen, I'm not talking about the mentally ill guy down the block who lives in a cardboard box and has a full blown relationship with a souvenir photo of the late princess Di. I'm not talking about a schizophrenic who stopped taking his meds either. We are talking about that voice in your head that might be telling you what you should have told your boss when they asked you to work late. The only problem is that was fourteen hours ago, and now that voice is so bloody loud and talking so bloody fast that you can't get to sleep. Are you clear about which voice I'm talking about? Good. Because it's the voice that said, "What voice?"

The real and important question is this: Is the voice friend, or foe?

Here's a common scenario:

You gain a little bit of weight, and that voice in your head says, "You know, you should go on a diet."

Suddenly, after much internal debate, you are on a diet!

Why is that voice, on the one hand, giving you all that flack about going on a diet, and then two seconds later that very same voice starts saying, "Hey, hey, look at that cookie... mmmmmm. Oh what's that? A bag of chips, some fries ... ice cream! Oh my god, is that.... No it can't be... CHEESECAKE! Come onnnnnnnn... You know you want it! Just one slice!"

You listen to the voice, and then what happens after you listened and followed that sage advice? Let me tell you: You go ahead and have a cookie, some chips, whatever it is. Suddenly that little bugger in your head turns on you like a doberman on an pork chop, yelling, "You are fat! You are lazy! You've got no self-control, you couldn't even resist having that cookie!"

Have you gone schizophrenic, or is this some kind of sick game that the voice is playing with you?

I know it seems crazy, but it is certainly a more productive way of seeing things: **Maybe your mind has a mind of its own**. What does that mean though?

Read on because it will start coming together after I talk about how thoughts and beliefs end up **fueling** your body.

Chapter 30

Band Aids® for Emotional Pain

Denial is a crappy defense...
It's so easy to point a finger at the down and out, seeing them as so different from us, the civilized functioning members of society.

Here's something you probably don't know about addiction.... We all have them! Some addictions just happen to be more socially acceptable than others. I know you are probably not addicted to hard street drugs, like John was. Maybe your addiction is more socially acceptable: T.V., cake, smoking, working, checking your email ... Maybe it's a combination of the above or something else that seems pretty harmless at first glance, yet in truth, if you just **have** to *have* it or *do* it—if this sounds a little familiar to you—then I'm sorry to tell you: You are hooked.

Maybe that voice in your head is telling you that I'm not talking about you, well sorry to say: Denial is a very weak defense, we all have our addictions.

The simplest explanation I can offer is that all of the addictions that we have, whether we are conscious of them or not, are there to distract us from the pain in our lives. We feed the addiction so we don't have to feel the pain—or at least so we aren't aware we're feeling it.

When a person reaches for that cigarette, drink or an 'illegal' substance that urge is usually a result of some disturbing and unacceptable feeling that we don't know how to deal with. So we get rid of the unacceptable feeling in ways we know will 'work'.

What's worth considering is: What if we stopped and checked in with our feelings before using a substance to alter our mood? Asking ourselves the simple yet powerful question of: *What am I feeling right now* has the potential to bring a new level of awareness to our habitual use of substances, or any other form of addictive behavior. In so doing we provide ourselves with the opportunity, the possibility, of making another choice. While by continually ignoring our feelings, we have none.

Before we go any further, I want to set something straight...Human beings have an almost universal desire for pleasure and escape. The most powerful pharmacy in the world is the one between your ears. Our brains naturally produce mind altering substances and these substances are what the adrenaline junky, habitual church volunteer, or chain smoker has in common with the heroin addict. All these, and a myriad of other habitual behaviors produce some kind of a high.

All addictions whether to substances, behavior, or thinking, sets in motion a chemical cocktail produced in the brain and is fed out into the blood stream.

You see, John the addict I told you about earlier is no different from you or me or anybody else who's running from their pain; realize, addiction is addiction is addiction. Just think about it. Whether it's emotional, mental, or physical, we all have some kind of pain in our lives. Whether we call them addictions or if you're just more comfortable with the term; 'habitual behaviors', most of us use them to avoid some kind of pain, or at least to avoid it to some degree.

188

If you want to begin reclaiming·mastery of your ego-mind, it might be time to begin dealing with your pain, instead of hiding from it. At this point, I want to be very clear in saying that right now I doubt you are too enthused about the idea that you might be addicted to some 'thing' or some behavior. However, it will be a lot easier to consider if you drop the stereo type of what you think an addict looks like. As much as you might want to pick this book up and throw it. I understand! This can be a big one to swallow, but stay with me because this is the path to mastering your ego-mind.

Still not convinced? Well, before you write me, this book, or anything else off, consider this: If you are not addicted, what part of you is so resistant to looking at the possibility?

I'll tell you what part, the part that's running the show, the part that uses unconscious addiction to keep you from owning your power... The ego-mind! Because if you look at a behavior and discover it's an escape, you could deal with it and then you would begin to gain mastery over your ego-mind, and let's face it, it's not going down without a fight.

At the basic level addiction, in whatever form it takes, is a search for immature and immediate gratification, (and we all do it, until we don't) it's like the needs of a dependent child who wants comfort.., NOW. To overcome being or getting hooked on a substance, behavior, or thought process there is a need to grow up, not in years but in maturity. This means taking on an adult role in life and dealing with whatever shows up in front of you. The point here is that it is not possible to 'grow up', while in denial, it is not possible to grow up without facing the pain that the ego-mind hides behind.

*"If you want to know where the ego is hiding
at any given moment, look into your pain.
The ego is always hiding behind it. "*

~ Dōv Baron

Now, I realize that you might not be jumping up and down with excitement at the prospect of discovering you are addicted. **However, as we all know: You can't deal with anything unless you are willing to admit it,** (whatever 'it' is). So I want you to stop and ask yourself a personal question.

I want you to ask yourself what kind of socially acceptable addictions you might have. Do you smoke? Drink? Volunteer? Do charity work? Overeat or spend? Socialize? I know you are thinking; *there's nothing wrong with at least some of these*, and you'd be right. In fact I'd go so far as to say none of them are, in and of themselves, particularly 'bad', when used occasionally. The challenge becomes when anyone of them is used on a regular basis to avoid a set of feelings that come up for you.

As I said earlier, the tricky part is recognizing and owning a habitual or addictive behavior, particularly if you enjoy it, and even more particularly if it's one that is socially acceptable and gets you accolades. Here's an example of one of those habitual behaviors that gets us the-old-pat-on-the-back and the 'what a guy/ what a gal': Yes, you guessed it:Stuffing emotions.

Society tells us we are strong when we don't feel. You didn't cry at the funeral of a loved one and they tell you how great you are doing. With that comment there comes a momentary rush of chemicals that are produced when we get approval, and without a need to run to the bathroom and fill the needle, we're off down the addictive path. Meanwhile, your cousin is feeling all her feelings of loss and we say she's falling apart. By the way, having a big dramatic response can be just as addicting as none at all.

Emotional addictions are a massive subject and I'll get more into that a little later in the book. For now, I want you to take out whatever you used to write on in Part I; when you asked yourself, "Why do I believe that" and start a new page. On that page, I want you to write down a few socially acceptable addictions you have or at least you suspect that you might have. This is important and if you want to get the most out of this book, it will only take about thirty seconds.

Done yet?

Here's the scary part, even seemingly productive activities like working out too hard, too often, or even eating so strictly you pretty much yell at yourself for looking at a cookie can become forms of addiction, if taken to a militaristic extreme. It just happens that some of the addictions we use to ignore the pain and fear in our lives—such as the ones I just mentioned—are more socially acceptable than others, so very few people are willing to call us on it.

Listen, you've come this far, and I'm proud of you for doing so (as the 'chickens' put this book down chapters ago). I know you want to get this so, be courageous. Ask yourself: What are, or might be, my socially acceptable addictions? And again, if you think it's nothing, think again. No one's looking over your shoulder, and you don't have to tell anyone your answers. Notice what you do or use to suppress your pain. Look hard. Because when you are not willing to look there, you are not the master of your ego-mind.

If you want to master your ego-mind, you have to look at and see your addictions for what they really are: A crutch. Listen up, it's not that painful. It's not even that difficult. In fact, once we get the ball rolling, it will feel quite easy.

The truth is, many of us grew up afraid to question their beliefs because they were punished or forbidden by adults (especially parents) just for asking 'why'. Well, guess what? You are no longer a child.

As an adult you now have the right to give yourself permission to question anything about yourself that you are not happy with.

If you are still hesitant, or unsure of yourself, know that I'm giving you permission as well—and I'm an adult, so you better listen!

Step up and realize that you have the right and are fully capable of looking at any aspect of your belief system and behavior and deciding if it's limiting or not. We all have the right to thrive, to reclaim mastery of our minds and of our lives.

Our friend John found out the hard way that in most cases addictions can end up being the source of more pain. Many adults never learn the skills required to address the problem at its root – they only learn to hide or dull the pain. Once we start ignoring or dampening the pain, our minds learn to ask for whatever we're using to cope with it because we've grown accustomed to it. While addiction can be detrimental, the capacity of the human body and mind to adapt to nearly anything is actually pretty amazing.

Case in point: Suntanning.

If you have naturally light skin and step into the sun for too long, chances are you will burn. If you have naturally light skin and spend two minutes in the sun one day, five the next, fifteen the next and so on, your body would begin to adapt and your skin would darken. The darkening of your skin is both an example of your body 'coping' with the 'result' of you spending more time in the sun as well as you 'training' your body to defend itself from more and more UV-Rays. The body and the mind are very capable of adapting; the challenge with adaptation is desensitization. That's why the heroin addict needed a hundred times more of the drug to get high than she did the first time she used.

In John's case, the use of drugs to soften the pain would be loosely likened to tanning.

Taking it one step further: Imagine that you would like to sit around all day in the sun, except you are *very* light skinned—I'm talking lighter than Casper the friendly ghost. So you lather up on lotion, then the sun makes you sleepy and you decide to take a short nap on the grass, thinking that you are protected.

Guess what would happen by the end of the day?

You are burnt like bacon in an iron skillet.

Likewise, if you had pain and decided to mask it through avoidance or suppression, in the long run, you are going to get burnt. You see, the coping method chosen to avoid the pain of being burnt rather than dealing with the issue at hand boils down to a matter of when are you going to feel pain, not if. Then, to top it all off, you also run the risk of becoming addicted to your coping method(s).

Another drawback to addiction is that at some point most people tend to lose sight of the very pain those addictions were masking or numbing in the first place.

There's this element of self-deception that goes on amongst those of us who tell ourselves that *we could quit anytime*, while others develop a new limited belief that they don't have the strength to quit. For those of you who believe they could quit anytime, I'm sorry but, why haven't you? I'm not asking to be mean, I'm asking because I want you to be honest with yourself. Why haven't you quit, whatever it is you are hooked on?

This is only the beginning of the extent to which pain and/or fear, when masked behind addiction, can turn into cravings, self-denial, or doubt about what's really going on inside. Those difficult emotions can team up with the voices in our heads and keep us stuck in a cycle. Really, that internal voice should be assisting you to make empowering choices, choices that help you to break free of your pain.

"All enlightenment starts with awareness, from this awareness we can see there are choices and only from the awareness that there are choices can we choose or choose again."
~ *Dõv Baron*

By having a better grip on what sorts of addictions we use and a clearer understanding of how we use addictions to mask pain, we can move on to how we were trained to lie to ourselves and others. Later we delve into how lying stops you from mastering the ego-mind.

Chapter 31

Lies:
To Thine Own Self Be True

Here's a riddle: "What is the one thing we always lie about when we say we are telling the truth?"

The answer is, when we say, "*I don't lie.*" To some degree we all lie and we do so on a very regular basis. I am not saying we always lie to be deceitful, although many people do. Most often we lie because it 'seems' more convenient.

One of the reasons we lie is to cover up some shame, shame about who we are or what we have done. At some level we believe that if we told the truth we would be rejected, and we might. So we settle for inauthentic relationships and we lie hoping that by keeping this secret part of us to ourselves, 'they' will love us. Sadly, the lying results in us not feeling very loved at all, because over time we feel even more unlovable for lying. This is one of the reasons why so many of us end up feeling lonely in our relationships; we feel like our partner doesn't know who we are.

*"The easiest thing to be in the world is you. The most
difficult thing to be is what other people want you to be.
Don't let them put you in that position."*

~ Leo Buscaglia

*"Being someone you are not and being genuinely happy
are mutually exclusive from each other."*

~ Dõv Baron

I'm going to make a bold statement here: We have all learned to be dishonest, not just with others but also personally. We were conditioned to point fingers, to blame others, and to avoid accountability at all costs. And by the end of this chapter, you will know why.

First ... Let's sift through some of your childhood memories until you find a time where one of your parents, grandparents, teachers, siblings, or any authority figure boldly told you not to lie and the important reasons why.

If you happen to pick a memory early enough, you will stumble upon a time where the you-as-a-child, did not fully understand what a lie was. Chances are, you-as-the-child isn't concocting some grandiose scheme of infamy. When you first lied, you did it because you did so—without much thought of the consequences and you probably weren't thinking that far ahead.

Regardless of why a child first lied, let me ask you: Who among us didn't have the idea that it is wrong to lie drilled into us?

I know that most of you grew up with pretty honest folks. However, for adults there was a type of lying that as kids we did not have the privilege to use. You know what I mean, right? When you-as-a-child asked the adults why they lied they would say that it was a "white lie" and that they were lying to protect someone else. (There's that protective lie crap again).

Let's face it. Call it like it is. A lie *is* a lie, is a lie.

I'm not saying that to tell a lie is some cardinal sin and all liars should be dammed, that's ridiculous. No, I just want us to be honest and call them what they really are: Lies.

Maybe when you heard adults lie they weren't big ones. Maybe you overheard them telling their friends that they couldn't go out one night because you or one of your siblings weren't feeling too well, when in truth you were absolutely fine, they just didn't want to go.

Maybe they were afraid that by telling their friends the truth, that by saying to them, "I'm sorry, we're not feeling up to coming out tonight," their friends might get angry or hurt. They might have thought that rather than explaining why they didn't want to do something, it would be easier to just lie. They justified the lies by telling themselves and/or each other that this way, no one had to run the risk of getting hurt.

You see how this is an extension of what we discussed in Part I about how we sometimes absorb beliefs in order to fit in? *It should. If it doesn't, check out, "Why would anyone adopt beliefs?" and "The manifesting mind in action."*

In fact, the acts of our parents, siblings, grandparents, or whomever, explaining to us the distinction between 'lies' and 'white lies' during our young, impressionable years, were inadvertently planting a seed within our ego-mind that, as we grow, blooms one day into a belief that as an adult, it's okay to lie as long as it's a 'white lie'—especially if it spares conflict or someone's feelings.

"Fear of conflict offers only an opportunity for resentment,
while dealing with conflict in a healthy manner
offers the opportunity for resolution,
compassion and intimacy"

~ *Dōv Baron*

How about this for another example of the lies in action?

Maybe you can remember one of your parents calling in sick to work, when they felt fine.

Honestly now, how can someone tell you not to lie when they are lying themselves?

Here's a sad while rather funny story: I can clearly remember my stepfather warning my brother not to start smoking.

Good message, right?

I'm guessing it would have been a little more effective if, while delivering it, my stepfather wasn't squinting from the smoke that was coming off of the cigarette dangling out of the corner of his mouth.

Here's an interesting and maybe even a little frightening point if you have kids of your own. The real psychology behind learning is that children learn more about what to do from *watching* their parents than from what their parents *tell* them.

Parents lie. It may not be malicious, but they all do it. They lie about how they feel about their own parents, how they feel about Uncle Bob or Aunt Sally, their friends or their neighbours. Most people even lie by pretending to be happy when they meet someone, even when they are not.

For most adults, lying is rather automatic.

Sometimes, adults will tell the people around them how great things are going in their lives because they are ashamed to concede they are not happy. They fear that if they were to admit things aren't going quite as planned, they might not be liked, and they might be judged or rejected. Others feel that their unhappiness might cause the people around them to see them as 'downers' or 'whiners', or even worse, that others would feel sorry for them. Afterall, 'frowners are downers and won't make friends', right?

Well, is it right?

How do you think beliefs such as those affect the life you are living today and everyday?

Have you ever had reservations about a co-worker yet were reluctant to say anything for fear it might cause tension? Or were you afraid that person or their friends might not like *you* if you mentioned anything, so you lied? Then again, I also bet you never imagined that being honest with them might lead to a friendship built on just that, honesty.

*"All great truths begin
as blasphemies."*

~ George Bernard Shaw

There is a risk in truth-telling. Then again, in Part I, under 'The six foundations of success', you did learn about how being able to speak your truth without hurting others, while being able to hear someone else's truth without the fear of being hurt or rejected yourself, is a foundation of mastery.

Are you starting to see a theme here?

Growing up we were told to 'own up' when we did things wrong, and when we owned up we were judged, shamed, or punished. So, naturally, most kids learned very quickly that telling the truth rarely had a positive pay off, and by watching adults, kids learned to be unaccountable, to find scapegoats...to lie.

To me, it's no wonder that through the lessons of experience, some kids have actually decided that telling the truth is dangerous.

I'm sure we all know someone who's thrown a baseball through a window and ran like the wind. And growing up, most of us knew that 'owning up' would have involved punishment of some sort. I realize the above example might seem minor, but if you were to add up all the little white lies, and all the times we avoided owning up because we were afraid of what might happen, you could clearly see how for many, it became the beginning of something that became unstoppable. It's like rolling a snowball down a mountain: It's not long before the avalanche of lies lays waste to everything that really matters.

This is what it boils down to: We were trained to lie to others first, and then we began lying to ourselves as adults by believing it was okay. *Worst of all, the lies we repeated often enough became lies we believed ourselves.*

> *"What a tangled web we weave,*
> *when first we practice to deceive."*
> ~*Sir Walter Scott*

Bobby: He's just having a 'lie' down.

Little Bobby was a phenomenal example of how we learn to lie, both to ourselves and others. Though this story is short, its meaning runs deep.

I'll probably never forget the profound impact 'Little Bobby' had on me after we discussed his life. When he spoke of his childhood, he didn't speak as the man he was, it was through the voice of the young, very impressionable boy he remembered himself being when he came home from school one day, *and seeing this...*

> One sunny day Little Bobby came home from school and found his dad on the floor, drunk, lying in his own mess. It wasn't the first time Little Bobby had seen this: It just happened to be the first time he was old enough to really notice. Little Bobby asked his mother with a blend of curiosity and concern that is natural to young children, "Mom, what's wrong with Dad?"
>
> His mom took a deep breath to regain some of her composure. She didn't look at him, it seemed more like she was looking through him.

Little Bobby immediately felt his mother's sadness as she avoided his eyes while covertly wiping her own, and she replied, "Oh ... nothing dear. Dad's not been well, he's just lying down for awhile."

What I'm going to ask you is this:
Do you think Little Bobby knew what a lie was? Do you think he knew the truth? How long do you think it took for Little Bobby to learn about lying?

The thing is, none of us want to cause any worry or risk hurting anyone's feelings, and most of the time that is the excuse we use to justify lying. When your parents lied about going out, in hindsight, you know it wasn't because they were evil. They just believed that the lie wasn't hurting anyone. But it did!

People lie to avoid dealing with the real problems at hand because they are afraid. When we get used to lying about the little things we are afraid of dealing with, over time it becomes easy to lie about the big things as well.

This again begs the question of what there is to be afraid of.

Chapter 32
How Lies Affect Us

I'm not going to take any moral high ground here. I don't believe that there is a big accountant in the sky, ready to tally up all our lies and deal us crappy things in life as a consequence, or punish us when it's all over. What I do know is that people get used to telling lies, especially if those lies were told to spare someone's feelings. Because we have all caught someone lying, we all know that people eventually lose track of their lies.

I'm sure you've seen this or something similar before. You are talking to a friend or co-worker who brings up this amazing weekend they had last month, when halfway into the conversation you remember that at the time they'd told you they couldn't hang out with you because they'd been sick and wanted to stay home! You can immediately feel your blood boil and there's a pretty good chance that just by looking at you they can tell they've put their own size nine in their mouth.

I know as well as you do, it's not likely that they lied just to avoid you. It was more likely that they already had plans with someone else, or needed a quiet night at home and didn't want to run the risk of hurting your feelings.

What it comes down to is, eventually most people lose track of the lies they tell and when they do, those lies that were supposed to be for the purpose of avoiding hurt feelings, end up generating many more. We lie because we don't want to cause or feel pain and we lie to avoid conflict. Healthy disagreement doesn't have to make anyone wrong. Telling your truth with honest feedback or response is one of the greatest gifts you can give your relationships. Some may say, "I could never be that honest." My response is that, until we are truly honest it is highly unlikely that one will ever experience true intimacy.

While the idea of lying to avoid causing pain to another is conceptually admirable, deep down we all know it's unnecessary to lie in an honest relationship. I'm sure that most of the time, just before you had mentioned the white lie you debated on telling it in the first place. I also bet that after you felt a bit guilty and wished there was another way.

Whether or not you feel guilty about telling a lie, the act of telling it causes a problem. The ego-mind (whom you will be introduced to in greater detail shortly) forms the belief that lying is 'OK' and 'necessary' **whether or not you feel bad about telling a lie**, and that really starts to mess up your QRF. (Why your ego-mind thinks it's necessary to lie will be fully explained in a few pages).

It's a pretty vicious cycle we get caught up in. Once we become accustomed to lying, we begin to convince ourselves into believing that lying is both 'OK' and 'necessary'.

Just let this sink in for a minute because there is a greater consequence: As a result of all this automatic lying we can end up not being able to trust ourselves or our intuition, because on the unconscious level we already know we are lying to ourselves and we are capable of doing it again.

Another point I'd like to make here is, as you've just noticed, if you are able to easily catch someone else lying about an amazing weekend they enjoyed, what makes you think you haven't been caught lying yourself?

Here's a different scenario, and an example of something you may have experienced yourself.

Have you ever been in a relationship where you looked at your partner and clearly knew that there was something wrong? Then when you asked, your partner looked back at you and gave you that dreaded one word answer: "Nothing."

Why wouldn't they admit something was wrong? Come on! It's as obvious as the snarl on their face that they were unhappy!

Was it about their work? The food in front of them? Were their parents getting on their nerves? Did it have anything at all to do with YOU? AHHHHHHHHH! Lies of omission are still lies and when we don't say, we leave the mind of the other person to go crazy making up all kinds of nonsense about what it 'might' be. I'm sure that if you've gone through that you know how much it truly sucks!

Wouldn't it be easier if they would just tell the truth? I'm sure you can understand how lying creates a whole other kind of pain which, given enough time, can ALSO create a new kind of addiction—like nagging, moping, or ignoring our partners' signals altogether.

Then again, maybe that person across the table telling that lie was you? I know you had a smile plastered on your face while you were reading that because you've been there. We've all been there.

Instead of being direct and telling people the truth of who we are and what we need; we do a dance with them and ourselves: 'The dance of politeness'. Meanwhile, we hope they will pick up on our subtle clues of what we're really thinking and feeling, and then we have the nerve to complain when they don't.

As mentioned, the rationalization we use for this game of not telling the truth is that we don't want to hurt anyone's feelings.

> To rationalize, you do just that.
> You make rational-lies.
> ~ Source Unknown

Even with all the rationalizing, let's be clear; all this lying doesn't work. It destroys relationships and it destroys lives. We may have been able to tell ourselves that we're protecting the people in our lives with these lies, but by now I'm sure that you've worked out for yourself that we only ever lie out of some version of fear.

Once again I'm going to ask you to think about who you need to share what you have just learned with. I know the moment you ask yourself that question someone springs to mind. However, please remember that the purpose of sharing what you've just learned is not to ram it down someone's throat, it is so that you can integrate it through sharing it.

To conclude this section I just want to point out: Lying sets us up to fail because when we start to believe our own lies, we lose the ability to trust our intuition. The result of that is that we feel as if we're left with no other choice other than listening to all the crap that our conditioned mind feeds us, the nonsense we didn't even want to believe in the first place!

I'm here to show you another way. A way in which you no longer need to lie; a way in which lets you trust your intuition again. And to get it, you have to reclaim your manifesting mind back from the ego. You just have to remember how.

Chapter 33

Intuition:
I've Got a Good Feeling about This

It's pretty straight forward, really. The mind is programmed with beliefs, some good, some bad, some useful, and some not. Your intuition, *your knowing*, is that part of you that acts like a compass which guides you towards or away from certain events and situations in your life. It even helps you out with your decision making—provided you know how to get in touch with it. When, as described in the last chapter, we operate from a place of self-deceit we stop that compass giving us a true reading.

I know for some people the idea of having an inner compass can sound a little confusing, but here's how I usually explain it in my seminars. Have you ever been in a real mess of a situation, something you didn't quite know how you got into, and even worse, had no clue how to get out of? You know what I mean. The kind of problem you didn't think you could solve on your own so you asked a friend. And when you asked that friend for advice all they could say was, "Uhhh, I don't know, *go with your gut feeling.*"

Granted, at first you might have looked at them with a half-grimace and thought, "Yeah,. thanks for all the help there, bucko." Except then, suddenly, *you get a feeling*. Something inside you... almost gave you a slight—I don't know—nudge, in a certain direction. What you probably hadn't realized is; according to scientific research there are equal amounts of neurons in the heart and gut as there are in the brain. So your gut really does know.

If you've ever experienced anything like that, wonderful! That's your intuition lending you a helping hand. If you haven't had that feeling yet, it's okay, because the exercises given to you throughout this book are here to open up your inner listening, to hear your intuition once again.

Now, first off, so there's no confusion, let's talk about what intuition is so you can begin wrapping your mind around the term.

When people have serious questions, instead of trusting what their gut—what their intuition—is telling them, they generally fall back into their habitual program of self-lies and addiction that they've been unconsciously running most of their lives. Remember, as I've already established, anyone who listens to their negative conditioning and relies on their addictions for anything gets to exactly where you are now.

The fact is, some of the people around you (not you, of course, after all, you are reading this) are unwilling to reclaim mastery of their ego-minds by challenging their limited beliefs and shutting up those negative programmed thoughts. They end up hearing negative, limiting thoughts all the time, thoughts like, "I'll never succeed at this" or "I'm not smart enough, or pretty enough, or successful enough..."

Comments like that, even if they are only running in your mind, are, excuse me, a bunch of crap. Thoughts and beliefs like that end up haunting you like a cancer, keeping you exactly where you are, getting you the same old jobs, relationships and problems etc in life.

How many times have you wanted more for yourself in your life? It could have been anything. Maybe you want to go back to school and your ego-mind is yelling, "I'm not smart enough" or "It's too late" like a broken record. I'm going to say it. **Bull.**

What about that diet and exercise plan you wanted to try and all you can think of is your failed attempts. Once again. **Bull.**

That's the kind of crap that will keep you stuck if you don't reclaim mastery of your ego-mind!

Do you know what Thomas Edison said after he created the light bulb? He said, "I didn't only create a light bulb, I first created one thousand ways to **not** make one."

It's time to be demanding with yourself and realize it can always get better! *It can always get better.*

Here's some more negative self-talk that I have brought up many times in my seminars. Ever hear this one before?

"If you don't compromise, you are going to end up alone."

Hey! Wait a minute. What's wrong with being all alone? It's better than being in some crappy relationship where you are never going to matter or be appreciated. Right? Well, is it right?

The result of all the 'self-lying' is that some people become blind. They ignore the signs sitting right in front of them that are pointing them in a better direction. Others ignore their gut feeling – their intuition, and many people have been ignoring their intuition for a long, long time. Way too long, if you ask me.

People wake up and go to jobs they don't like every day because they've been told, sometimes even by their friends, "It's never gonna happen dude, it's just never gonna happen for you. Life just doesn't work that way." So what happens? They stay stuck. They believe the lies that have been spoon fed to them and in turn they start lying to themselves by believing the lies are true. Those people have chosen to believe .that they will never get anywhere in life, and with an attitude like that, you won't get anywhere, ever, will you?

Look at reality around you and decide for yourself: I've met people all over the world who waste their time dating people who are not right for them waiting for their partners to change. Trust me, it's never going to happen; they are not going to change. To reference my earlier analogy, it's as if you are ordering steak from a vegetarian restaurant... It's just not going to happen.

When people choose not to connect with and listen to their intuition, life can appear easier, because if they actually listened to their gut, they would have to stop taking other peoples' advice and begin taking responsibility for themselves. See, if you don't listen to your gut, life appears easier because then you don't have to change; something *out there* has to give. It's the world that has to change.

Remember what I shared with you in Part I? *You are the common denominator in all of your experiences* (See Part I in the section titled 'The common denominator'). If you are noticing patterns, then it's not the other people—**it's you**. You are the common denominator.

Remember Forest Gump? "Stupid is as stupid does," right? Let's re-phrase that. Stupid is as stupid keeps repeating what doesn't work. It's not quite as catchy but it's definitely true. Repeating anything that doesn't work while expecting a different result the second time around... or the third... or the two-hundredth.... is just, not bright.

> "Insanity is, doing the same thing
> over and over again
> and expecting different results."
> ~Albert Einstein

Hear me out here. I bet you've hit yourself on the thumb with a hammer before. Hurts, doesn't it? I'm sure every time you picked up a hammer since then you were *much* more careful around your fingers (or your toes!).

I've got some breaking news for you. It's as equally dumb to keep expecting somebody or something else to be different when you are always doing the same thing—when in fact, **you** are the one that needs to change.

Therefore, if you are *tired of hitting your thumbs with a hammer, **you** must be the one to change. You are the only thing that can change.* You can start by noticing your addictions, challenging your beliefs, and changing what keeps you from thriving.

Speaking of beliefs ...

I'm Sure I'm Right, This Time ...
So why do we keep doing it? Why do men and women all over the world keep metaphorically banging on their thumbs with hammers, refusing to change, constantly repeating what doesn't work?

We do it because there's a belief behind our behavior.

Let me put it another way ... .

Chapter 34

Behavior is The Best Demonstration of Belief

If you want to know what you really believe, then take a good look at your behavior. Whenever I'm asked to explain how behavior demonstrates belief, I tend to think of this one lady in particular.

Denise

Denise had a dream; she wanted to start her own catering business. She was a fabulous chef, by the way. I should know because I had her cater some events for me.

Anyway, she arrived one day and told me about her business and how it wasn't growing the way she'd imagined, even though she was using my EFM Audio Technology™. She went on to say she was kind of thinking about going back to her old position—thinking about getting her old J.O.B. back. (In case you don't know what J.O.B. is, it stands for Just Over Broke).

I looked at her and thought to myself, "All right, that's fine, let's take a look at what her behavior is so I might get a glimpse into what her beliefs are."

We started talking. I asked her to walk me through one of her typical days so I could take a look at what was going on in her life.

She said that since she didn't officially have a job, she figured that it would be okay to sleep in a little later.

As I settled into my chair to get more comfortable, I asked her, "Tell me about that. How do you begin your day?"

She relaxed into her chair, took a deep breath and said, "Well, I get up around nine and I have something to eat. I get a cup of coffee, and then I read the newspaper for about an hour. I read some stories, the comics, the horoscopes ... those kinds of things. Then I watch a little bit of tv."

Her eyes widened as she said, "Oh! And I like to read a bit of personal development. You know, self help books and tapes, so I read some of that."

"By then it's about lunchtime," she continued. "I grab some lunch and usually have a look through the paper again." This alone had me concerned, but I've got to tell you, it gets better or worse, depending on your point of view. She continued: "This time I look through classifieds and I kind of look for, well ... I find myself looking through the jobs section, looking at, you know, the jobs I used to do."

I said, "Alright," and for a moment, I paused, looked down, really thought about what she was saying to me and I hoped that at least by saying it all out loud she'd get it, after all she is a very bright lady. Sadly, that was not the case. As I looked back up at her I said, "What else?"

She never skipped a beat, "Well, I'm looking around for places where I might apply. You know, give them my resume. Let them know that I sort of have this catering business and give them a little brochure, or whatever."

"And after that, what do you do," I asked.

She smiled and said, "Well, after that I watch some Oprah."

To be honest I wanted to scream; "Hello, wakey, wakey!" But instead, I waited. I returned a smile as she continued, "Well, I like to watch Oprah. What's even better about it is nowadays I can do it in my 'jammys'."

I said to her, "Do *you* believe you can be successful in your own business?"

"Oh yeah!" she beamed , "Absolutely! I know I have the skills, but it's just that the business isn't coming in."

I firmly and quickly replied, "I'm afraid you are wrong. Your behavior demonstrates your belief, and your belief is that being self-employed means that you can sit on the couch and watch Oprah in your 'jammys'." No one gets to be successful in their own business by watching 'O' and flipping through the classifieds, no matter how many times they use EFM Audio Technology™ .

> *"God gives us the nuts
> but he does not crack them."*
>
> ~ *German Proverb*

Remember: **"Behavior demonstrates belief"**.

There was more to that session, a lot more. Except the rest has to be cut out because I'm pretty sure you can see what direction she was heading if she continued down that path. Keep in mind, that was an example of just one of her limiting beliefs.

Another thing you might have noticed while reading about Denise is she also demonstrated that she clearly believed that she couldn't make it in business on her own. That's why she kept looking in the classifieds for positions in her old line of work.

So many people live lives just like Denise, saying they have a dream while waiting for a miracle. Having said that, please understand I believe that the miraculous happens every day. However, the miraculous is not a passive process. You have to be fully involved in order to bring about your miracle. To be fully involved you must take action and that starts by recognizing that if you don't master your ego-mind and each of the six foundations we talked about in Part I, then **who you are today will always be who you were yesterday.**

If you want to master your life, you must first master your ego-mind. You must pay attention and notice the signs in front of you. You must discover and obliterate the beliefs that just don't work for you if you are going to ever live the life of your dreams. And you must be honest about what you are doing that simply doesn't work.

> *"Your Life depends upon how honest you*
> *are willing to be with yourself about your life.*
> *Like it or not it's time to stop bull*
> *shitting and do what it takes:*
> *Now!"*
>
> ~ *Dõv Baron*

Now, I'm guessing that at this point some of you are asking the question, "Where do our beliefs come from, and why do we keep doing what doesn't work?"

Well, earlier I explained to you that you get your beliefs from your family, your environment, the media, and your peers. I want to go deeper than that. So, let's go deeper.

Chapter 35

The Mad Chemist:
Your Ego Mind

A little while ago I promised I would introduce you to your ego-mind. So, say hi! Your ego-mind is the one who has been in charge of gathering up all your beliefs and filling them into your unconscious, like a serial killer trying to hide the bodies in a swamp.

I think that you might already be ahead of me as I now go through the ideas that are so deeply relevant for you and for me in beginning to master the ego-mind. I'm sure we've both been guilty of hanging on to things that we know we should have let go of? Things that if we had released sooner, would have brought us, or allowed us to regain more freedom. True?

As I'm sure you've noticed, so many people just don't know when to let go and move on. This happens in personal relationships where the relationship has simply finished, everything has gone completely flat. It's not mean, cruel or abusive; it's just dead and neither party is prepared for the freedom that separation will bring.

This hanging on is not limited to personal relationship, it happens in business with customers and clients. After the many years I spent

221

working with small business people it becomes blatantly obvious that there are some customers who should simply be let go of. These are the kind of customers who are just not worth the time and effort being spent on them to justify the amount of profit being made from them. Is this hard? Sure, but it's also totally necessary if the business is to not only survive but thrive.

Are there other areas where we are holding on to something that is now outmoded, where there are new versions of the programs we are using, but we are still holding on to the old ways, like life itself depended upon it?

Why do we hold on? The answer is simple yet deeply engrained. We hold on because we've always done 'it' like that. Which is a statement of fear, what might happen if we didn't do it the way we've always done it? Check for yourself: Do you have stuff that is hanging around in your home, stuff that is there for some sentimental reason, but you know in your heart of hearts you will end up dumping it, maybe not today, but certainly, one day? Perhaps that day could be today? What is it that you are holding onto in your life that may be preventing you from exploring new adventures?

One of the reasons we hang on is because of our conditioned thought processes, we hang on while telling ourselves, and to some degree believing, we have no other choice. In fact nothing could be further from the truth. We always have a choice! Even if the choice we are making is to tell ourselves that we don't have any. Bottom line is: However difficult the choice is, however hard the road we must travel following that choice, we still always have a choice.

Might it be worth taking a good hard look at your personal and professional life and realize by some serious thinking that perhaps you are unwittingly suffering from the ego's grip? Realize that it is now time to let go?

Here's an analogy that may help: Imagine the ego-mind as that stubborn old man we've all met at least once in our lives; loud as a motor boat and grumpy as an ox. He tends to be pessimistic about changing anything. He has a 'proper' order to *do anything*; right down to exactly how much butter belongs on a piece of toast for breakfast and what time you have to eat it. Heck, even by shifting the time he would normally eat would cause a 'ruckus' so large that you would think you were trying to saw his leg off with a jagged spoon.

You get what I'm saying right? The kind of grump that can't even play solitare without having perfectly straight lines of cards or the old lady that if even one napkin has been moved on the table that's never been used in years (in a room no one's allowed in unless there's plastic on the furniture), that hell might just break loose.

That's the kind of 'stubborn' I'm talking about here; the kind where at times it can seem like getting him to change his ways, his beliefs, would be like trying to squeeze water from a rock.

In some cases, he hasn't changed in thirty plus years and he's rather proud of it. (After all, why wouldn't he be? He's survived this long, right? And he's obviously happy and fullfilled, isn't he?).

Don't get me wrong, I'm not wanting to paint a negative picture; he's not all bad, at least once you understand him. Nonetheless it is of vital importance to you and your levels of success and joy that you do get who and what he is.

Your ego-mind is just like that grumpy old man—it has always helped you survive, and it's proud of that. In fact, its strongest argument for not changing is you are alive; therefore what it does, works. However, if this grumpy old man of an ego is stubbornly clutching onto old negative and limited beliefs of what you are capable of, he's never allowing you to *thrive* either; never allowing you to grow into your own unlimited potential.

Deep down, on some level, you've always felt there is a better, easier way to move through life, haven't you? If you could only get through to the part of you that stores your beliefs, what I call your ego-mind, or who I playfully refer to as 'the grumpy old man'.

The Science behind Your Beliefs, Made Easy
I want you to understand that all the beliefs people have about everything in their lives create a certain neurology within them. In case you are unfamiliar with some of the words I'm about to use, I'll explain them as I use them, so everyone can end up on the same page (pun intended).

Let me show you exactly how this works:

Neurochemistry, the Chemistry in Your Brain
Please excuse me taking a moment to explain what Neurochemistry is and if you are already familiar with its meaning, as I said, it is important that everyone's on the same page.

Neurochemistry isn't a hard word to understand once it has been broken up into its smaller parts. Let's start with the first half, neuro. We put neuro in front of any word when we're talking about topics that have to do with the physical parts of the brain.

And **chemistry** is, well, chemicals (just like in high school).

Slide the two words side by side and you can instantly see that when we say *neuro***chemistry** we are talking about the *chemicals in the brain*. That wasn't too painful, was it?

In this section, the interactions between of all of your perceptions, beliefs, and the chemicals that accompany them all fall under one word, *neuro***chemistry**. Each part will be explained as we get to it, so it can be very, very easily understood. You will see.

Back to basics. In order for any of us to survive, we need to have a system in place that allows us to recall and interpret *all* the events that happen in our lives. Remember we were designed with an automatic system in place between ages zero and about six. I'd like to take the opportunity here to point out that remembering an event and interpreting it are separate actions. Just keep reading and you will catch on fast.

The ability to both remember and interpret information allows us to create a *'belief system'*, which is a short way of saying 'a structured way of perceiving reality'. A good example of a *belief system is*, 'in the morning, the sun will rise from the east', or 'apples grow from certain trees'.

If you didn't have the ability to remember and believe, you would be facing two major problems concerning the above statements:

- You wouldn't know the sun would rise in the morning.

- And you wouldn't be able to believe that apple trees grew, well … apples.

Remember what I just told you though and don't confuse your ability to remember the past with your ability to interpret it. These are two different functions. The ego-mind (the grumpy old man) remembers

225

past events, except his real job is to create **belief systems** from those past events. If he didn't, you would *only* remember that the sun rose every morning as far back as you can recall. You wouldn't be able to believe it would rise again tomorrow, which could potentially make living life rather complicated.

Here's my question for you: Again, who else are you going to be sharing your new understanding of the ego-mind with over the next few days? You do know don't you? I thought so.

Chapter 36

Why Your Neurochemistry
Can Be So Hard to Change

If we go back to the example of the sun rising in the morning and how apples grow from certain trees, you can begin understanding why changing ANY belief can become so difficult.

That grumpy old man in your mind believes that every morning the sun will rise and that if you want to eat, if you want to live, you better believe that the sun will rise again tomorrow and the days that follow. The grumpy old guy says you will want to know this so you can find your way around this world, and if need be find an apple tree if you want to eat an apple, because there aren't any apples coming from rocks.

Back to the neurochemistry. Look, the problem here is that if someone's mind is filled with negative disempowering beliefs such as 'I don't deserve love', or 'I don't deserve wealth', or even 'things will never get any better', the ego-mind will fight to keep those beliefs in place just as hard as it fights to maintain beliefs such as 'the sun will rise from the east in the morning', and 'apples grow on apple trees'.

Your ego-mind, that grumpy old man, does NOT understand the

difference between beliefs that keep you alive so that you can function (such as 'fire is hot so don't touch', or 'glass sliding doors are still solid objects so don't walk into them') and beliefs that hold you back while making you miserable (such as 'well, that's just the way life is' or 'life is a struggle').

I often put it this way: **your ego-mind only helps you survive, it doesn't help you thrive.**

The ego-mind can't help you thrive because it doesn't understand the difference between surviving and thriving. He wasn't built to make choices about what you should or shouldn't believe. Instead, he takes a 'truth', makes a **belief system** out of it, then fights to the death to maintain it. If a new belief tries to take the place of the old one, it's fought against tooth and nail regardless of whether it's better or not—whether it keeps you stuck or moves you forward. First come first served, is how the grumpy old man sees it. He doesn't have the capacity to understand the difference between surviving and thriving. Only you do. And as we said, true, long-lasting change can be difficult if you don't have the necessary tools and understandings that allow you to communicate with your ego-mind.

This is what I meant when I said we all run 'programmed beliefs' and 'programmed limited beliefs'.

The way the ego-mind maintains beliefs is similar to a plane on autopilot. You set your altitude, direction, and speed, hit a button, let go of the control stick, close your eyes and rely on the program you set. What's more, that program runs until you change it, or until you slam into a mountain. The only catch is that most of us aren't familiar with how the control panel works—heck, most of us have had our eyes closed so long that we aren't even aware there is a control panel.

As you can imagine, autopilot is an amazingly useful feature—as long as the destination you are heading is where you truly want to go. The beauty of autopilot is that once we have the right destination in mind, it allows us to get there with minimal effort. You just dial in what you want then sit back and enjoy the ride—eyes wide, no struggle.

Surviving or Thriving
Please understand that the ability to create and maintain beliefs for ourselves is a natural part of our survival. Yet since the ego-mind <u>cannot</u> distinguish between positive healthy beliefs and negative limiting beliefs, **it has no choice other than viewing any attempt at changing any belief of any kind as a survival threat.** The ego-mind operates as if it has no choice other than to treat all beliefs as essential, because the ego-mind perceives that if you change, you might not survive. So the problem ends up being that the persistence of your ego-mind can prevent you from allowing yourself to thrive.

It's time to not only survive, *it's time to thrive.*

The truth is if you don't change, you will die—maybe not physically, but definitely mentally, emotionally, and spiritually.

If you are tired of merely surviving and want to start thriving, then it's time to start living your life the way you want to live it by at least challenging your beliefs with the techniques I have laid out in this book.

How the Ego-Mind Can Hold You Back
How does the ego-mind keep us from making the changes that we need to live our dreams?

To keep things the same, the ego-mind creates and must maintain a closed system, meaning nothing must get in, even at the level of being able to question the faulty system.

How does it do this? By appearing to be open, while having an automatic dismiss sequence that slams down a disguised steel gate on what should be an open mind.

What is the automatic sequence that slams down the steel gate? Well, it's not very complicated, but it is very effective. The automatic dismiss sequence is three little words. And those three words may have already fired off several times while you were reading this book. If they did they locked out whatever you were trying to let in. These are the three words that have echoed in all our minds at some point in our lives and they are extremely dangerous to the open mind, *"I know that."*

Those words are what some psychologists refer to as a defense mechanism. The old man is threatened by change and "I know that" is his best defense when he catches you considering new ideas and new actions that might lead to new beliefs. The steel door comes down to the sound of: ***I know that.***

Those are the words that keep people stuck in life because the ego-mind, that grumpy old man, thinks like this:

"Who you are right now, is who you were yesterday, and that's all you are ever going to be because that's how we survived this long. Who you are is who you were, and that's all you are ever going to be."

I'm here to tell you: He's wrong!

Let me say it again. Wait, no, let me yell it out to you:
"HE IS WRONG. Who you were yesterday is ONLY who you were

yesterday. Today YOU can choose who you want to be right now and for tomorrow."

> *"Today you can choose who you want*
> *to be for tomorrow."*
>
> ~ *Dõv Baron*

If it were true that you are nothing more than your past, then tomorrow *nothing* could change; not your beliefs, not your perceptions, not your thoughts. And something is changing right now because by reading this you have already taken the first step in changing who you are today, to live the life of your dreams, tomorrow.

Back to the science of it...

Chapter 37

Neuropeptide Cocktails
for Everyone

A few paragraphs ago you learned why beliefs are necessary, and read about how they are formed. The next step is to learn how beliefs not only *reside* in the unconscious—but how they have a physical effect on the brain, and every cell of your body as well.

There is a part of your brain known as the hypothalamus and one of the functions of this part of your brain is to produce chemicals in the form of *neuro***peptides**. As a result of the hypothalamus doing its job you have chemicals running through your body that matches up with every belief and every emotion you own.

Remember how we defined the word neurochemical? We will define this word the same way.

Neuro: We put Neuro in front of any word when we're talking about topics that have to do with our brain. To understand peptides, we have to understand another word, **protein**.

For most people when they read the word *protein* they start thinking chicken, beef, maybe even tofu. That's not quite what we mean here.

It's true that protein, can be chicken or beef, except what I'm referring to here is protein on the chemical level.

When I say *protein*, I only mean fuel for our cells. (Pay close attention to the word fuel. We're going to use it again shortly, and it's going to be a big point!).

Use your imagination and picture a couple of proteins floating around (imagine two floating tennis balls). Grab some crazy glue, stick enough of them together, and you will get a peptide. Simply put, combine a few proteins, and you get a peptide.

Put **neuro** in front of **peptide**, and you have, well, brain food.

Hold on, I'm not asking you to learn any difficult chemistry here. All you need to understand is that every one of your beliefs creates a series of chemicals inside of you. That series of chemicals is called a *neuropeptide chain*. And if you can understand that, then you will have no problem following any of the upcoming science and re-claiming mastery of your ego-mind will be like a warm summer's breeze.

Now remember, every belief and thought you have triggers your brain to create a unique series of *neuropeptides* which join together in a specific sequence and then this particular *neuropeptides cocktail* then releases into your body.

Let's check out what your body does with that neuropeptide.

How Beliefs Fuel Your Body
Ok, now that you have a sense of how your brain creates neuropep-tides, I want to help you understand why neuropeptides affect you.

The brain uses beliefs and thoughts as "triggers" to create chemicals (neuropeptides). Those neuropeptides are then released throughout your body. To put it in a more useful way, every moment you believe you deserve love (whether it's a conscious or unconscious belief), your brain uses that belief to create a chemical that matches your belief of love and then releases it in your body.

Your beliefs become the blueprints for all the neuropeptides you create.
Look at that statement carefully, as it's rather pivotal. Beliefs become the blueprints for all the neuropeptides we create, so you better start keeping an eye out for what you choose to believe, because what you believe is becoming fuel for your body. I'll expand that point in a bit.

Let's do a quick recap to see where we are and where we're going with all of this.

First, you have a belief, and that belief causes a chemical (neuropeptide) to be created in the hypothalamus and released into your body. Then what?

In your body there is something that absorbs those neuropeptides. There is something inside you that literally eats neuropeptides for breakfast.

Remember that word, fuel?

Cell Receptors: We Eat Neuropeptides for Breakfast
Scientists found that everybody has what we call cell-receptors all throughout our bodies (or in this case, neuropeptide receptors).

These receptors act a little like sea urchins. As neuropeptides swim through your body, the cell-receptors just grab them and eat them. Your cell receptors are literally grabbing your beliefs and absorbing them all throughout your body!

Your body is constantly producing more and more cell receptors to accommodate all the neuropeptides you are continually creating with every thought and emotion that pops into your mind. What's interesting is that this production occurs regardless of which beliefs you experience most often, be they positive ('I succeed in all that I do'), or negative ('nothing I do works out right').

The human body is good at adapting. So, whatever program you allow to run in your ego-mind, your body will mirror.

With that said, if you are constantly mulling over negative thoughts and beliefs, your body will create cell receptors designed specifically to consume those miserable neuropeptides that match them (figuratively and literally). On the other hand, if you create an abundance of positive beliefs, your body will create a bounty of cell receptors hungry for happiness to eat those positive beliefs up instead.

There is a catch, though. Cell receptors are very picky about what they consume. For example, if most of your life you carried a belief that money is hard to come by, then you would have a lot of cell receptors that only want to consume one type of neuropeptide: The exact neuropeptide that carries the blueprint of 'money is hard to come by'.

This puts us in a vicious cycle. We may have the occasional intentional thought that we deserve 'more happiness', and that thought WILL create a neuropeptide that has the blueprint of 'more happiness'. Unfortunately, if we've been carrying around any negative or limited unconscious beliefs about happiness, we won't have enough cell receptors available to eat up that positive belief to create an impactful change.

That is why the tools you were given in Part I are *sooo* important—unless you begin shining a spotlight on the beliefs you are carrying around in your unconscious, all the positive thinking in the world won't make a lick of difference. This is also what I meant when I said 'fuel' earlier! Your beliefs are literally feeding your body.

> *"A feeling sparked in your mind will translate as a peptide being released somewhere. Peptides regulate every aspect of your body, from whether you're going to digest your food properly to whether you're going to destroy a tumor cell."*
>
> ~ Candace Pert

So that begs the question: What's the next step?

How do we break the cycle?

Well, before we go on, if you don't mind, I want to remind you that what you've just learned was both insightful and powerful, wasn't it? So, just like before; think about who you need to share that neuro-peptide information with. As always, I'm sure someone came to mind right away. Remember, it's good to share what you learn because in sharing very often that's when we really get it ourselves.

Chapter 38

I Mean…What Do You Mean?

Remember earlier I said that the only common denominator in your life is you? In a moment, I'll show you an example of how we interpret information, and then you will realize how you can start breaking the cycle of the same old stuff showing up over and over again.

Except before we do that, I want to give you a break from the science portion of this book and make sure you understand the major point we are leading up to: **Your beliefs determine your reality**.

Simply put, your beliefs are the filters that interpret, or as I will show you in a moment, act as *lenses* that can distort incoming information. I'm going to say that again because it is very important to you. Regardless of the analogies and the metaphors used in this book, the key point is this:

Beliefs determine your reality because they become the filters and lenses that distort information.

The reason we unconsciously distort information is because as we learned earlier, the ego-mind (the grumpy old man) needs to make sure that once you have beliefs, you see all other events in the world as proof that your beliefs are correct. Again, remembering that from the ego-minds point of view, the filtering has helped you to survive.

That last paragraph might confuse some people, so let me clear up any uncertainty.

Once the ego-mind—once your grumpy old man—owns a belief, not only does he fight to keep that belief alive, he distorts all incoming information so that you see life as a reflection of that belief.

There is a reason why this happens, and before we get into that reason you need to first understand the ways people distort incoming information.

While you read about lenses and maps and see why we distort information, I'd like you to use another technique that develops your intuition, because ultimately it will help our progress here.

As you read the next few pages, keep this idea in mind: "**The ego-mind is constantly distorting information that is coming in.**" Open your mind and imagine a few ways that your ego-mind might distort information, and while you are at it, how you might begin breaking that cycle. (Here's a tip; if you hear the words *I know that* in your mind, or if you have the urge to resist doing this, then your ego-mind is distorting things right now!).

A few sentences ago, I made a strong statement, "Your ego-mind distorts all incoming information to maintain your beliefs." This process is best illustrated by a story. It just happens to be one of my favorite stories because it always makes me smile.

Ever been on a vacation to England? If you ever find yourself in

England, you will want to make sure to leave your old beliefs behind, and open your mind up to some new ones.

Imagine you are now in England driving down any old street and the light is turning red. As you are waiting for the light to turn green, you happen to see a guy walk by in a British military uniform. You find yourself caught up in the excitement of traveling abroad and smile at the soldier while proudly giving him the 'V' (peace) sign—a sign that some of us tend to believe stands for 'victory'.

The British soldier looks back at you, and you notice by the expression on his face that he is *really* upset!

I'm going to bet that unless you are a Brit, or you've spent a significant amount of time in Britain, you are completely baffled about why this guy might be so upset.

Well, as it turns out, the victory sign in the U.K. is the same as the 'bird' in America. And the bird is not exactly a huge compliment in America.

The point of this story is to illustrate how the environment people grow up in shapes their current view of the world. Most of the beliefs people own have been passed down from their parents, the history books we've read, our peers, and the media. The beliefs we adopted from the people around us then get projected into our present as if they are unquestionably correct, and through these preconceived notions we go about creating our future.

You've probably realized by now there is another way.

You now know you have the choice to challenge your beliefs, and see whose beliefs they really are. You can either live the life of your dreams or you can live in the shadow of others.

To start to live the life of your dreams you must master the Six Foundations. You can only master those six foundations by examining the beliefs you have been holding about each of them. In mastering those foundations you will reclaim ownership of your manifesting mind.

Nelson, Roger, Martin and Rosa

I have to say, when it comes to what can be achieved by challenging commonly-held beliefs, several individuals clearly stand out. Their lives are an inspiration to me, and they have all changed the beliefs of many others around the world. Some of them you will remember and some you might have forgotten, while all have changed our lives by challenging the status quo and in so doing changing what we have believed.

Nelson Mandela

Not that long ago, it seemed as if that there was no way to end apartheid in South Africa. For those who don't know, apartheid is a policy that maintains segregation and discrimination based on race. It's a severe form of racism.

In order to truly understand the courage it took Nelson Mandela to stand up to his convictions, you need to fully comprehend the depth to which apartheid was engrained in South African culture.

When it came time to vote in South Africa, the colour of your skin determined how and where your vote would count. For example, if that system was running in the U.S. and you were African American your vote would only be counted in, as they put it back then, the 'black' community. Let's say the same was true for Hispanic, Native American, and white. The policy enforced such extreme forms of segregation that you couldn't even seek education or employment in communities outside of your own 'color' because your status was based entirely on your ethnicity.

Just think about it: Apartheid was not only an enforced policy in South Africa, for many at that time it was also a chosen and enforced belief system.

Nelson Mandela was fighting against a nation that believed equality was measured by skin color—and that way of life was defended by militaristic and political forces.

Imagine the courage it took to wake up every morning and be required to fight hand, tooth, and nail for equality, for happiness. Mr. Mandela could have adopted the beliefs of the others around him. He could have found a way to move to a different country and walked away from it all. Instead, he chose to speak his truth.

Nelson Mandela let his truth ring and resonate in the ears and hearts of anyone who would listen. He stood up for his beliefs, the beliefs he chose for himself. *He* chose what it would take to make him happy.

Obviously it wasn't an easy path to take. The man spent 27 years in prison, and was constantly attacked both politically and personally for many years before, during and afterward.

I know that chances are you are not attempting to overthrow an entire socio-political structure (although you could do much worse—there are people with far less savory aspirations). Yet, in the end, Nelson's unwavering belief in himself and his divine right to be, earned him the right to choose his happiness—the same right we all have.

Roger Bannister

Most people don't know that up until 1954, nobody believed there was a way to run a mile in under four minutes. Well, nobody except for Roger Bannister.

Until Roger Bannister proved them wrong, scientists had told the international community that a four-minute mile was impossible. Doctors claimed that if anyone ran at that speed or faster, their lungs could collapse and joints could shatter. The world was told and believed that the human body could not handle it. Up until that point it was "truth."

On May 6, 1954, in front of three-thousand spectators, Roger Bannister did what they said was impossible and ran a mile in three minutes 59.4 seconds.

Not only was the record broken but also a belief that the world held as "truth" changed in that instant. His record breaking run resulted in that record being broken an *additional six times* in that year alone. You read that right: **Six times.**

What the entire medical profession believed, what the entire world believed, was changed in one brief moment by a man who refused to succumb to limitations placed on him by others.

Nowadays, you can't even qualify to be in the Olympics unless you can run a mile in under four minutes.

Think about that for a moment. Roger Bannister was not an exception to the rule. He was someone who refused to believe the rule and the limitations other people put on themselves. What is absolutely fascinating is that once he broke that barrier, it was broken for everyone around the world. After all, if he was the only one who could break that four-minute mark, then it wouldn't have been broken **six more times that year, would it?**

When someone accomplishes something like that—when they do what everyone believed was impossible—they expand our consciousness. They expand what is possible for all of us.

> *"Every time someone does something that you believed*
> *was impossible, it gives you another chance*
> *to realize that anything is possible."*
> ~ Dōv Baron

What would South Africa be like today if Nelson Mandela listened to the presiding beliefs of a large number of racists? For that matter, what about Roger Bannister, Rosa Parks, or Dr. Martin Luther King Jr? What would the world be like today if they hadn't stood up and spoken their truths? Do you think any one of them allowed someone to dictate what they should believe or what they could achieve in their lives?

Then why have you? ˇ

Oh you say, you are not a politician or an athlete—well neither was Rosa. Rosa Parks was just a lady traveling on a bus who decided she'd had enough of the status quo.

Let's just suppose for a moment that you now have THAT kind of unyielding drive in all your activities. What are you doing with your life? Where are you going? What are you achieving?

I know it can simply seem like words on paper. You might catch yourself saying, "But it's different for me as I'm no Rosa, I'm not saving South Africa, or the ozone, or whatever."

And no one's asking you to.

What I am asking you to save is: Yourself. If you want to change what seems impossible into *what is possible* in the blink of an eye, then you must change your beliefs. And just so you know, it does happen that fast, in the blink of an eye. I want you to think back to Part One of this book where you looked at what you've accomplished. I asked you to focus on those accomplishments, to really step into those feelings and take pride in what you've done and who you are.

Now, let's take that exercise to a higher level, so as to propel you to greater and greater levels of success.

> *"There is no real success without the risk of failure.*
> *If you never risk failure you will never*
> *know the real heart pounding joy of success."*
> *~ Dōv Baron*

Right now, get out the pad or journal, or whatever you have been doing these exercises in. On a fresh page, I want you to write the words: My Everest.

As you probably know Mount Everest is the highest mountain on the planet. And just like those other 'impossible' barriers it was believed that no one could climb it.

On May 29th 1953, the later to be knighted, Sir Edmund Hillary was the first man to conquer the seemingly unconquerable Mount Everest.

Can you imagine the ongoing squabbles taking place inside that guy's head? At some point or another I'm sure he replayed the belief systems of the time: "It's too high, no one's ever climbed it, it's impossible. You are crazy to even try, you are going to fail."

In all likelihood when the weather got treacherous on his third attempt, his mind and possibly his body would have been screaming for him to; *give up this ridiculous dream.*

However, Sir Edmund Hillary had a relationship with himself that forgave the past 'failures' and held strict boundaries about whose belief systems were going to run his life. As a result, after three previously failed attempts he finally did it; he conquered Everest.

In an interview the media said, "You've conquered the mountain," and Hillary said: "No, I've conquered myself."

Chapter 39

What is Your Everest?

The Exercise:
Write down the thing that seems like a mountain that you must conquer. Maybe it's being open to having a romantic relationship again. Maybe it's reaching a certain financial outcome in your bank account. Maybe it's getting yourself in shape, running a half marathon, or shedding some extra weight. Maybe it's starting your own business or going for that promotion. Whatever your Everest is, write it down.

Now, once you have written down what your next Everest is I want you to think back to some of your previous ones. What have been some of the things you have done that at one time or another, before you completed them, you would have thought they were impossible mountains to climb?

Once you've written some of them down I want you to think about scaling your next Everest by thinking of it in just those terms. In order to conquer Everest, Sir Edmund Hillary, would have to have had a plan. He would have had to execute that plan and he would have had to travel a certain distance every day in order to reach the top. In other words, he didn't conquer Everest in one go, there were a whole series of steps that needed to be taken to reach that outcome. What I'm sharing with you here is; it's no different for you as you climb to your peak.

You want to know something? It's a little secret between you and me. If you are reading this, you want to change. Do you know how I know that? It's because you are reading this.

Ok, that was obvious. But nonetheless, it's true.

Unless you are one of my family members reading this because I gave it to you for Christmas or your birthday, I'm willing to bet that you would like to change your life in some way for the better. Knowing that the ego-mind sees change as 'death' makes it seem difficult, like an uphill battle. I'm here, however, to wake you up and tell you it's not an uphill battle. I want to show you how change can be seen as exciting, invigorating, and dare I say it, *pretty simple*.

The 'how' will be described in Part III under the heading, the Equation for Manifestation™. WAIT! Don't go flipping there yet. Before you get to that, you need to understand how our perception of events affects the neurochemistry in our bodies, and how by changing our perceptions we begin seeing our beliefs—our lives—in a new light. How we begin doing that just happens to be the heading of the next section.

Chapter 40

Information Filtering

Two ladies are sitting in a coffee shop chatting when the young guy who works there leans over them and accidentally spills a carton of milk. Profusely apologetic he tries to clean up, but one of the ladies is furious, she screams at the young fellow, providing him with a verbal list of all the things that is wrong with him and his establishment.

Meanwhile, the other lady quickly jumps up out of the way of the milk spill and, in so doing, makes sure none of the spilled milk lands on her. She reaches down to assist the other lady who is deeply embedded in her tirade. The second lady is calm and unruffled by the event while the first lady looks a little like one of the establishment's espresso machines... steam is coming out of her ears.

Why is it that the same event happened to both ladies and one of them is completely unfazed. Has she just returned home from meditating at a temple in Tibet? Maybe. There again, why was it such a big deal for the first lady? Has she just had a bit too much caffeine for her own or anyone else's good? Again, maybe.

The fact is: Events, whatever they are, on their own have no meaning. We are the ones who give any situation or circumstance its meaning and in so doing we decide if something is good or bad.

Interesting you say. No, powerful, I say. Why? Because in the process of reclaiming your manifesting mind there will be some things you will decide that you need to change, things that your ego-mind will want to stay the same. The good news is, because we are the ones who get to decide the meaning of anything; change can be perceived as exciting rather than stressful. Be absolutely clear when I say "we" I don't mean the media, your friends, or family, I mean **you**.

You decide if the events that go on in your life make you happy or sad. This point might be best illustrated through an example. Happily, this example also demonstrates some of the concepts we've discussed up to now.

Let's say you are sitting around a coffee shop somewhere, maybe the one where the milk just got spilt, you overhear two people talking, and one of them mentions that they just got out of a long-term relationship. From your vantage point you can't see this person and so you don't really know from their face how they feel about the break up.

Now, there are several different re-actions you might have. The majority of us might feel badly for them, knowing how rough a break up can be. There could be some folks that would get excited for them. (And for the record, we might call those people vultures). The rest and even some of the previous two groups would likely fall into the 'glad it isn't me' category.

You might be asking, what's my point?

Well, the point is that no matter what your re-action is, you are re-acting. And that re-action is based on a belief you have formed about 'break ups'.

The phenomenon of breaking up may be universal yet re-actions after the break-up will differ from person to person.

Let's take it one step further. No event, even a break up evokes a universal emotional response for everyone. In fact, you are the one attaching meaning to all the events in your life. May I suggest that you better seriously consider taking hold of that concept, really letting it sink in, because it's a major point! It's so huge, that I put it in bold on the next line. I really did, look!

It's the truth: **No event in life has any meaning other than the meaning we attach to it.**

To boot, there's some science supporting that fact:

Neurochemists recently discovered that every time anyone witnesses an event, a polypeptide chain is created and released because they have a belief about that event. (Whether that belief is in their conscious or unconscious awareness doesn't matter, the inner pharmacy goes to work).

Another thing you should know is that regardless of whether or not the event witnessed was enjoyed or not, a particular polypeptide chain is still released.

Now, consider this next point very carefully: Regardless of whether you enjoyed what you saw, or it made your blood boil like a lobster in a pot, the polypeptide chain your hypothalamus released in love or in hate, are nearly identical.

I'll say it another way: **Peptides released in excitement and peptides released in fear are almost identical**. At a neurochemical level these things that we may have considered as opposites are close to identical... Freaky isn't it!

I understand that can be a little confusing for a few people, but just follow along with me here. By the end of this example you will understand everything clearly.

Roller Coasters: Friends or Foes?

I'm going to guess you've probably taken a ride on a roller coaster before. If you haven't, I'm assuming you've been too afraid to try. I understand, I'm not a fan myself, while my wife loves them. Since you don't have a roller coaster in front of you right now, I would like you to imagine there's one right there. Can you imagine that roller coaster and honestly tell me that the roller coaster is emitting a vibe you can feel that is somehow informing you that it's either scary or fun?

Did the roller coaster call you up on the telephone before you came down to the amusement park and say, "If you ride me, I'm going to scare the warm apple juice out of you!"

I'm guessing it didn't. Actually, I'm pretty sure that you received no vibes and no phone calls directly from any roller coaster, ever.

So where does your interpretation of fear or excitement come from?

If it's not the roller coaster calling you up and saying, *fear me*, or if it's not something from out there, doesn't that only leave *you*? Once again: Wouldn't that mean that: *The only common denominator in your life is you?* After all, if the roller coaster can't tell you it's scary or fun, then something inside of you must be telling you that, right?

Like I said a few pages back, whether it's roller coasters, break-ups, or whatever: No event in life has any meaning other than the meaning you attach to it.

So, how do we attach meaning to the events in our lives?

Chapter 41

I Can't See the Map,
because I Can't Find My Glasses

One of the ways we attach meaning to the events in the world around us is by what I call *looking through a lens*.

Picture this:
You've seen those sunglasses people sometimes wear, the ones with colored lenses? If you were to pretend that someone was standing next to you wearing a pair of red-tinted glasses, and you were both looking at a white wall, would they see the wall in the same way as you, or would the wall appear to be tinted with at least a little more red for them?

I'm hoping you concluded they would see a red or pink-tinted wall, or we're going to need to send your imagination in for a check-up!

Ok ... following me so far? Fantastic!

I'm sure you hear what I'm saying here, that it wouldn't matter what the two of you looked at. Whatever your friend with the red glasses was looking at it would always have a touch of red in it, while you would be seeing its true colors.

My mother has worn glasses all her life. As children my siblings and I would often find that my mother's looking for her 'stolen' glasses as a great spontaneous source of entertainment. Oftentimes mom would take an impromptu nap and upon waking up, in a less than fully alert state would start stumbling around looking for her glasses. Eventually she would shout at us kids, demanding to know who stole her glasses. All through this fiasco we would be holding back our laugher as the 'stolen' lenses stared back at us from the top of my mother's head. Because she couldn't see them, for all intents and purposes they didn't exist!

The lenses we wear are the ones we cannot see and the truth is we are very, very rarely without them. The invisible lenses we wear are the beliefs we carry with us. We would like to think these lenses are completely invisible but often times they can be seen better by others than by us, the person wearing them.

The meanings we attach to the events in our lives are tinted by the color of the lens we wear. So, if you happen to know someone who doesn't like how they see the world, you could always suggest they change their lenses, which of course, is not as easy as slipping off an old pair of glasses.

Maybe this short story can shed some light on the kind of power beliefs seen through the limiting or destructive lens can have on us.

Have you ever walked down the street and smiled at someone? Then, in return you received a look? Just a look, that's all it was, although for some reason you got the distinct impression that this look meant, "Go screw yourself," or something similar?

What if your impression was wrong? What if the person you looked at, the person you smiled at, was friendly? Maybe they were even a little interested, although a bit embarrassed, caught off guard perhaps and they didn't know how to re-act.

You do realize that any impression you felt was only on account of the glasses you were wearing at the time. See, you attached a meaning to the re-action you witnessed, just like the case of the break-up!. Maybe what that person felt was embarrassment, maybe they were thinking of something completely different or something very annoying and they didn't even notice you. But the lenses you were wearing were labeled 'rejection', so that's what you experienced.

You were the one attaching meaning to that event and you did it in a millisecond based entirely on your beliefs—on your negative beliefs.

It comes down to this:

> *"If you don't like what you see in the world,*
> *change the lenses through which*
> *you see the world."*
>
> ~ *Dōv Baron*

I find in my live events that about half the room nods and laughs after that example, while the other half stares at me like deer caught in headlights. So, here's another way of looking at it.

Chapter 42

Maps:
Another Way to Look at Lenses

Another way we attach meaning to the events in our lives is through the use of what I call *maps*. Hold on, don't run to your car and tear up your road maps. That's not quite what we're talking about.

This is what I mean:
Everyone, including you, has what I like to call a 'survival map'.

Simply put, a survival map is the combination of the beliefs and behaviors people have. To put it another way: Your survival map is your life, except it's *your* life with all the meanings *you* attach to all the events in it.

It's sort of like getting a map to all the restaurants in your area then grabbing a red pen and adding in notes about all the good and bad places to eat, based on what your friends and family have told you. Think about it, if this were the case, generally speaking once you've marked a restaurant as bad you are not to likely to eat there are you? In fact, you will probably tell all your friends not to eat there, either. Now remember, you may never have even stepped in the door of the place. Your opinion is purely based on: Someone told you that they perceived a bad experience in that restaurant, or maybe they didn't, or maybe it was their mother/brother/son/friends-nephews-best-friend's-uncle that said it was bad.

Doesn't that seem awfully similar to how we adopted most of our beliefs? Some we tried, most we simply took on because other people said they already 'tried that, it doesn't work'. You and I both know just because I may love Indian food doesn't mean you won't dislike it, or vice versa. So wouldn't it make sense that you need to try something new out yourself and see what happens rather than putting your experiences in the hands of another?

Anyway...Back to your survival map.

While reading this section on maps I want you to keep asking yourself, "What might be my survival map?" One of the ways to find out is to ask yourself: "What is my 'normal'?"

Growing up, we had no idea what was good or bad, healthy or unhealthy. We had no idea what to believe. The only way we were able to get through the first part of our lives as children was to adopt our parents' and familial belief systems.

Without our parents, we wouldn't have learned valuable lessons in life such as to eat our greens (though, I still need to work on that), not to play with fire, and to stop hiding Grandma's teeth. More relevant to our discussion here, we also adopted their beliefs about love, relationships, money, health and anything else we might throw in the category of success.

For a lot of us while growing up, certain beliefs were not to be questioned. In some cases, all family beliefs were beyond question. For many, beliefs about a certain subject, like love were treated much like beliefs about the sun rising in the east. You just didn't question them. For a long time you may never have even considered that they need to be questioned.

As we grew older, the habit of not questioning beliefs could have become a belief of its own. In some cases we had spent so much time learning *from* others we had stopped learning *for ourselves*. Many of us even stopped believing we could learn for ourselves.

> *"We have carried our beliefs like valuable jewels*
> *because for a time they served us in some way.*
> *It is the willingness to recognize when that same belief*
> *that once served us now restricts us and we let it go,*
> *then and only then we are free."*
> ~ *Dōv Baron*

Let me clarify what I mean by learning from others here.

Earlier, when you asked yourself where your beliefs came from and whose beliefs they were, did you take it one step further and test out if those beliefs were absolutely true?

Follow along with me here. If we were to take a common belief that the world holds, the belief that 'money is hard to come by', (or as I often heard growing up, 'Money doesn't grow on trees') is the belief "money is hard to come by" true for everyone all around the world? Is it written in stone? Genetically passed down generation to generation?

Tell me now, **what has to be true for that belief to be true?**

Let me give you a clue. In order for that or any other belief to be true, you have to MAKE it true for you. You have to choose to believe it. And as you know, if your belief is that money is hard to come by, you are creating a neuropeptide chain to be released into your system with that belief as its blueprint. You are literally feeding your body that belief because that is how our neurochemistry works!

In turn, those beliefs are creating a resonance field that will keep making money hard to come by, *for you*.

That belief gets demonstrated over and over again in your life through your behavior because you allow it to be embedded into your unconscious—to be held onto by that grumpy old man, repeated to you time and time again as he waves his cane at you.

I'm not saying that saving money is a bad idea. Of course not! What I'm saying is that if you think about money and right away you are *afraid* that there won't be enough, or if you 'remind' people that money is hard to come by, you are re-enforcing that unconscious belief. All the while, you are re-creating the circumstances necessary to generate more of the neurochemistry that carry the blueprint for 'money is hard to come by' in both you and the people you are preaching to.

After a while, that belief becomes a point on your map of survival, or if you prefer how I explained it earlier, a lens through which you see the world.

Oh! Here's a really frightful thought: If you have kids who hear "money's hard to come by," while they grow up, what notion do you think will form in *their* unconscious? Remember, when under six years old the information goes direct, no filters, straight into the unconscious mind.

Makes you want to gulp a little doesn't it. It's profound how much power we carry around and yet rarely use for our growth. Again, think about who you need to share that with. Who comes to mind that would find what you just discovered fascinating? Someone always comes to mind, it may be colleagues, friends, family the people you deeply care about. Share the knowledge if that helps you to really get it.

Back to the point at hand: I'd like you to take notice of the word I used just a few moments ago to describe some people's attitude toward money: Afraid. To be afraid is to live in fear, and as you read in Part One under the heading: 'It is your divine right to have the life you want', fear leads to anger. Anger leads to hate. Hate leads to suffering. Or if you prefer, to put it bluntly, if you live in fear, your QRF will draw events to you that re-enforce that fear over and over again, BOTH because you are literally looking for it (through your lens) and because you begin to resonate on that 'fear level'.

The trouble is, once your ego-mind believes that 'money is hard to come by', the grumpy old man will file that belief away with the same importance as beliefs such as 'the sun rises from the east' and 'apples grow on apple trees'.

From then on, your ego-mind will take *every* opportunity to remind you that money is hard to come by just as strongly as it will remind you that the sun is rising from the east tomorrow morning. It will remind you until, of course, you decide to change your beliefs.

Just for the record, we're talking about changing the belief that money is hard to come by. Because let's face it, no amount of belief will change the direction the sun will rise. We're not talking fantasy here!

I don't know about you, but my manifesting mind now thinks the belief of 'money is hard to come by' sucks the big hot dog!

Anyway, back to your survival map ...

As you grew older, certain beliefs became real to you. They became normal. They became if you will, "cities" on your map of survival.

The problem is that as we attempt to navigate terrain towards a rich and fulfilling life, most of us tend to still use the same outdated maps we used in our childhood. Sure we've tweaked them a little if only to argue that they are not the same, but essentially, they are the same maps to the same place.

If you're twenty-five, thirty-five, or sixty years old and you're still using those old maps (beliefs) you were given as a child, something worth considering is that you may have got those maps from people who never had the courage to live their dreams. Chances are you won't get where you want to go in life using someone else's map, particularly if you are carrying the map of a dream crusher rather than a dream builder.

I'm not saying that all your beliefs hold you back. I just want you to ask yourself which beliefs are holding you back from living the life of your dreams, and then obliterate them.

Not taking the time in your life to check whether or not your map is still guiding you to the right destination is like following Chris Columbus's directions to India. By the way, he never got there. It's worth noting here that is the reason why the first nation's people of North America were called Indians.

It just doesn't make any sense to keep doing what doesn't work!

Chapter 43

The Physics of It

We're going to get deeper into quantum physics in Part III. Meanwhile, you will be surprised at how easily you will understand these introductory concepts. I'm going to begin by presenting to you two brilliant minds that have reshaped the way I and many others think.

The first of these brilliant minds was a man by the name of Werner Heisenberg. Werner was one of the forefathers of quantum theory. In his early years he taught the theories put forth by Albert Einstein and then went on to expand them. He won the Nobel Prize in 1932 for a theory he created and is now known as "Heisenberg Uncertainty Principle."

The second is Anais Nin, a Cuban-French author and diarist.

Heisenberg's Uncertainty Principle states that by simply observing something, just by looking at it, both you and the thing you are observing are changed in some way.

Did you absorb that? Simply by observing, by looking at something, *anything*, both the observer (you) and the observed (it) are changed in some way.

Confusing, enticing or just plain weird, it does make you think. When I first came across Heisenberg's uncertainty principle I spent weeks thinking about, not just what it said, but what it might mean in my own life. On one level what I saw within this work was that Heisenberg understood that the reality I see depends on the lenses I'm looking through and the map I'm using to navigate the terrain.

Here's what Heisenberg himself wrote: **"What we observe is not nature itself, but nature exposed to our method of questioning."** Do you see what I mean about lenses and maps?

Hold that quote from Heisenberg in your mind while you read what Anais Nin wrote, "We don't see things as they are, we see them as we are." This simply means that the world we see is a reflection of our beliefs.

This is the point we were making earlier when we were talking about how your ego-mind uses maps and lenses to distort all incoming information to match your beliefs.

Here, I'll clarify further. In our lives, we're not seeing evidence of what reality is we're seeing evidence of *our* reality. We filter out what doesn't fit into our model of reality. Like Heisenberg said, *what we observe is not nature itself, not reality itself, but nature exposed to our method of questioning.* And to reference Nin, our method of questioning is a reflection of who we are. Therefore, as the Simon and Garfunkel song goes: *We see what we want to see. We hear what we want to hear and we disregard the rest.*

I know YOU don't want to see constant struggle and 'lack of' in your life, yet if your ego-mind unconsciously believes that's what life is all about, you will end up seeing exactly what your ego-mind wants you to see.

**Bringing the Lenses, Filters, Maps, Physics, and Chemistry ...
Together**

Let's pretend you are looking at an opportunity right now, whatever it might be, though you are looking at it through a lens of low self-worth. Let's say I'm looking at that exact same opportunity, except I'm looking at it through a lens of healthy self-worth.

Are we going to see the opportunity in the same way? Of course not. **Of course not.**

In this case, our ego-minds have different belief systems, so we are seeing the exact same opportunity through completely different filters and different lenses; using different maps.

My ego-mind would encourage me to pursue my dreams regardless of what the world thought. My ego-mind (it's now well trained) would not be telling me that there isn't enough, or that things don't work out well.

I'm not saying that I don't have a grumpy old man. I'm just saying I don't view him as grumpy anymore because I learned how to speak to him. He still holds on to beliefs with the same die-hard conviction as your grumpy old man, it's just that his beliefs drive me forward so I can live a life of what I referred to as *Full Spectrum Success*. (In case you don't remember what *Full Spectrum Success* is, take a look at Part I under "The Six Foundations of Full Spectrum Success").

If you are still looking at the world through lenses of 'not enough' money, time, good guys, good women, then you can't even see all the wonderful opportunities that are often right in the palm of your hand.

Because believe it or not, some of your beliefs are actually limiting the amazing possible experiences that you could be welcoming into your life if you began seeing the world through different lenses!

Right now your brain is releasing a cascade of neuropeptides as you are reading this. Here's what that means. While you are reading this, your ego-mind is constantly filtering every statement through the lenses you wear to see how it fits in with your current beliefs—your 'normal'... So it might be worth checking your 'normal'.

There are actually a few things happening simultaneously.

First, every time you read a statement you release a neuropeptide chain based on how you *feel* about it, the information you read. Then you compare what you've read to your current beliefs, which releases more neuropeptides—the ones linked to your current unconscious beliefs.

I can imagine that some of you just read that and had an ego-mind yelling "This is too complicated!" or "This will require too much effort to learn, and you never follow through anyway, so don't bother!" I'm also willing to bet there are more than a few of you who have read parts of this book and said, "I know that!"

Well, if any of those thoughts have run through your mind at any time, that's a surefire sign that you need to start using the techniques in this book and reclaim mastery of your mind because this stuff isn't complicated, in fact it makes perfect logical sense, when you let it.

Look, do you have an opportunity in front of you, right now? Something staring right back at you that you hadn't fully allowed yourself to see yet? Something you are not hearing properly because you've been filtering out all the good stuff that doesn't yet fit onto your map of reality? Knowing what you've been learning throughout this book, do you now feel that you might be wearing lenses that block you from fully experiencing opportunities in your life?

If you want to start living the life of your dreams then you have to put on a different pair of lenses. Rename your survival map from 'not enough' to 'options for thriving'. Either way, you have to be willing to do whatever it takes to get it done.

Keep this at the forefront of your thinking: Your ego-mind sees all change as a threat, and it's informing your neurochemistry of what's in the filing cabinet labeled "beliefs we defend", then, using those old worn-out beliefs it will run your life until you learn to master your ego-mind.

If you are unwilling to challenge your ego-mind—challenge your be- liefs —then you might not even see opportunities right in front of you if those opportunities seem to threaten the ego-mind. When you master your ego-mind, you learn to talk to your ego-mind so that the neuropeptides you create, the lenses you wear, and the map you hold work with you to take you to the all the right destinations.

What's more, if and when you go off track, these new maps get you right back on track the moment you decide to pick them up again.

We talked a little about fear, earlier. You've likely heard that they say; the greatest fear of all is the fear of death. Well, from my research I have discovered that for most people the greatest fear is the fear of re- ally living, living passionately, living dynamically, *thriving* ... .

People are bloody scared of having to draw a new map to live wide open in a world abundantly full of opportunity and adven- ture. Too many cling to the shore line of 'desperation harbor' when the island of their dreams awaits them.

They are scared to death of thriving, so scared to live passionately that they stay in their little humdrum lives when there's so much more they can be; there is so much more you are capable of being. If that has in any way been how you have been operating I want to remind you of something that is a fundamental truth: "You are a diamond. You are a magnificent being. Tear off the lenses and become who you really are."

> *"We are never less than what we become*
> *yet always much more than we will ever know."*
> ~ *Dõv Baron*

Why are people so scared of thriving and living life passionately? Because those around them might judge them or might not like them. They might say, "You know, you are a bit too much for me dear— you are a bit too much." They are choosing to *fit in* rather than *stand out*; choosing to *follow* rather than *lead*. I could come up with about 20 more ways of saying that, except I think you get my point. They learned that it might be painful to step into the light and shine like a shooting star, or that it's scary, or both.

Either way, whatever the reason: Remember: It's your life. Live for them, or live for you, it's your call.

I know without a doubt, and again, with more than twenty years of experience, that living your life for *them*, whoever they are, will never, EVER bring you long-term happiness. **To be truly happy you must find out how to break those adopted limiting beliefs you've taken on, and you can begin doing that right now.**

Remember, behavior demonstrates belief so let me give you a bonus.

Before I go on any further, I'm going to lay down another exercise, an exercise that will help break some of the more subtle, addictive beliefs that you demonstrate in your behavior. These are some habits that you may not have noticed until later.

For the next few days pay attention to your habits. For example, notice which shoe you put on first, left or right. Then ask yourself this question, "If there was a belief behind this behavior, a reason why I put this foot in first, what would this belief be?" Now, I know some of these exercises may sound corny at first, but just give it a go—there is nothing to lose. And you may be very surprised by what you will learn!

Once you become comfortable doing that (and honestly, even if you are not comfortable with it!), take the next step and ask yourself why you do most of the daily things in your life in the ways that you do them. Which arm do you put in your shirt first? Better yet, notice something that doesn't have to do with left and right, like where you tend to sit on the bus or at the dinner table. Here's a random one: How about which side you start to brush your teeth from. You may notice almost all the things that you are doing are done automatically, habitually and unconsciously.

Life on Autopilot

We think we are free thinkers, but you can't claim to be a free thinker if you don't bother to think. Is it really hard to believe that most people's lives are on autopilot? Ok, then let me ask you, when was the last time you had to concentrate on walking (and being drunk doesn't count!)? How about breathing? I'm betting this question only just now brought your attention to your breathing.

273

You will be surprised at how unconscious beliefs play out in your behavior.

Mastery is When 'You' Do It

I'm sure by now you realize that the mind mastery program is a complete system for finding, revealing, and obliterating what's really been holding you back from living a life of what I call Full Spectrum Success.

Ultimately, this work is not all about paying attention to your breathing, or noticing which shoe you put on first (although this is a start). It's about realizing that most of your life you have been on autopilot. This autopilot has kept you alive—I'm not knocking it. I'm just saying that you can program in a new destination so the autopilot works entirely for your benefit, not only keeping you alive, but helping you to thrive.

You have to understand, simply reading these words and remembering them is not enough. Being able to quote them to your friends and loved ones, or strangers you meet isn't going to create the kind of change you are really looking for. You have to take action. I said it before and I'll say it again:

Chapter 44

Knowing is One Thing, Doing is Another

Doing represents wisdom.

Facing your ego-mind can sometimes be tough. After all, that cranky old man sure is stubborn, but he can change. Change is easy if you start taking small consistent steps.

Take one minute out of your day and do a couple of the exercises we talked about in Parts I and II. Question some of your old beliefs. Those tiny steps can and will make a massive difference over time. Remember that old saying, **a journey of a thousand miles begins with one step.**

Anybody can sit around and imagine what it might *look* like to live a healthy life, with loving relationships, peace of mind, and a fulfilling career that offers wealth, but experiencing it...mmmmmm ... now *that* requires action.

By noticing your habits and challenging your beliefs daily, you may begin seeing those now-imagined pictures of a fuller, brighter reality becoming even bigger, vibrant and clear as a bell. You will also find this happening every time you take action and practice these exercises.

At this point, your ego-mind may be chirping up in the background with stuff like, "I'm no Roger Bannister, I'm no Rosa Parks, and I'm definitely not the next Martin Luther King. I'm just me!"

I'm here to tell you **it doesn't matter who you are, or where you came from**. Do you really think Nelson, Roger, MLK, or Rosa thought they would have that kind of impact? No matter who you think you are, if you practice these exercises, if you begin to look at your beliefs and change them, one small step at a time, you will change your life.

Some regular people, just like you and me, wrote to me to tell me how this material I've been teaching for over twenty years and sharing with you here has changed their lives.

Testimonials

> *Dear Dov,*
>
> *You are of the very few faithful, industrious and magnificent self help people that I have ever come across. Actually I am growing weary and leery every day from any mass thinking "guru" or "idea" or "belief." I am more into that this dream landscape is my own creation. If I create something, I also have the power to de-create it. Simple.*
>
> *I also must mention here that I don't dwell in this weariness too much. I just smell it, snuff it, recognize it, discard it, design what has to be there instead.*

Thank you for being the honest person you are. I am happy to have you as a soul partner in my own universe...

Jonathen from Amsterdam, Holland

***

Dear Dov,

I also must mention here that I don't dwell in this weariness too much. I just smell it, snuff it, recognize it, discard it, design what has to be there instead.

Thank you for having the courage to be who you are, so that I can gather my courage to do the same! Thank you also for showing me, by your example, how to say how you feel to the people you love. I received some coaching from you many years ago, and, more recently attended an Attracting Force weekend, what powerful experiences they both were for me. I especially appreciated the the evidence that was gathered to show how powerful I am.

Louise from Alberta, Canada

***

Thank you so much Dov for such an important and impactful reminder of what gratitude can do for us in our lives. Thank you for all you have done for me through your programs. Thank you also for being a role model for me and showing me how to have compassion while speaking the truth and saying the hard things that need to be said that inspire growth in so many people.

I am truly grateful to you for supporting me in my continual growth.

Blessings and Abundance

Barbara Lynn from Victoria, BC

***

Isn't that great?

Here's another one.

Hi Dov,

I am thankful for meeting you many years ago in my last teenage years.

I vaguely remember attending some introductory seminar of one of your programmes. However, for whatever reason your style of teaching did not resonate with me then and for reasons unkown to my conscious mind now I kept the brochure so I have a picture of you :-)

In recent years I re-discovered you in the internet arena and ...have no idea how re-discovered you but I am so grateful that I did.

The funny thing is I've actually discovered your style of teaching resonates with me strongly and in recent years in some tough personal times I occasionally tuned into online audio recordings. Just listenting to them alone has led me to some insights into some personal issues to deal with to truly living the life of my dreams. These insights I was not picking up from other teachers I was in more contact with regularly.

In the same time I slowly learnt the need to actually have mentors as generally in life I've tried to do things on my own but I'm realising that can only get you so far.

I recognised the teachers I was listening to more than you I was personally not making any significance progress with.

This year the opportunity presented itself to purchase your online coaching program. I am working with it right now to apply this knowledge into my life.

This has only been the start of this journey for me choosing you as a true mentor. I never really thought about the need for mentors and I'm glad the previous teachers at least made me realise the need for such a role in a persons life even though they did not become that for my journey going forward. I'm grateful for their role on my path to this point.

The more I listen and read of your quantum-meta-psychology the more I realise I could have not have attracted a more ideal mentor than you. As us Aussies like to say you are fair dinkum and the real deal as a mentor. I look forward to learning more from you and one day attending one of your live events in person as I know there is so much more depth to what you have to offer as a mentor than I see on offer in this era of "The Secret" and magic pill type teachings that are prevalent all over the internet.

I just felt compelled to say thank you for your authentic and deep style of teachings at this time and keep on keeping on. You are a true inspiration Dov! I am grateful for your presence in our world ...

Shaun Bates from Australia

***

Amazing isn't it? That's the kind of stuff that just sets me on fire. That's the stuff that makes me very, very happy and really, that's what makes this worthwhile to me.

Listen, I am passionate about what I do. Over the course of decades I've personally used the system that I'm teaching you in this book and in my workshops to change my life and the lives of the thousands of students I've worked with around the world. And we have had enormous success with it.

Honestly, I've seen people's lives change in a heartbeat—just **BOOM**. They go to lunch and they come back different. This material really works. And if you allow your mind to open up and really absorb it, if you are willing to put on a new pair of lenses, I can show you how to take action to live the life of your dreams. Don't you owe this to yourself? You've come this far. Start taking action. Practice the exercises and start living your dreams.

I could literally fill books with examples of people just like you who have used what I'm teaching you to change their lives dramatically, though it won't make a lick of difference until you decide you are ready to begin taking ownership of your mind.

More than twenty years ago I made an important decision. I decided to become the master of my own destiny, to master my ego-mind. As a result I've created my own personal version of the full spectrum of wealth and abundance. Honestly, I've never looked back. But let me be clear that decision is an easy one 'to say', while the follow up had its challenges. You see for me, there was a time in my life when I was so sick of things being the way they were and I was no longer willing to put up with it. I was no longer willing to be a victim of circumstance. Simply put, becoming the master of my own destiny became 'the' most important thing in my life, and as a result I was willing to question every aspect of my reality in order to do that.

When I look at the students I've worked with over the years and I see the massive positive changes in their lives I know my sacrifices were worth it. What I can also tell you is that when I look at those students who have had the most significant shifts in their lives, they are the ones who just kept chugging along. They kept doing what they could each day to gain mastery, they scaled the mountain one step at a time and each of them is clearly enjoying the view from each new level they reach.

So the question I ask you is, "What about you?"

Do you want to join the people who are really reaching for this and who understand that they can choose to master their lives? If you say yes, and that's totally up to you, you need to take the first step in that life-long journey towards mastery.

Remember this: Mastery is when you do it, not just when you know it.

I'm not going to lie to you. I have no idea how you ended up reading this book or wanting to attend my seminars. I just want you to realize how far you have come, and I know that you see that this is what you need to get your current life, your current reality, off of life support and to make it juicy – *to make your life really juicy.*

When indecisive people – folks who have not yet made up their minds about what they want in life – get confronted with something that actually has the potential to change their lives, to make a massive difference to their lives, often they are like a deer caught in headlights: They get stuck.

When you are trying to make a decision that differs from your usual pattern, and you get stuck, that is the ego-mind saying, "Oh gosh, don't change. Everything is fine. It's ok. I'm all right. I'm fine. AAAAHHHHHH!"

Like I said, they get stuck. That's because they've not chosen to reclaim mastery of their mind. Get un-stuck. *You must reclaim mastery of your ego-mind and your life, and you must do it now.*

I truly hope you are one of the people who make the decision to step forward and do that. Throughout history there have been people who have really pushed the boundaries of what is possible. I talked to you about Nelson Mandela. I talked to you about Roger Bannister. Those are some people who have pushed the limits. They've done amazing things. And so can you.

We call them charismatic individuals, charismatic leaders. We call them enlightened beings. You know what I call them? I call them people who have mastered their minds.

They are people who have questioned the status quo. They've questioned the beliefs that have been imposed on them by their environment. *They are also people who have embraced choice.* Do you see that? They've embraced choice. They have chosen to choose. They've also chosen to honor their new found beliefs even in the face of every rejection.

Let me explain this huge contradiction. The people who have made the greatest difference in the world, whose ideas and actions have moved millions, are the same people who have had the cojones to stand up and face massive rejection.

Even when the odds were stacked high against them, these people were willing to rise up, ask for more, and ask for better. They weren't people who gave in to that cranky old man, plagued by the doubting voices in their heads seeking to keep them from following their dreams —or the cranky old man coming out of others.

They stood up to the world, they claimed what was theirs and were willing to go out and fight for it.

They didn't always begin their journey with the support of those around them. This is because – and I know you've heard this before – misery loves company. **Do not expect people who have given up on their dreams to support you in yours.** It just doesn't happen. Like ordering steak from a vegetarian restaurant, it just doesn't happen.

I've said this many times throughout my life: Fate is no friend of yours. Fate, luck, it's just the QRF you have built, in action, or for some people, in non-action.

I look at life as being relational and I consider myself to be a relational person. I place value on relationships. I'm suggesting to you that the very quality of your life and, by that, I mean the success you experience on every level, is dramatically affected by the quality of your relationships. Are your relationships authentic? Are you really showing up, giving it your all? Are you delivering on who you are—allowing people to witness your courageous authentic self? And just as importantly, are you spending time with miserable people looking for company?

One of my fundamental personal relationship laws is this: Only be in relationships that add value to both people. Don't spend time in relationships that are one-way, where you are doing all the giving and they are doing all the taking, or vice versa.

Also, be willing to give what you are asking for. If you want more love, give more love. If you want more commitment, be willing to give more commitment.

Sorry to be repetitious but this is something you will really want to drop right into your subconscious ...

Whatever it is that you want in life, give more of it and you can get more of it.

What this does is set up a resonance for you to accept more of what it is you are putting out. You are not coming from 'lack of' or a place of fear or greed; you have this energy, this quantum field that says "There are lots! See! I can give it away! I'm not attached to it." Because you are not attached, lots of it comes back to you.

Let me clarify a bit. Sometimes we don't give as much as we would like to because we're afraid that we won't get anything in return. It's almost as if we're waiting for the world to show *us more* before we *give more*. That type of thinking will keep you in a nasty bind because it is founded on a belief of 'lack'.

The truth is that abundance is all around us. *You* have to change before the world will change. If you don't believe me, look at your own life and the lives of the people around you. Has the world changed much since you've been following that old map?

So if you want more love, give more love. If you want more commitment, give more commitment.

Now let's do a quick review of what we've covered because you will be blown away by how much you've learned. We've covered a ton; I recorded twenty-seven points that we have gone over in Part II.

Chapter 45

A Quick Review of Part II

➡ All human beings have the potential for addiction. Some of our addictions are socially acceptable and others are not.

➡ Addictions are all about soothing and numbing pain—coping with our pain. Pain comes from fear, and facing pain can be as simple as knowing how to ask the right questions about what you believe.

➡ I suggested that maybe your mind has a mind of its own, and that is what's behind the negative voice you sometimes hear in your head.

➡ I shared that 80 percent of your thoughts are negative and repetitive. So you really need to pay attention to your thoughts as they are merely the regurgitations of your beliefs.

➡ We're trained to lie, particularly to ourselves, and that sets us up for getting more of what we *don't* want. We get caught in a vicious cycle where we start to believe that lying is necessary. Then, because we unconsciously know we're lying to ourselves, we end up not being able to trust ourselves and our intuition.

➡ You learned that dishonesty comes from wanting to be liked; we're desperate to be liked and *fit in* and that sets us up to lie. In time we become so used to lying that we become deaf to our own intuition. Lies destroy the things we are trying to protect by lying.

➡ I suggested that if you keep doing what doesn't work—if we remain limited by our addictions—we stay stuck. Using an addiction to cope with the underlying problem rather than facing the reality of the situation has you repeating the same pattern over and over again, never moving forward. Stupid is as stupid does, over and over again when it doesn't work. Stop hitting your thumbs with hammers.

➡ I gave you an example of how you can get a deeper understanding of your behavior by paying attention to what you are doing and asking yourself what the underlying belief is.

➡ I noted that beliefs, by design, can be difficult to change because your ego-mind thinks you will die if you change them. Take my word for it, you won't die; he won't kill you. You can get the technology to change beliefs that aren't serving you, and your life will get better and richer for it. (Really, when it comes down to it, once you are on the right track you will *want* your ego-mind to defend your beliefs enthusiastically because you won't want to get de-railed!).

➡ Remember those three words that keep you from living the life you dream of? In case you don't, they are "I know that." The life you've been dreaming of, the things that you want most, your heart's true desire—those visions are not in your mind by some fluke or accident. They are your soul crying for the expression of who you really are!

➡ It is our beliefs that determine what is possible or impossible for us. Beliefs are filters that distort your reality.

➡ We learned a new medical fact, that the states of being terrified and excited are actually neurologically very, very close – they are almost the same. No event in life has any meaning other than the meaning you attach to it.

➡ To your body/mind, 'normal' is only what you grew up with. Normal is the comfortable feeling you get living the life you live because neurologically (neurochemically), as far as the cell receptors and neuropeptides are concerned everything is all right, all is normal. Normal is not necessarily healthy. So take a look at what you've accepted as normal and what you determined to be abnormal. When you begin examining that your entire life can shift in a moment.

➡ Take those glasses off! You are looking at life through lenses— these are the beliefs and perceptions you've been carrying around, and they color your world. There is nothing you see that isn't tinted and often tainted by your beliefs. If you look through red lenses all you see is a red world. We don't live in a red world. We live in a beautiful, magnificent, colorful, and abundant world. Take off the lenses and see it!

➡ You have a choice, either you run your ego-mind, or your ego-mind runs you. If you let it, the ego-mind's fear will run everything and will stop you from making the empowering decisions that you need to make.

➡ What it all comes down to is: You are either waiting for your ship to come in or you are getting help to build one.

My question to you is: "What are you going to do with this knowledge and the exercises you've been given so far?" Are you going to sit on your butt cuddling your excuses, or are you going to take action and become the master of your manifesting mind? Decide what you are going to do.

Decide now, I promise that looking back to this point in your history you will see now as the point where everything changed for the better.

As I will always do, I'm going to challenge you to take action with what you've learnt. Take action, apply it to your life. Again think about who you need to share what you've learnt with. Think about who came to mind right away, and think about which part you are excited to share with them. Remember that sometimes we need to share something in order to really get it ourselves.

Today, allow yourself to imagine what your life could look like if you had mastery over your mind. Before we hop into Part III, I want you to consider something.

Having mastered your ego-mind, what would your life sound like? What would be the sounds that surround you? Would there be the sound of the ocean? Would there be birds singing? Maybe there would be children laughing. Perhaps the voices that have been holding you back finally fall silent. What would your life feel like if you'd mastered your ego-mind? *Would you feel, now, that sense of being really on purpose with everything you do*? Would you feel at peace knowing you were in the right place at the right time, doing the right things, if you now mastered your ego-mind?

If you mastered your ego-mind, would you feel more love, for others and for yourself?

You know, one of the ladies who trained with me about four years ago said that after the Quantum Mind Mastery™ program she was walking around and people kept asking her, "Who's the new man in your life, who's the new man in your life?"

She was actually getting kind of miffed with these people because she wasn't seeing any new man.

One day, after relating this to me, she realized she had been exhibiting a resonance of love. Having mastered a part of her relational foundation for the very first time in her life, she was in love... with herself. This is something that can happen when you master your ego-mind.

And on that note, I would like to begin Part III.

Part III

Chapter 46

Making It Real

As I said in the beginning of Part I:
Goooooooood Mornnnnnning!

Welcome to Part III. This is a whole new level of waking up. The fact is you are already a different person than you were when you first picked up this book. You see once you know, you cannot pretend you don't know. Once you've been awakened the old dream is broken and with it the illusion that the one dimensional reality is all there is, is gone forever. My sincere congratulations on making it this far. Congratulations on your commitment and your dedication to your growth and with that let me once again repeat a heartfelt: "Good Morning."

Before we dive right into the last part of this book, I'm going to give you a quick preview of what you are going to find. Consider it a little mind marinade to soak your old beliefs in.

First off, in this part of the book you will learn why some people inaccurately feel there's something wrong with them and how their friends may actually be holding them back.

We will also look at how those ever-popular personality tests get in the way of re-claiming mastery of your ego-mind.

Further along, there's a lesson out of a book James Earl Jones (the voice of CNN America's Cable News Network and Darth Vader from the Star Wars movie series) wrote, which is another real life example of how the perceived impossible is possible.

You will discover the key elements to creating long lasting change and how, under certain circumstances, change can be absolutely instantaneous.

I'll also share with you what I call the "S.H." principle.

Oh, and here's a big one. You are going to uncover the vital contents of your own QRF and even more about why you have kept attracting the same old dreary junk into your life.

We will be going into detail about the technique that led many of you to read this book: The **Equation for Manifestation**™. When we get there, you will be completely stunned by how easy-to-use this powerful technique can be.

Finally, you will see that there are four obstacles that keep you from manifesting the life of your dreams, and I'll present you with the three character traits possessed by the truly successful. Alright let's kick off.

Chapter 47

See It and Say It

I'd like to start by expanding on two of the techniques most of us have heard about: *Visualization and affirmation.*

Many of us have at one time or another repeated a set of affirmations while trying to visualize our lives differently and doing some goal-setting along the way.

I know that growing up I spent many-a-night picturing my life very differently than what it was back then: Lying down in the Bahamas surrounded by beautiful beaches, clear blue oceans, and well… you get the point. As I was saying, if you are one of the many who have tried those techniques, you've probably noticed that generally, they don't work that well.

Frankly, I believe the use of affirmations and visualization alone has the same potential for success as a child putting on a red cape and jumping off a bed hoping to fly.

Consider this: If affirmations and visualizations did work and that was all we truly needed, we'd all be living the life of our dreams perched on top of Mount Awesome, married to the partner of our dreams, doing the work that fulfilled our hearts and souls (mind you, a few of us would not be working at all!). We'd all be springing out of bed every day, eyes wide open, excitedly screaming YAAAAHHHHOOOOOOO ... Though realistically, that's just not the case for most people.

And here's why:

"There really is no 'Out There' — Out There"
Dr. Fred Alan Wolf

There is nothing *out there* that's going to make things right; On the other hand, there is nothing *out there* that's going to make everything wrong, either. There is nothing outside of you that can change anything. If your unconscious beliefs contain elements of 'lack' or 'unhappy' etc., it's your *unconscious* which is programming what may be a bleak future.

In Part I (under the sub-heading Unconscious Deserving) and throughout this book, I shared how we all unconsciously create our own luck through what I termed *unconscious deserving*.

In a nut shell, there are many people in this world running around with crippling, limited beliefs such as 'life is a struggle' feeding into their QRFs, messing up their unconscious deserving. Faulty beliefs such as those eventually become the lenses through which we see the world, which in time become the roads we follow on our map of normal.

Now wait, don't blame the word 'normal' here. Making things 'normal' isn't good or bad—it's natural. The only time making something normal could be considered 'bad' is if it's hurting you, hurting others, *or holding you back.*

Do you remember Suzanne's story from Part I? Her 'normal' was a belief that the women in her family were unlucky. She demonstrated that belief by pushing away the one guy who treated her in the way she'd only dreamed of, while moving towards her abusive mother (who, might I add, just happened to be living with that belief as well. Any idea where she adopted that belief?).

As we've noted, beliefs are demonstrated through behavior. In Suzanne's case, the act of pushing her boyfriend away demonstrated the unconscious belief that when it came to the game of love, the women in her family lost. That same set of behaviors show you, if you look carefully, how her beliefs caused her to see life through the tinted lens of 'unlucky'. Remember the deep-seated belief she carried with her? The one that stated the women in her family tend to be unlucky, especially in relationships?

Look, there was nothing outside of Suzanne to cause her to have one bad relationship after another. There was no one *out there* constantly giving her the evil-eye, putting some kind of curse on her—making sure that all she could find was crappy unfulfilling relationships—nor was there anything *out there* forcing her to push her boyfriend away.

The belief she held about men set up her *unconscious deserving* to attract the men that treated her poorly while pushing away the ones who treat her well. Her unconscious deserving also justified her beliefs about 'bad luck in relationships' that her ego-mind held so dearly.

Like I said, there's nothing 'out there' making things right or wrong.

As you may be noticing, the unconscious beliefs we allow ourselves to own are breathtakingly powerful. I'm sure you can now get how Suzanne's beliefs colored her life in many profound ways—not necessarily for the better.

297

In case you haven't guessed yet: The belief that she was unlucky, especially in relationships, was passed down through her mother and her grandmother, and through countless other generations.

The people she grew up with maintained that belief, so Suzanne had to make it normal in her life because she needed to *fit in*. Not only that, until she was nearing her teens, most of the beliefs her family held went straight into her unconscious, becoming belief systems. That poor girl then spent her life re-living and re-acting the same way all the women in her family did, until, of course, one day we sat down together, identified what was holding her back, and she made some new, positive choices.

Interestingly, Suzanne's story is also a prime example of how 'maps' we adopt as children can influence our lives today. (If you don't remember how maps are drawn and used, refer back to 'Maps: Another way to look at lenses').

So, once again, if you haven't looked at the beliefs you've been carrying with you, do so now. You will be surprised at what you learn about yourself.

As a quick refresher, since we're already talking about unconscious beliefs, I'd like to share another powerful way you can identify some unconscious beliefs that you might have in this very instant.

Are your comfortable? Snuggle into that chair for a moment and think of a situation where you re-acted one way, but would have liked to have acted differently. Choose any situation: Maybe the time your boss asked you to work late and you begrudgingly caved in, or maybe the last time you stared at a cookie and could have sworn if you didn't have it, a little piece of you would die inside.

Think back to that time just before you re-acted the way you wish you hadn't and notice if you had a sense that there was something impeding you, something you couldn't quite see or hear. Something you couldn't fully wrap your hands around...

That, my friend, is an unconscious block.

Ask yourself what was going on that made you re-act the way you did. It could have been an unsettled feeling or a sense of impulsion, anxiety, or fear ... . Ask yourself if behind that block, however it chooses to exhibit itself, is a belief that you might not be fully aware of yet. In fact, it is 'the' belief which causes you to re-act that way and gives you the same old *crapola* every time that situation, or even anything similar, comes back into your life.

Remember in Part I, when you asked yourself, "Why do I believe that?" and then later "What has to be true for that to be true?" You can use those questions as a hammer to break down those blocks and see what's lurking behind.

By the way, if your hammer isn't big enough and you're still stuck, come to one of my workshops because I bring a velvet covered wrecking ball!

Chapter 48

Action versus Reaction

There are one-and-a-half very important points I want to tackle in this section. I say one-and-a-half because they are so closely related that they can't truly be considered two separate points.

The first is the reason I've broken up words like 're-act' and 're-action'. The second is how that applies to our beliefs.

When I say re-act, I literally mean to act again. Notice that when you re-act to something, you are not *choosing* the following action and/or emotion, you are doing or experiencing it as an automatic response to the initial event.

On the flip side, when you act—regardless of how many times something happens to you—you *choose* the 'response' you are going to have —even if the action you choose is the same as the one you chose before. It's the fact that it's not automatic that keeps it from being a "re-action."

When we're not aware of our beliefs, we re-act to circumstances, with little sense of choice in the matter.

Unconscious beliefs cause you to 're-act' the same way you always have, getting you the same results over and over—much like hitting your thumb with a hammer, shouting or mumbling a few colorful words, and then hitting yourself with the hammer again while expecting a different result. Or if you prefer a real life example, you can remember how Suzanne *re-acted* when it came to relationships.

When we keep doing what doesn't work, when we keep 're-acting', it's like wanting to step into a new area of your life and seeing a big brick wall. Then, walking towards the wall, banging your head against it repeatedly, trying to bash your way through.

When you are re-acting to events in your life, you are not taking the time to consider alternatives.

I'd like to express an important point here: It isn't stupid to bang your head against the wall in an effort to break through if you never knew there was another way. Please understand, it doesn't make you stupid to keep "re-acting" that way if you never even knew there might have been a door you could have walked through or a window you could have opened.

Besides, the truth of the matter is we've all had times such as those in our lives. I know I've certainly had times in *my* life where I've been banging my head on the wall not noticing the doorway; and there is a doorway that will get you through.

So ask yourself this question: Where in your life are you banging your head against a wall trying to get through? Where, with just a little bit of guidance, could you find the doorway and painlessly get to the other side? Trust me, your thumbs and forehead will thank you for it.

Needless to say, when we look at our lives and see that the picture we have in our mind's eye differs from the picture we're living, we can end up feeling like there's something wrong with us, or we become depressed and down on ourselves. That's when we lose sight of our dreams. Whatever you do, don't do that. Do not lose sight of your dreams.

It's not you. There's nothing wrong with you.

> *"Every leader, every genius, every star must face*
> *the pull toward mediocrity.*
> *The pull that will keep you from your own brilliance*
> *is the need to be accepted. Remember no greatness*
> *was ever achieved without opposition."*
> ~ *Dõv Baron*

Don't give up on you. *Listen to me.* Do not give up on you. Instead, give up on those limiting beliefs, or even better, **obliterate** those limiting beliefs because there's nothing wrong with you—it's the beliefs that don't work.

Chapter 49

Self-worth, Self-Esteem, and What's In-between

I'm sure you've heard the saying 'success is a journey not a destination'. Well, what I'm about to share with you here assists you in truly understanding what that statement means beyond the cliché and into something truly meaningful for you.

Where we are going here is dealing with something that gets you passionately enjoying every step along the way. As you will see, when I realized the truth of this subject, life took on a whole new meaning, often pressure melted away, stress simply disappeared, and it will for you, too. Now you will discover the number one mistake that most people make that costs them a fortune in self doubt, destroyed relationships and loss of income. When you avoid this mistake your earnings soar beyond your wildest dreams and you will finally get what you rightfully and intrinsically deserve.

Here's an important truth, the code has finally been cracked on this and once you know the truth you can no longer be lost in the ignorance of why you were not getting what you wanted. It's something that so many of the outstanding individuals of our time and throughout history have at least intuitively known and has allowed them massive success and yet so many people get it wrong, because they don't understand why it works. In this extensive explanation you will finally have a step by step process to shift your conditioning away from empty goals to getting any result that you want, and what you should know...it's not what you think. Using what I'm about to share, you will make more money, gain more freedom, and you will use it to gain control of every thought and every action the minute you hear this method. How often have these or similar words been echoed?

"Oh my god, what's wrong with you, don't you have any self-esteem?"

There's a good chance that at some point in time you've said something like that, or at least thought something like it, or even worse had something similar said to you. Apparently, self-esteem is the great cure all for almost anything we can imagine. However, let's face it, the whole idea of self-esteem went main stream as long ago as the mid seventies, it's not like it's a new subject. Why do so few people seem to have enough self-esteem and why is it that someone can seem to destroy it so fast? And more importantly is self-esteem what we really need, or is there some other missing ingredient?

Hang on while I share a personal story that will take this a little deeper.

In June of 1990, my speaking career was beginning to show some real promise and I was being featured on popular radio and television shows and traveling all over the place to present my programs.

Needless to say, my hectic schedule was taking its toll and I decided to take some time off to engage in a sport which I found completely exhilarating... Free-climbing.

In case you don't know: Free climbing is essentially **mountain climbing without the aid or security of ropes and harnesses.** Yes, I really was that crazy back then particularly so, because I was by no means an expert in the sport.

To make a long and quite gruesome story short, I went climbing that day with a friend of mine and as I was approaching the summit, **I reached to grab hold of a rock which in turn dislodged a bigger rock which hit me square in the face. Ahhhhhh!**

My grip on anything solid or stable was gone in a moment and I was sent plummeting down the rock face for approximately 120 feet (about twelve stories) to kiss the jagged rocks below.

As you can well imagine, falling one-hundred and twenty feet, traveling at approximately seventy miles per hour and landing on your face is something pretty much any fool can do. **It's the surviving, getting up and recovery process that takes all the real effort.**

Needless to say, with my jaw smashed into five separate pieces and many more de-facing injuries the **numerous reconstructive surgeries that were required on my face put an abrupt halt to my speaking career.** As a result, the wonderful teachings and knowledge I so desperately wanted to share with the world were put on the back-burner while I began **what felt like a very slow and impossible recovery.**

I won't pretend to be macho about the whole experience, **to say the least, it was truly humbling**. In fact, the pain and emotional turmoil of losing what had been my face and the scars of creating the 'new' face were enough to drive me into a deep and very dark depression. The feeling of hopelessness assailed everything else to the point where **I was ready to give up all hope of ever getting back on the platform and speaking in public again.**

Before I fell, you could have asked anyone and they would have told you, and quite rightly, that I had great self-esteem. The fall destroyed that self-esteem and as a result after about six or eight months I gathered some of my students around me in order to make an announcement.

I'm sure many of them were expecting me to not only say that I was coming back, but also when I was going to do so. These people who had loyally followed my teachings, who had attended my seminars and who had worked one-on-one with me, sat in my living room waiting.

The atmosphere in the room was palpable, a mixture of anxiety and excitement; *why had I asked them to attend this meeting and what would I say?* Was I going to share some deeply profound story of 'going to the light'... *what was it all about?*

Looking around the room I was sure to make eye contact with every single person there. It was suddenly easy to see: In their eyes I saw not only the kindness and spirituality of souls on the path; I saw the thing that I had refused to see before I fell, the thing that had compelled me to call this meeting...

I thanked each of them for not only the kindness and support they had shown me but also and more importantly the lesson that I so deeply needed to learn. With that said, I made my announcement to dropped jaws and wide eyes: "I quit!"

"What do you mean, you quit. Are you saying that you are still recovering and you need more time, are you saying...?"

I stood up, gently asking everyone to leave and repeated to each of them that, "I quit!"

I was done; I had learned what I needed to learn. As a bonus piece of guidance for you, let me say: **When you are truly done learning something, move on!**

Reading this you might be thinking; *what the heck is this guy talking about?* After all it's fairly obvious that we're reading his book? I'm guessing that maybe you are thinking, *well, I guess after his announcement he decided to make a comeback?* If by some chance that's what you are thinking, you would be only somewhat correct. But you say; *that's ridiculous, once again, I'm reading your book.* Maybe you've even attended one of my workshops since the fall. In order to make sense of what's going on here let me bring us back to where we started in this chapter with our discussion about self-esteem versus self-worth in order to make sense of my quitting and coming back *without coming back.*

Remember I said that I had gathered this group of people together and thanked them not only for the kindness and support they had shown me but also **the lesson that I so deeply needed to learn**? I said I had made sure to make eye contact with every single person because, in their eyes I saw the thing that I had refused to see before I fell, the thing that had compelled me to call that meeting. So, what was that thing that I saw in their eyes? The answer might shock you... I saw my self-esteem!

How could I see 'my self-esteem' in 'their eyes'?

In that moment of looking in their eyes, I had realized, as much as I 'so desperately' (another clue) wanted to help 'them', what I wanted more was what I had believed they could give me. Up until the fall, it had never even crossed my mind that there could even be some unconscious motive driving the work I was doing. How could that be, at the time of the fall I'd already been teaching for a good few years and studying for many more? The answer is simple: No one seems to teach the difference between self-esteem and self-worth.

Unlike self-worth, self-esteem is something we consciously or unconsciously pursue getting from others. When we say *self-esteem* and *self-worth* most people think they are the same thing with two different names. Although there are similarities, there are some very important distinctions between the two.

Let's start with the one most people have a pretty good grasp on, the supposed cure all: *Self-esteem*. It 'appears', (there's your next clue) that when we have lots of self-esteem we feel good about ourselves. We may appear to have 'bags of confidence'; maybe even that *I can do anything* air about us. However, as I'm sure you are aware, self-esteem is fragile for one simple reason; if it comes from others —it can be taken away by others, too.

Self-worth however, is internally based. It does not require anyone else to feed it nor can it be taken away by another. Other people can build or damage your self-esteem; however, only you can build or damage your self-worth.

Side-bar: Do you like watching the Oscars? Apparently millions of people do, so here are a couple of great examples of what I'm talking about from the Oscars. See if you can tell whether each of these people is in self-esteem or self-worth:

In 1999 Roberto Benigni won the Oscar for Best Actor in the amazing movie: "Life is Beautiful". Upon the announcement of his win Benigni did not do the; oh so humble, head bowed down, dignified saunter to the stage, followed by the kind of patronizing speech that can so often be the case at these ceremonies. No, instead Benigni leapt from seat to seat on the backs of the chairs, arms above his head in joy. The applause rang out and he quite literally hopped onto the stage where he delivered a speech that for him was clearly heartfelt and appeared to be unrehearsed.

Accepting his Oscar from the movie industry legend and fellow Italian actor, Sophia Loren, he said:

"This is a moment of joy, because you are the image of the joy.
I feel I want to dive into this ocean of your generosity, this
hailstorm of kindness and gratitude for you."
~ Roberto Benigni

Take a moment to think about how Roberto Benigni received that Oscar in the context of self-esteem and self-worth. Which place would you say he was coming from?

Not sure yet?

Okay, let's try another example.

In 1985 Sally Field, wins Best Actress for her spectacular portrayal of Edna Spaulding alongside the equally brilliant Danny Glover and John Malcovich in the movie 'Places in the Heart'. Unfortunately, I have no memory of how Sally Field entered the stage. However, I do remember her deeply emotional response to receiving the Oscar. Clutching her Oscar with both hands, the tears were visibly flowing down her face when she said:

"I haven't had an orthodox career, and I've wanted more than anything to have your respect. The first time I didn't feel it, but this time I feel it, and I can't deny the fact that you like me, right now, you like me!"

~ Sally Field

Both in their own ways very powerful acceptance speeches, wouldn't you say? Still not sure, who's displaying what? Don't worry; it often takes a while to know the difference between displays of self-esteem verses a display of self-worth. Especially because a person can give both of them lip service and to the untrained eye there is no difference.

Okay, that brings us back to the story of my fall and how it relates to the difference between the two: Having realized that I had unconsciously been helping everyone else in order to feed an insatiable hunger for self-esteem, (and it's always insatiable because as one person builds it up, another can take it away and that means there's always a need for at the very least, a top up). Anyway, having realized this and some other significant things about myself, I realized I could not go back to being 'that kind of a teacher'.

Let's remember our definitions because I believe I can help you get crystal clear on the difference between the two and how Roberto and Sally demonstrated either self-esteem or self-worth. Self-esteem is external. (That's a very important point). We get self-esteem from others. However, it's important to remember that self-esteem is fragile for one simple reason; if it comes from others, it can be taken away by others.

Self-worth however, is internally based. As I said, other people can build or damage your self-esteem; however, primarily you are the one who builds or damages your self-worth.

If you think of it as a flow of energy: Self-esteem requires an inflow of energy as there's a wanting, a needing. While self-worth is an out flowing, and there's an expression, a giving. One is about getting, (self esteem) and the other is about giving, (self-worth).

Self-esteem is the value you allow others to put on you. It's what other people believe you deserve at the minimum and/or maximum, whether it's 'financial' worth, 'love' worth, or any other 'worth' you can think of, it's all externally determined.

Self-esteem can also show up as confidence in one's own abilities, as much of that is directly feedback related.

Although they appear closely related, there is a difference.

Here's an example:
Let's say someone has a job in which they make $60,000 a year, and

they are looking for a new position with higher pay. If that person had unconscious self-worth issues, they may have an unconscious belief that they don't deserve to be paid more than what they are currently receiving while at the same time having full confidence that due to the feedback, their current skill level surpasses the $60,000 range.

On the other hand, while this person may not unconsciously believe they deserve more than $60,000, they also may not unconsciously believe they deserve less than $50,000. They might not take a job for less than $50,000 unless they decided there was no other option, and life would have this odd way of making sure that they would be within their standard range in no time.

Like I said, self-esteem and self-worth are very closely related. I'm sure you can see how having great self-esteem doesn't necessarily mean that this person has high self-worth, although if one's low the other's probably not doing that well in it's own right. Got it? Good.

Now, if somebody has unconscious *self-worth* issues, do you think those issues are going to interfere with their beliefs about whether they can fulfill their dreams? Do you think those issues are going to get in the way of them believing that this book can help them to fulfill their dreams? At this point, do I even have to tell you what I think the answer to that question is? I can pretty much see you smiling and nodding your head in agreement. *Of course those issues will get in the way.*

Chapter 50

You Are Not Your Beliefs

L isten, if you are afraid to do something, no matter what it is, if you are afraid to do something, that fear you are feeling is coming from an unconscious and sometimes conscious belief that says 'you can't'. Chances are, you may be telling yourself 'you can't' because there's a belief that there's something wrong with *you* rather than that *there's something wrong with the belief.*

It's not you!

We spoke earlier in this book about how most of what we believe is not our own it is simply something we adopted in an effort to "fit in". For many of the people I work with at my workshops, the big surprise is that they are not their beliefs—rather, they have been *limited* by their beliefs.

Give yourself permission and ask yourself, what might be the unconscious limited beliefs holding you back, and what are you going to do to obliterate them? Remember, no one's looking over your shoulder; it's just you and this book.

We are all friends here, right?

I'd like to talk about how 'friends' and personality tests can inadvertently hold us back. I don't know about you, but I can certainly remember a couple of times in my life when I was trying to change something, to step up to the plate and really grow. You know what I mean: *I wanted to become more for myself, because I wanted it, no, I deserved the right to try and get it and become 'more'.* Do you know what the people around me did? Do you think they threw me a party saying "Congratulations! You are going to succeed!"

Not quite.

Maybe you can relate to this: They made comments like, "Oh, that's a good idea, *but you are just not like that,*" or "*that's not you.*" "Life just isn't like that." "You are too *this,* you are too *that.*" "You have a responsibility to your mom, dad, brother, sister, uncle, wife, employer, guy next door, whom you haven't even met but if he knew what you were thinking of doing he'd tell you how it REALLY is!"

AHHHHH Crap. All of it, crap.

What I didn't realize then is that if we let ourselves listen to crap like that, we end up absorbing those statements and making them into beliefs. Some of us may even say to ourselves, "Yeah, I guess that's true, I guess that doesn't really sound like me, so what's the point of trying?" If we let ourselves think like that, then we run the risk of falling back into the trap that we're trying desperately to climb out of.

The interesting thing about beliefs is that we tend to want to be surrounded by those who believe what we believe. What that means is that when you decide that it's time for you to grow you will have to examine your beliefs and without any particular intention to challenge anyone else, this will most likely be seen, heard or felt as a threat.

Beliefs whether inherited or authentic become our map of the reality they refer to. For example, let's take someone who is heterosexual and considering entering a romantic relationship with someone they just met: This person has certain beliefs about the opposite gender. Those beliefs and a whole stack of supporting beliefs become their 'map' of the territory known as relationships.

However, there is something very important for you to realize...In the words of Polish-American scientist and philosopher Alfred Korzbski, "*The map is not the territory.*"

What this means is that our perspective of something, or our re-action to it, is not the thing itself. A simple example is: Your opinion of a particular person, whether favorable or unfavorable, is *not* that person; it's simply your own representation of a concept you have of that person and not the person themselves. Many of the limitations we hold about ourselves and others come from these maps. What we believe we are actually capable of either doing or being comes from confusing the map with the territory. Think about it this way and it will make perfect loigical sense: Could you say that you've experienced Paris just because you have been through a map of Paris? You don't need me to tell you the answer, do you?

For the purpose of clarity, let's take this a little deeper.

Chapter 51

Personality Tests: Roadmaps of the Past

How many of you at one time or another have taken a personality test? Maybe you've taken one on the web or had a professional run you through it. In all likelihood, if you have been through one of these tests, your hope has been to get a greater understanding of yourself.

Whether it's been done for work or play, the result tends to be the same. At the end of the test you find out that you are a (I'm making up fake results but I'm sure you will get my drift), TPK or you are an MLJ. Maybe you are blue with a red top or you are a four with a five wing. (Or any other sequence of letters or numbers, that supposedly signify who you 'really are"). And then, whether 'your life' is read off a piece of paper or it pops up in some window on the web, the end result is usually the same. Most people end up nodding their heads and saying, "Oh yeah, that's me, that's soooo me."

A major problem with personality tests—or any test that tells you who you 'are' for that matter—is that they become a really solid excuse not to change. They become a cozy reason to not do anything at all about you or your circumstances. Not only that, half the people run out after receiving their results and start telling all their friends that '*this* happened' in their life because of the J portion of their MLJ profile. Or they decide that the people they've drawn into their lives as friends or relationships suddenly 'make sense' because it's right there on a piece of paper!

When you think about it, when you *really* think about it, doesn't that sound like an excuse the ego-mind would grab on to, to justify whatever decisions we've made in our lives – regardless of how they served us—just to make itself feel good, to keep you trapped?

Let me explain to you why tests seem so accurate.
Those tests—and you've heard me talk about this next point throughout this book—are based on your behaviors. And your behaviors, as you learned earlier are a demonstration of your beliefs.

The problem with a test that's based on your current behaviors and your *current* beliefs is that it's only telling you who you were up until the moment you wrote the test— *not who you could and will be.*

Think back to what I said earlier in Part II (when you were introduced to the ego-mind), "Who you were yesterday is ONLY who you were yesterday. Today you can choose who you will be tomorrow." Recognize that, and *you* take back the reins that determine where you are going and when. Recognize that, and you are back in control of your destiny because you know that you can change your beliefs, which changes your unconscious deserving, which changes your QRF, which changes what you attract into your life.

What tests, friends, parents, and strangers have said or will say about you is not and never will be the final word on who you are, unless you allow it. They may have a map of who they perceive you to be but that map will never fully represent the total territory of who you are or for that matter can be.

Statements you have repeated to yourself and heard from others that place limits on your potential by securing you within a defined box, are only glimpses into the unconscious beliefs that were working in the background up until now.

In our past when we said, "Oh I guess *that's* who I am," that was the ego-mind speaking for you, trying to protect the beliefs it holds so dear—it was the ego-mind's valiant attempt to stay safe and survive. Unfortunately, it's also the same defensive action that keeps you from truly thriving.

So, if the people around you are throwing curve-balls at you every time you begin to take action (or if your ego-mind is throwing curve-balls at you when you even *think about taking action*), get the tools to start knocking those limited ideas out of the ball park. Learn to work with your ego-mind so the beliefs it files away with *the sun will rise tomorrow* are helping you thrive. If you are willing to simply accept tests or statements that only define who you were up until a moment ago, *then you are making a commitment to staying stuck*. And that's a commitment I'm sure neither of us wants to make.

Earlier in Part II of the book you learned some neurochemistry. In that section you learned that the thoughts you have trigger your brain to release neuropeptide cocktails throughout your body which carry the blueprints of your unconscious beliefs. Those peptides become the fuel and food for your body. Just as it is with all food, limited nutrition leads to limited health. *Limited beliefs lead to limited lives.*

I want to be crystal clear about those tests, your friends, and family and anyone else who ever told you who you were. They are not out to get you. There are some brilliant psychologists and psychiatrists who have written some amazing personality tests that are wonderful tools. Your family and friends are also well-intentioned; they are looking out for you as best as they can.

Tests and people may be able to accurately tell you where and who you've been *up until this moment, but they can't tell you where you are going*, if you decide you are going somewhere else.

In fact, friends, family, doctors, and personality tests were all written by people, and those people *see the world through their own personal lenses and filters*. If the lenses they see you through are colored with a limited tint, they are only seeing you in the way their ego-minds want to see you because there are no exceptions to the rule: Our ego-minds see what they see.

With that said, I don't think that a group of doctors woke up one morning, came together and thought, "Hmmm...how can we screw people up today?" The same way I don't believe, drug addicts like John, wake up wondering how they can make their lives more difficult. Your friends aren't consciously trying to mess with your head and hold you back when they say, "You are not like that, it's just not you." They are doing it because that's what they know; that's what they believe is best for you. In some cases they are touring through life with old maps, just as lost as anyone else. They are only trying to help. But as the saying goes 'it's the blind leading the blind'.

I want to reiterate that because when I say, "I believe" it doesn't make it the truth. I'm just telling you where I'm coming from so you can see another perspective, so you can see life through a different lens, discover your unconscious beliefs and challenge the ones that don't serve you.

My belief—and again this is just my belief—is that when people put these limitations on you, they are not doing it to screw you up, they are doing it because they actually believe it's in your best interest. But it's not in your best interest. It's a framework that holds you back and you are much bigger than that framework. You are much greater than that. I'll say it again—over and over until you believe it. "You are a diamond. You are a magnificent being. Tear off the lenses and become who you really are."

When we accept as gospel what our friends, family, or personality tests say about us, we put a cork on our capacity to evolve. The next moment becomes just as limited as the last, and so on, until of course, you now decide to change something.

Let me prove to you that people get limited ideas stuck in their minds.

Growing up we hear things like, "Oh, you were a very shy kid."

Kids are told that at five years old. Now they are eighteen, twenty, thirty, FIFTY! And they are still shy! I meet people that STILL, at 40, swear they are shy and constantly make statements like, "Oh I'm shy, I know that because I was a shy kid. My mom tells me that all the time!"

To boot, every time they attempt to become more, or break-free, the same people who told them they are shy all their lives remind them once again they are shy, re-enforcing that limitation. Then whenever they fail at an accomplishment, they can blame it on shyness. And to top it all off, when they succeed, the people around them congratulate them in spite of their shyness saying words like, "Wow, pretty good for such a shy person."

You have no idea how many times I've heard people give praise and scorn to 'the shy'. If they've heard it often enough, the people who have been called 'shy' have had that belief filed away with "the sun will rise from the east" as far back as they can remember. Their ego-minds have been defending that 'shyness' with a passion for the last twenty, thirty, and in some cases fifty years!

Shyness is not a truth. It's a learned behavior that has its roots in a belief. And for so many people, it is a very limiting belief.

How do I know that it's only a belief and not written in stone and handed down by the gods? Because many shy people have been known to overcome their inhibitions to lead social and outgoing lives.

There is no gene at birth that predicts 'shyness'. Genes may *contribute* to conditions like muteness, deafness, or blindness. And it is true that growing up with any one (or several, like Helen Keller) of those conditions can offer someone many opportunities to develop personality traits like shyness. But conditions like blindness, deafness, and muteness are not the cause of shyness, or any other personality trait for that matter. Ultimately, it's our perception of the world through the lenses that muteness, deafness, and/or blindness cause that has us feel like shyness is destined for some of us. And here's proof ... .

Chapter 52

James, Walt, and Albert

One amazing example of how conditions aren't the cause of personality types is James Earl Jones.

At five, James became functionally mute because of an incredibly severe stutter. He didn't speak for nearly eight years. Let me remind you that I'm referring to James Earl Jones, one of the most recognized voices on the planet. Where would the television network C.N.N. be today without James Earl Jones telling us that C.N.N. is the most trusted name in news? What would Darth Vader have been like with the voice of Jerry Lewis? Those familiar and distinct voices – are the voice of James Earl Jones. Where would he be, a boy who was functionally mute, a boy who had a stutter, if he had sat back and said, "Oh, that's just the way I am. Must be genetics!"

Deep down, James must have realized at some point that being functionally mute did not relegate him to shyness or lack of confidence. It didn't define him. It did present challenges above and beyond what most of us encounter, yet in the end he did not let it determine the course of his life. He broke out of the shell that the stigma of a stutter created. And as just said; he became the host Voice of C.N.N. and every Star Wars fan knows his voice as that of Darth Vader.

Do you know that Walt Disney tested 'slow' in school, or that he was fired from a newspaper in Kansas City for being "Non-creative." What about Albert Einstein, did you know he tested 'learning disabled' and his professors told him he'd never make it to university? I wonder, what are names of the guys who tested Walt and Albert? None of us remember them, do we? We do, however, remember Disney. We do remember Einstein?

So you see, we're only as limited as our ego-minds allow us to be. What that means is that if we can get into our unconscious minds and change those beliefs, then we become expansive. We become more than what we were one moment ago. Comments from the people around us and personality tests show you where you were up until the very moment you took the test or heard the words. They don't show you who you are or where you are going—unless of course, you allow them to. Again, I remind you to think about where James Earl Jones, Disney, and Einstein would be (no better... where would we be) if they had believed what they were told about themselves?

The bottom line is we need to create belief systems to survive. You already understand why the ego-mind has to defend your beliefs. After all, knowing that apples come from apple trees helps us survive. It's not hard to see how eating and surviving go hand in hand. Unfortunately, if someone were to also believe that they are shy because 'it's just the way they are', or that they don't deserve healthy relationships, or good health, or happiness, then the ego-mind is working against them, not with them.

All those personality traits (like shyness or quietness, angry or a downer, etc) that family, friends, and personality tests claim for you may be true, but at best, they are based on the past. *And the past does not automatically determine the future.* You can change if you want it badly enough. If you need it badly enough—whatever it is—you can change your beliefs so you can allow yourself to have it—to be it.

Whenever I talk about traits such as shyness, creativity, confidence, or anything like that, I'm reminded of a lady I counseled years ago who, in the process of working with me, realized that there was something about her that was very creative that she clearly was not in touch with. I gave her some homework to do over and over again. Because she believed in the process of what we were doing, she fought against her own resistance and kept at it. When I said to her, "You know, there's something about you that's incredibly creative", Do you know what she said to me? She said, "I don't know what you are talking about. I can't finger paint. I can't even draw a matchstick man."

The home assignment I gave her allowed her to examine the confines of the limitations of what she perceived creativity to be and to *explore her map of the world*. We began by examining some of the unconscious beliefs she had about herself. It turned out that she grew up in a very stodgy English ex-patriot family who didn't place much value on creativity, so of course she naturally adopted the beliefs of her surroundings in order to survive. She wrongfully assumed that she was completely uncreative because that's the belief she needed to adopt to *fit in* with her family. That's how the ego-mind works; it helps us survive in our environment.

I'll just expand those last few sentences to be crystal clear.

While growing up, one belief her family held firmly was that creativity was unimportant. So, in order to *fit in*, she suppressed her creativity by convincing herself she wasn't at all creative. The combination of her family's belief that creativity was worthless and a child's natural need to fit in had her ego-mind create beliefs that fostered and reinforced the perceptions of the people around her (even adults have that need to fit in). Once she believed that she wasn't creative, this became a reality, and it blocked her. Once we explored the reasons behind her belief and drew some new points on her map of the world, she began to thrive creatively. This example is not unlike that of Suzanne who grew up believing that the women in her family are unlucky.

I'm telling you this because I've now been to not one, two, or three, but *four* of her exhibitions. I've been to four of her exhibitions!

Her work is up in the galleries and I have several pieces of her art in my home. It's an interesting career path for somebody who thought that they had no creativity. Isn't it pretty amazing for someone who once believed that they couldn't draw anything other than matchstick men?

> *"If you want it badly enough you can get it.*
> *If you have the desire to be it, the desire to learn it,*
> *and the willingness to do whatever it takes,*
> *then you can become it."*
> ~ *Dōv Baron*

Consider this: The only obstacles in the way of you living the life of your dreams are those unconscious limited beliefs that you have. You simply have to be willing to face them, then change them.

Whatever you believe you are capable of being—whatever it is—the freedom to live your dreams stems from your unconscious beliefs. These unconscious beliefs make up what I called in Part I, *unconscious deserving*, which you will recall are the beliefs you held in your unconscious without question; beliefs that you weren't even aware you had.

Remember the beliefs that form your *unconscious deserving* feed into your QRF, attracting to you what you want—and what you don't want —in your life, that's why you can end up with a whole bunch of people, situations and circumstances that you would never consciously choose.

Chapter 53

From the Impossible to the Possible

I told you earlier that in June 1990, I fell off a mountain. I was told by numerous doctors, nurses, and all kinds of "experts" that it was impossible to survive a fall that far (especially landing on rock). Well, here I am, almost twenty years later, on a computer, writing about that fall. Clearly, I survived. What I would love for you to really get into the very core of your being is this: *The impossible is possible, if you want it badly enough.* This is especially true if you are willing to begin believing in yourself, as I had to begin believing in myself. You will discover that when you truly want it this badly, you'll move mountains to get it, and the best part is that you don't have to move a mountain. All you need to do is begin by shifting one pebble at a time. Start using the exercises I've laid out and watch the mountains begin to crumble.

Terry Fox

Most Canadians know who Terry Fox was—a national hero. In 1980, Terry Fox began what became known as the "Marathon of Hope". He did what most thought impossible. For those of you who don't know, Terry Fox was a one-legged man with a degenerative form of cancer who ran a marathon of forty-two kilometres a day for a total of—just listen to this—five thousand three hundred kilometres. **5,300 km!** Most people carry a belief that says this would be impossible for themselves WITH two fully functional legs, let alone for a one-legged man. Are you picturing that? Imagine a one-legged man with degenerative cancer running down that road ahead of you. That man was Terry Fox. In this incredible journey and process he raised what was then a massive, **twenty-four million dollars** for cancer research.

Was it impossible? Clearly not. Terry showed us it's not impossible. And if you remember, so did Rosa Parks, Nelson Mandela, and Roger Bannister.

Desire, Willingness and Placebos

Some of you might have asked by now, what makes 'it' possible—what really makes it possible? What separates 'those who do' from 'those who don't'. The answer I give to you is this: *Desire* and the *willingness to learn*. Having a burning desire, and an unwavering willingness to learn whatever you need to learn, make the impossible, possible.

One of the major psychological drives of human beings is to win. Or at the very least to not be thought of as a '*La-hooser*'. You know what I mean....No one wants to be thought of as a loser. However, there are several problems that lay hidden within this drive to win or be seen as a winner.

Let me explain what the problem with this drive is and how you and I solve this problem/inner dilemma so as to experience so much more of what life has to offer.

The challenge people face is this: Because they want to win, because they feel a drive to win and because they don't want to lose, as strange as it might seem, they set their sites far too low. In many cases way below what they are truly capable of and end up with as

Henry David Thoreau put it: *Living lives of quiet desperation and going to the grave with their song still in them.*

Whilst you and I would certainly resist any suggestion that we have been or are leading lives of quiet desperation there may be some real advantage in examining how bold we really are. Maybe we all need to be willing to honestly look at how driven and willing we are to live a life of noisy achievement. These are questions of the highest value, especially when so many are telling us to not be 'big headed' or 'too big for our boots', etc.

That begs the question, how? How do we get out of the prison known as the comfort zone? To start, let's examine why people don't give it their all, why when they actually could they don't step off the edge and fly. You and I want to examine this to make sure that we aren't being held up and hindered by the same reasons. Having talked to thousands of my students in my various live events around the world over the years, it appears there are a number of key reasons as to this lack of will to step up and achieve something worthwhile, and give their lives purpose.

Of course there are our old enemies, fear of failure and its equally ugly sister, fear of success, that stop people really stepping out of their comfort zones. Often those two are the undercurrent of those who would say that any major goal is certain to be unachievable and they can offer an unending list of reasons why. Others say they are busy, they don't have time to decide what they want, which actions to take to get 'it' whatever 'it' is, or let alone do something about actually achieving their desire.

Most people don't do what it takes for a couple of reasons but here's the big one: Comparison.

Write this down, tattoo it on your brain:

"All comparison is negative!"

~ *Dōv Baron*

If you are comparing yourself to who you 'should' be there is a very high chance that you will spend a good amount, if not all, of the energy needed to fulfill your purpose beating the crap out of yourself. If you are comparing yourself to another, you are doing one of two things; you are either making yourself better than them or you are making them better than you. Either way one of you has to be minimized. There is nothing productive about comparison and worse of all, it keeps us stuck.

Give up comparing and begin to see yourself as a unique individual. Yes, you have your faults, but there again so has everyone you ever compared yourself to and so does everyone you've ever looked up to. Remember this: Comparison is sabotage!

What you need in order to really step off the edge, to make 'it' possible and to re-claim mastery of the ego-mind are a *burning desire* and the *willingness to learn*.

Let me give you a real world example: Walk into any hospital around the world and you will see that there are people getting diagnosed with all types of deadly cancers and other debilitating *dis*eases. If you listen closely, the first thing most of them will ask is, "Well doc, how long do I have to live? How long have I got left? How long before I'm..." What they are actually doing is asking the doctor for 'the map' as if it was the territory of who they are. Those people are finding out how much longer they have left to survive. They've almost commited to staying sick, living with it, playing the cards dealt to them—or as I would say, leaving it up to 'fate', 'luck', 'Karma', or 'Gladys, Fred or God' for that matter.

On the other hand, there's a second group of people in the hospital. The type of people you read about in newspapers. The ones that friends and family call 'lucky' or 'survivors'. While some doctors write off their patients 'success' over the *dis*ease due to a great response to the treatment, thereby minimalizing the patients mental and emotional state during the entire process. If you were to become a fly on the wall and pay really close attention to the survivors, you would most likely hear them demanding, "Tell me about the ten percent who survived." "Tell me what they did, who they saw, and who they spoke to."

You find that, as soon as they found out the name of the *dis*ease or diagnosis, they generally sponged up all the information available from any source imaginable about it and/or had the belief that they would overcome it, find a cure, get results, change their lifestyle habits and patterns. They would do anything required to get better; to become better, including changing their perception of the *dis*ease or themselves. Those people have the *desire* and the *willingness* to learn. They'll do what it takes when it's time without question or hesitation.

When it comes to illness we tend to 'believe' that the illness is something that is out of our control, and all too often we give that power to those we have been conditioned to believe have all the power… the doctor! Now please understand that I have nothing against doctors, without them I'd be a lump of hamburger at the bottom of the mountain I fell from. No, what I have a challenge with is when we abdicate our own power to directly affect and impact our own health.

As I'm sure you are aware, in the early part of this millennium there was a lot of hoopla made about the Human Genome Project. It was believed that once the Human Genome Project was completed we would have what it would take to discover why everyone is what they are and why some people are 'predestined' for certain *dis*eases. It was all very exciting, until it was discovered that genes were in fact NOT the answer. For example: The Breaking news story of the discovery of the 'breast cancer genes'; however, what the media failed to point out was: *Ninety-five percent of all breast cancers are not due to inherited genes.* In fact, only five percent of all cancer and cardiovascular patients can attribute their *dis*ease to the heredity of genes.

Can you grasp the implication, despite what you may have *believed*?

DNA does <u>Not</u> Control Biology!
You may be asking: "How does belief fit into any of this?" Well, this is just the tip of the iceberg. I'm pretty sure you've heard of the *placebo effect*. For years whenever that term was used it was used in a derogatory manner, meaning that whatever was put down to the *placebo effect* seemed to mean 'it didn't count'. What medical research is showing is that in many ways the placebo effect may be the thing that counts most!

A placebo as many people know is a 'sugar-pill' (meaning it contains a harmless substance) that really shouldn't help the body any more than any other harmless substance or sugar you might put in your mouth and swallow. In other words the 'medication' (which is not a medication at all) is taken by the patient without them knowing it is only a placebo. Here's where it starts to get pretty fascinating: There is a massively growing body of evidence showing that many human ailments are at the very least relieved by these placebos.

Remember the patient 'believes' they are taking medication while in fact they are only taking the placebo. And here's where things get a little wacky: Many of the patients taking placebos will experience the common side effects of the pill 'they think' they are taking.

The fact that you believe the pill will work makes it work. Bottom line, as Dr. Lipton puts it: *Your belief controls your biology.*

In medical science there is a corresponding effect known as the 'nocebo' effect. If someone believes the worst, or is given a poor prognosis they are far less likely to get well. The latest scientific research shows that the placebo effect accounts for a substantial percentage of *any* drug's function. When clinical trials use dummy pills 35%-40% of people will report improvements despite there being no active ingredient, except of course: Belief. Beliefs really can make people well and they can just as clearly make someone sick!

> If you really want to know more, I highly suggest you get your hands on Dr. Bruce Lipton's book, 'The Biology of Belief'. It is without doubt one of the most informative and interesting books I've read and having met Bruce on a couple of occasions I can tell you that he is a wise man of great integrity.

Now, knowing what you have just discovered or re-discovered in the paragraphs above, I ask you; is it really luck that 'miraculously cures those who survive terminal illness'? Was it fate that they would get a *dis*ease and then recover a short time later? Was it karma showing a loving hand for living such a good 'proper' life? Or was it the fact that instead of finding out what the 'survivors' did, they found out what the 'thrivers' did?

Survivors let the world decide how it's going to happen based on generalities. Generalities are usually based on beliefs of the people around them (the nay-sayers, the Downer-Debbies or the people who want to invite a few more guests to their pity party). They don't realize their successes and failures in life are *a result of how you cope*, as John had earlier said.

Where-as 'thrivers' understand that if you are willing to ask the right questions of yourself and the right people to get the tools that you need to thrive, then the odds are MASSIVELY stacked in your favor to achieve anything it is that you want—be it Physical health, Financial abundance and security, Relational and emotional honesty, Intellectual stimulation, or the Wisdom to put knowledge into action.

Are you seeing the difference between the two attitudes? *Desire* and *willingness* are extremely powerful key elements in getting you where you want to go and critical for getting past unconscious limited beliefs that keep you from your desires.

Chapter 54

Old Dogs with New Tricks

I'm sure you know this old saying, "You can't teach an old dog new tricks." If you have believed that or if you've ever been told that people can't change, *especially if you've been told* that *you can't change,* ***you've been lied to.***

Anyone who wants it badly enough or anyone who has the desire and the willingness to learn, can and will change. You will soon discover that under the right circumstances, change can be absolutely instantaneous. ***Pow!*** Just like that!

The obstacle is most people don't call their limited ideas and beliefs what they really are. Instead, in most cases, they clutch onto their old limited beliefs like grim death and that causes them to see the world through colored lenses.

You are already intimate with the ego-mind and how it has most of us looking at the world around us through filtered lenses, constantly seeking out evidence that all the beliefs it holds so dear are true. Through that distorted portrayal of reality some believe they found *the truth.* The real truth about that is this: *It's not 'the truth'.* It's not the truth because the search is limited.

339

I wonder how many times this has happened to you: You are facing some dilemma, you've racked your brain to come up with a solution and after all that you finally reached a decision. Let's pretend that decision is; bankruptcy. As far as you can see there's just is no other way, this is what you have to do. Then feeling less than great, but nonetheless clear that there is no other option, you go about your business. While you are out you bump into a friend who you trust enough to share your predicament and the corresponding decision that you have come to. Out of nowhere, without any premeditated thought, your friend says something that offers you a solution that had never even crossed your mind: Boom! You are catapulted out of the limited idea that bankruptcy was the only solution.

Listen, your ego-mind is looking out at the world for evidence of what it *already* believes to be true, filtering the rest out. That makes the search limited because the beliefs used to govern the search are limited. And when the beliefs are limited, *the life being lived is limited*. The ego-mind sifts and sorts, that's what it does, so the challenge is that without our guiding what it sifts and sorts very often it throws out the baby with the bathwater.

If you only ever see what you want to see, if you are only allowing yourself to look for evidence of what you already 'know to be true', then your ego-mind wins, a*nd who you were yesterday will be who you are tomorrow*. I don't think you want that. *You are more than that.*

I'll give you another example of how some people only see half of what's out there. Let's pretend you are watching a murder mystery on television and due to some technical reason half of the screen is blacked out while you are trying to figure out who the murderer is. It's going to be pretty hard, isn't it? What you are seeing is only half the evidence—it's only half the picture.

That's what it's like living in a world with an ego-mind that's looking for evidence that purely supports the past. The ego-mind is looking for evidence of what it *already* believes to be true. It's looking at the past to justify your present and future and saying, "Oh yeah! This is just like it's always been! Can't you see? It always ends up this way. Aunt Sally and Uncle Bob were right! Mom and dad always told me… and they were right!"

Fortunately, it's not that way…

You have choice. If you are tired of getting the same poop, (remember that's a technical term describing more of what you don't want) in life, then put on a new pair of lenses, draw up a new map, and do whatever it takes. Take in a new world through a new vision. You can do that. Take away the screen that's blocking half the picture. Open up the full screen and see what is really, truly there.

One gentleman I worked with, who by normal standards was extremely successful, couldn't manage to hit the million dollar mark. I worked with him for a period of just six weeks, and in that six weeks we were able to uncover the beliefs that were in his way. He hit the million dollar mark six weeks to the day. And that is not an exaggeration. In six weeks he broke that million dollar mark, just by discovering and obliterating his unconscious limiting beliefs.

Another lady I worked with had spent years of her life in relationships that just didn't work, kind of like Suzanne . You see, her flaw was that she was nice to a fault.

You've met people like that before, right? Since she was a child she committed herself to pleasing *everybody* at all times. She *always* put others first. And whenever she did anything for herself, she ended up feeling selfish and guilty.

Throughout her life she had been involved in some very emotionally abusive relationships, and the sad thing was that she didn't even recognize it.

What shocks me every time is that some people who are in abusive relationships—and trust me, she was—don't even know it.

Why do you think that is?

Quite simply, they've got these unconscious beliefs that were based on what they've had to make normal in their lives, so it becomes 'normal' to be in an abusive situation. They end up saying, *"Oh I'm fine, it's normal. That's just how it is. You don't understand, see I said ... and I should know not to say that because that pisses him off. I mean he always tells me when he gets home from work all he wants to do is... and I didn't listen, so it's not really his fault. And anyway, we apologized to each other and worked it out."*

I'm telling you, some people have 'abuse' marked as points of normal on their map. Hell, in some cases I swear people mark abuse and struggle as 'points of interest' on their map of survival.

What you will really want to understand is this: These are NOT stupid or ignorant people. Very many of them may be as educated or more educated as the person reading this who's thinking; god they are stupid. Remember what John said much earlier in this book.

> "Being hooked isn't about being smart or dumb; it's about trying to cope with a pain you don't believe anyone can ever understand!"

Well, being hooked into a dysfunctional even abusive relationship is no different, it's about coping with the pain you don't believe anyone can ever understand, it's about doing what has, with time, become normal for you!

Let's get back to the lesson here. One of the ways in which this lady's partner would be abusive was by being controlling. He would tell her what she could and couldn't do. In fact, she even told me that she wanted to come to one of my programs and he was insistent that she couldn't because it would be very selfish on her part. *God forbid she ever do something for ... herself.*

So many times I hear lives being lived like that, and it still sends shivers down my spine.

Why would anyone allow their desire to please others to be used against them? Imagine what it must feel like to live a life like that, day in and day out? I won't even go into how many times I've seen parents use guilt against their children, even when their children are fully grown adults!

One of the goals this woman told me about (and she hadn't told anybody else about it because she felt it was very selfish) was that she wanted to own property.

Can you believe that?

Her ego-mind and the environment around her created a belief in her that told her it was selfish to own property! Well, we took care of that by working together and discovering the unconscious limited beliefs that she had held for so long, beliefs she accepted as normal.

As a result of the work we did, within a reasonably short amount of time she got right up, made the necessary changes, and left the abusive relationship. By the way, she now owns property. I still smile when I remember how when she told me about all the accomplishments she had made in her life, her face glowed with pride and happiness. One huge change was the choice to be in a very healthy, stimulating relationship where she is respected and treated as an equal.

Let's face it, the only thing in her way was the only thing in *your* way: Her acceptance of limiting beliefs. Or the desire and willingness to do whatever it takes to remove them.

When you gather enough desire, willingness to learn, and wisdom to put knowledge into action, you too will make changes. Now, you can change those limiting beliefs and you can change them by getting up, sitting down, lying down, whatever it takes, just make the time to practice the exercises right here in this book. Or, if you feel you need further instruction, you can change these beliefs in as little as three days in one of my programs. www.AttractingForce.com/bookbonus

I know there are a few of you out there who bought this book at one of my seminars or experiential workshops and you are using it as a reminder of just some of the material we covered. Others who haven't met me yet and don't know anything about where these concepts have come from should know that I didn't just make this up. The knowledge in this book, the knowledge you are hopefully turning into wisdom by living it, has come from twenty-plus years of trial and error, experience and teaching.

I want to take a moment and tell you a little more of what you could look forward to if you decide to now take the next step and meet me at one of my experiential workshops, as well as a bit of what I'm all about.

You know, many people while reading this book and while in my live events have these what some call 'ah hah! Moments'. I know that those of you who've joined me in person know what I mean. For those who only know me in these pages, an 'ah hah! Moment' occurs when you read something, that at first sort of sounds right, sounds like *it could be true*, then ... all of a sudden it hits you like a Mack truck on the freeway! Something snaps, something pops up right in front of you and you think, "That's it! That's it! It makes sense!" I believe those moments are wonderful, I really do. Still, I've given up the idea that they are a 'currency'.

'Currency' may seem a little out of context here, but allow me to explain.

In my programs, there used to be a currency given out every time people had a breakthrough with me. We used to count up how many 'ah hah! moments' participants would have and the tally would be used as a reminder to mark where people were before they attended my events, as compared to where they are upon completion.

I would hand out currency after you have an "ah hah! moment" that was jaw-dropping or when you had a revelation, an insight, where things snapped together like puzzle pieces and you realized something about yourself that was holding you back.

Without doubt those moments are sensational! Yet, I'm more interested in giving people the skills, techniques and tools so that life is a constant 'ah hah'! One moment after another. I believe that after you leave my programs it's important that you keep getting those moments over and over again, realizing that the limits to what we can do in life were nothing more than an illusion.

As I write this I'm thinking about a call I had with a friend of mine this morning who was telling me about a friend of hers she had brought to one of our introductory events. My friend was asking her if she would be attending another upcoming live program and her friend said that even though it was six months since she had attended her original event she was still having breakthroughs. In fact she had been in an extremely stressful work situation and everyone around her was having some kind of meltdown while she was for the first time in her life, the calm in the storm, as a result of the tools she had received from attending this one event.

Now, we're going to take a look at something I cover heavily in my seminars—a principle that for me, sometimes, *says it all*. I call it the S.H. Principle.

Chapter 55

The S.H. Principle

Just so you know, S.H. stands for Shit Happens, and I mean it as I said it: It's life, *Shit Happens*. I just happened to say it a little more elegantly in Part II when I said, "*Everyone has some kind of pain about something in their lives, that's just the result of being alive; although, the trick is to have way more joy in your joy-to-pain ratio.*"

No matter how spiritual, metaphysical or angelic we try to be, the bottom line is there is stuff that is going to show up in your life that you just can't explain via your normal conscious process. (As I explained earlier in the book most of what's going on in our lives is coming from the unconscious). What that means is: You will bring into your life (mostly via an unconscious process) stuff that really challenges you. And I'm here to share with you that challenge is a good thing.

Throughout Part II of this book I explained that despite all the importance or unimportance we put on an event: *Events have no meaning other than the meaning we attach to them.* That is true for challenges we perceive as well; it's just a matter of perception.

The fact remains: You can learn through either joy or pain. So when something challenges you in life, you can look at it through the same-old lenses of doubt and fear, or see it as an opportunity to turn some of the knowledge in this book into wisdom and experience another chance to grow.

That can best be illustrated through an example:

Some people (let's call them group A) re-act to challenges negatively, so they avoid them, mostly out of fear—you might have heard it said, or said it yourself as, "I like to avoid confrontation."

Others (group B) look at challenges as exciting because they know they are an opportunity for personal growth.

To group B, challenge means they are going somewhere, learning something, *being something other than hum-drum and uncomfortable (or scared)*.

Take a look at the meaning that is attached to each of those points of view. Be honest and ask yourself, which group would you feel better belonging to? Come on now, be honest.

Where would you put yourself; in the group living in fear, constantly avoiding opportunity, or the people walking, leaping, and running through life, excited to be alive? Because really, the way you act or re-act to a challenge in life determines your ability to face and conquer it. And notice I gave you the choice of acting or re-acting. *How you act or re-act to a challenge*, because I'm sure most of us are tired of *re-acting* to life with an automatic programmed fear.

If you have the *desire* and *willingness* to learn what I'm teaching you through this book and in programs, you will develop a skill set and tools to reclaim mastery of your ego-mind because, as I said to you, life is going to throw curveballs at you; so you better have the skills to knock them out of the ballpark.

Now, back to the S.H. Principle. When the S.H. Principle comes into play, does it throw you off? Of course it does. It might throw you off for a minute, it might throw you off for ten minutes, and in some cases, it might throw you off for a lifetime. But if you have a set of skills and tools it will only throw you off for a little while.

We all have to accept this fact: Life is going to throw curveballs; Sh*% Happens. In order to play the game right, you have to learn a set of skills and get the appropriate tools because everything that is coming to you in life is being thrown at high speeds. So get in the game!

I wonder how many of you reading this have been observers in this game we call life? How long have you watched from the sidelines or up in the rafters? Have you ever had a friend, co-worker, family member... or ever known someone who accomplished something in their life that you wanted? It could be anything: Got the job you always wanted, met the girl or guy of your dreams, or living the life you feel you deserve, anything! Have you ever asked yourself, "What do they have that I don't? When will it be my turn?" Maybe you even attributed it to a dice rolling deity called luck or fate.

It's time to read the signs on the walls. It's your turn now! Listen to me. It's your turn! Right now you are learning the skills and the mindset to *be anything*. And if you haven't done any of the exercises I've laid out in this book, then put the book down right now, and do one. Why? Why do an exercise now? Because, you've asked the question, and some of you have asked countless times, "What do they have that I don't?" The answer is: *The right tools and the desire, willingness, and motivation to get off their ass and do it.* After all, it's hard to build a house if you don't have the right tools and the willingness to get up off your rump and build it; and it can also take a long time to build the house on your own.

I know you have desire; we all have desire because we all have dreams. So that leaves willingness. Look, you are reading this book, aren't you? You've gotten this far, right? Even for those of you who've said, "I know that" or "I'll do the exercises later," *you are still reading this.* So even if your ego-mind is trying to procrastinate and justify why you can't or shouldn't and blah blah BLAH ... you have already begun to change because you picked up this book. And by picking up this book you took one of those small steps we talked about earlier: One of those small steps that take you where you want to go.

That's all it takes. Who you were yesterday is now different than who you are today. All you have to do is to keep going. Keep taking those small steps. Start or continue on with these tools I have given you here. And if you need more help, I'm here. Both in these words and in my programs.

I'm making a safe bet that there are a few of you out there who are looking at this and thinking, "Whoopee, more motivational affirmations and wishful thinking. Been there, done that". Well, for those of you who think you see that, know this:

I'm not only here to motivate you and make you feel good about the choices you've made in life up until now. I'm here to give you the tools and the knowledge to allow you the choice and the ability to reclaim mastery of your mind and of your life.

At the Baron Mastery Institute (www.BaronMasteryInstitute.com), we don't only want to make you feel good now, we want to teach you how you can make yourself feel good anytime. If you find it difficult to keep up with these exercises on your own or you want to take it beyond what is covered in this book, then I'm here to make you another promise. As you know, because I've kept my promises throughout this book, I will do what it takes when you come to see me to make sure that you don't only learn these tools and mindsets, you master them.

Now back to the S.H. Principle.
If you don't have the tools to deal with life when S.H., your ego-mind will have you 're-acting' the way you always have in your past. All those re-actions are triggered by the meanings you attach to the sh*% that happens at any given time. The meanings you attach to the events in your life cause your neurochemistry to fire off, which pushes you to re-act the same old way you always have, thus at the end of the day, getting you more of the same old *crapola*.

Another way of seeing it is like this: People interpret everything in their lives, (including what they believe to be sh*%) the way they do because of the unconscious beliefs they carry. And you will recall that the beliefs they have about all the events in their lives make up their quantum resonance field (QRF). Because you've gotten this far in this book you understand that your QRF holds the contents of your emotional history, which creates your resonance, which is also your inner genie (you remember how we discussed our inner genies in Part I). That resonance generates a quantum energy/frequency which gets broadcasted into the universe, and as you know, if that frequency isn't in-line with what you 'consciously' want, then that same frequency will draw more and more opportunities for the same old sh*% to come into your life.

I know for some people (but not you, of course) all this can seem over-whelming and confusing, especially all squeezed into one paragraph like that. But all you have to understand is that when you change your QRF, you change what you are sending out, (ordering) from the universe. You, by reading this book, and doing these exercises, have already started changing your QRF!

Chapter 56

Pleeease Don't
Play It Again Sam!

You may recall that I mentioned I wrote a dissertation on Quantum Resonance Fields, and I referred to those fields a few times a paragraph ago. In case there is some confusion left, I'll take a moment and explain how a QRF works in a little more detail. Also in Part I, I promised that in Part III we'd get into a little more physics. Well, I'll now fulfill that promise by linking local and non-local communication to your QRF.

So, here's an analogy in line with what we discussed in Part I under, 'Putting Quantum and Resonance Together'. Think of your QRF as a radio station that's broadcasting out across the universe. With a normal radio station, the further you get away from the station, the weaker the signal being broadcasted becomes. That's called a *local* field, a local broadcast.

The QRF is a *non-local* field, which means that it's broadcasting as strongly right here in front of you as it is across the universe. The problem is that you are not always in conscious control of what's in that field. And as I said, if you think of how radio stations broadcast songs, you can understand what I mean when I say that your QRF is broadcasting a playlist. The playlist just happens to be a result of your ego-mind playing the records of your history.

Now, you may want your radio station (your QRF) to play contemporary tunes. You may want it to play the good stuff that you are focused on bringing into your life in this moment. However, if you are not taking control and mastering your ego-mind, then a lot of the time it'll play the old stuff—the stuff that, chances are, you are sick of hearing. And the result of playing old records (emotional history) is that you keep getting more of what you don't want.

To use the same analogy, what this means is that you keep attracting people, events, and experiences into your life that are in tune with your station audience. If your playlist is broadcasting punk music, then you are never going to attract the Mozart type of person. No matter how much you 'say' you want Mozart experiences, it's just not going to happen—like your chances of getting steak at a vegetarian restaurant. Or to bang that nail home, you keep attracting that which resonates in sync with you.

So, if I want to hear classical music and I tune in to your station and it's playing punk, what am I going to do? I'm going to get turned off—I'm going to be repelled. That's exactly what we do when our unconscious beliefs aren't in sync with our conscious desires—we repel what we consciously want. We have to learn to get in sync. We have to learn to change the dial.

In real life, as in the world of radio broadcasting, you will only attract the people, events, and experiences that energetically match your QRF. If your station was playing a punk playlist, your station is going to attract a lot of punks to it, right? It's simple logic. Therefore, if you are resonating lack, struggle, pain or anything else you'd say you don't want, then there's a spectacular chance that you are going to keep attracting to you more and more opportunities to have exactly what you say you don't want.

The QRF works much the same as a magnet; a magnet will attract metal and not plastic.

You should also know that human beings are both broadcasters and receivers. To return to our metaphor: We're not just radio transmitters; we're also the listening public.

When we meet up with somebody else who's broadcasting on the same frequency, there is a *wave match*. When those waves match, it's called *attraction*. We feel pulled to them, we literally *feel in sync* with them and that's what resonance is. As a side note, if you are tired of crappy unfulfilling relationships, yet somehow keep finding yourself attracted to the type of person that inevitably gives you the same old crap you left the last one about... I would take a hard long look at your beliefs about Relationships and if you now decide, I also teach two programs called, "Quantum Soul Mates for Singles" and "Quantum Soul Mates for Couples" dealing in that one specific foundation. (www.QuantumSoulMates.com/bookbonus)

Throughout this book and in my programs I always take time to explain the concept of resonance completely because it's so unique and critical to getting what you want. Personally, I feel it's one of the most missed and misunderstood links people have been talking about. This is where my teaching takes off from the work that you may have done before, and it's through understanding resonance that you open the doors to understanding *why* life is the way it is.

Chapter 57

Resonance;
a Personal Understanding

The easiest way to understand *resonance* is through example. Very early in this book we spoke about luck... Do you know anybody who thinks they are lucky? One thing lucky people tend to say is this, 'I'm really lucky'! 'Lucky' people are the ones who go out, buy a scratch-and-win .... And guess what? They win! And you know what? They *are* lucky, though not for any magical, mysterious reasons. The simple fact is: They are resonating luck, so they are lucky.

I know in Part I I emphasized that it's not a matter of luck. I still stand by that, though I want to add something here that in Part I most people might not have been ready to understand.

Like I said, most people think luck is something dolled out by fate or karma or some other mystical force. I don't believe it works like that (and remember, this is only what I believe). To me that luck is a mindset—a collection of positive or beneficial beliefs and healthy expectations about yourself, your situation, and the future that result in being 'lucky'. It's that combination that has you resonating *luck*. That's what I meant when I referred to 'what people have mistakenly called luck' in Part I.

They've got a saying in Australia to describe a 'lucky' person that goes, "If they fell in a pile of sh*%, they'd come up smelling of roses." That's a reference to somebody who has a resonance of everything going right.

Here's what you need to get: Resonance is not true for some people and false for others. It's true for *everybody* and *everything*. This is where the physics you've been learning up until now comes together.

Everything has a resonant field that contains quantum information. It's broadcasting that information out all the time whether you are aware of it or not, whether you want to or not, and whether you like it or not. And everything around you is 'listening' in on what you are broadcasting. If it's *in sync* with what you are broadcasting, you attract it. On the other hand, if it's Mozart you are wanting and you are playing a punk playlist, well you can work out what will happen ... .

All that energy—that quantum field energy—that we're all broadcasting is held in something Carl Jung called the *collective unconscious*. The Collective Unconscious is where all knowledge, known and unknown, is contained. (By the way, for those of you who don't know, Carl Jung was a psychiatrist who is paramount in today's understanding of psychology).

Edgar Mitchell was one of the first astronauts to stand on the moon. David Bohm was a student of Albert Einstein as well as a famous and very renowned physicist in his own right. These influential men, and authors such as Michael Talbert, Greg Braden, Fred Allen Wolf and an extensive list of others in the quantum physics field call the collective unconscious the *quantum hologram*, the quantum field, the field, the zero point field and a whole list of other names for the same thing.

However, what Jung, Mitchell, and Bohm etc. are all referring to is a realm of knowledge out there that's beyond anything you consciously know. When we clear our minds of all the old, limited beliefs we carry, we allow more of this universal intelligence into our beings.

There are no exceptions to the rules.

While you can allow more of this infinite intelligence and divine intelligence to come into you, you should know, most of the time we're full. That's because we've all got old ideas taking up space in our minds. And part of how we stay full is by using those three words we talked about throughout this book that keep people stuck. We say, "I KNOW THAT!" everytime someone tells us something we already know (yet lack the wisdom of doing). We all can usually recite what book we read it from (sometimes even YEARS ago), or who we heard it from. It's really not that hard to know something.

You see, what someone is saying between the lines when they utter "I KNOW THAT" is this, "I'm going to hold onto the information that I have even though it may not be working for me—even though it may be holding me back." So no space is made. No space is made, if you will, for more of this divine intelligence to pour in.

It's that simple.

It's like holding up a full glass of water while asking me to pour in some more. If it's full, it'll just spill out on the table. Granted, *some* might make it into your cup, just not enough to launch you towards your dreams.

*"There is a difference between knowing the path
and walking the path."*

~ *Morpheus*
The Matrix (movie)-1999

This is the mysterious bridge between science and spirituality people have been talking about.

Some of you know I traveled the world to study with different spiritual masters. The lessons I received from my teachers didn't always seem like lessons when they were given to me. This was because I'd ask a question and the answer I'd receive would explain nothing at all – it was a bloody riddle. I was expected to go away and work it out on my own until it came to me.

Hopefully, I'm doing a better job of explaining concepts to you here.

Anyway, I had to get my knowledge very experientially. To be honest, I've invested enough of my time trying to imagine *the sound of one hand clapping and what a tree would sound like if it fell in the forest when there's no one there to hear it.* I guess that's why I'm very keen on doing my best to explain to you why as well as how.

Implementing what it is you learn here is vital because one thing I learned is that *doing* teaches you lessons that knowing only hints at. In fact, I know that if I didn't actually experience what I learned first hand, I would be walking around this world knowing a hell of a lot while actually *achieving* very little. The reason I'm not asking you to sit around contemplating why every snowflake is different is because there is a faster way to start taking control of your life, and this is it—use the tools, challenge your beliefs.

360

Where am I heading with this? Many years ago I was studying Buddhist philosophy under the guidance of a man I had come to have a lot of respect for. This man stood out for me because he refused to accept that he was in any way better than me or anyone else for that matter. One day after I had been questioning him with the intent of understanding the way he saw the world I was presented with a particular teaching. In the style I had referred too, I was given this teaching without any further explanation, it was simply given and I could and often did, say what I thought it meant, but I certainly wasn't getting any input on my interpretation. This profound teaching was in its way one of the things that most dislodged my limited ego-mind's view of the world. Here's what Fryer Jessop shared: *"The murderer lives in me."*

Maybe you can imagine the expression on my face when I heard that. And if you can't, here's a mental image for you: Picture a child opening up a birthday present expecting a dream to be realized, and instead, getting two pairs of socks, one pair of underwear, and a book explaining the amazing adventures of a turtle and a hare... it would be a cross between unimpressed and frustrated.

Now, my normal rational re-action to *the murderer lives in me* would have been, "Wait a minute. I'm not a murderer, that's not me! I'm just not like that." And BAM all my defensive mechanisms would kick right in. In fact, there was a time in my life when anything that didn't pass through my filters of the world or points of view that were different from my own would cause defense mechanisms to kick in.

What I didn't realize then is there were two lessons in that riddle, two very big points.

The first of those points was this: Don't judge, because you just don't know. This was a simple lesson, an incredible lesson, and very well-valued. Understand it. Got it? Good.

The deeper learning within this is the lesson that is now embracing quantum physics, something the Buddhists have known for millennia; we are not separate. Quantum physics is now showing us exactly what spirituality has always demonstrated and what the most profound spiritual teachings have taught for hundreds and even thousands of years.

Chapter 58

There is No Separation; We are All Connected

I don't think you will find too many people who thought or think Einstein was anything other than a genius. What few people had realized was that Einstein was every bit as much a philosopher as he was a scientist. One of the major reasons that this side of the man was barely even noticed for so long was that for many there could be no marriage between the subjects. To many linear thinkers, science/mathematics and metaphysical philosophy were worlds apart. However, Einstein did not feel this way and often shared his spiritual philosophies with those close to him. You see he understood that we are much greater than the restricted ego-mind's concepts of who we are.

"A human being is a part of a whole, called by us 'universe', a part limited in time and space. He experiences himself, his thoughts and feelings as something separated from the rest ... a kind of optical delusion of his consciousness.
This delusion is a kind of prison for us, restricting us to our personal desires and to affection for a few persons nearest to us. Our task must be to free ourselves from this prison by widening our circle of compassion to embrace all living creatures and the whole of nature in its beauty."

~Albert Einstein

Isn't that powerful? Let's just take a look at a few of the profound messages within this quote. *"He experiences himself, his thoughts and feelings as something separated from the rest ... a kind of optical delusion of his consciousness."* The ego-mind creates separation between you and everything else and in so doing imprisons not only you but the belief of what you are actually capable of. He then goes on to say: *"Our task must be to free ourselves from this prison by widening our circle of compassion to embrace all living creatures and the whole of nature in its beauty."* In this part of the quote he challenges us to go beyond the confines of our ego-minds' separateness and judgment. I wonder if Einstein and I had both been given the same insight: "The murderer lives in me?" Makes you think, doesn't it?

Everything is connected to everything else at all times. At a base level, we are all vibrating, frequency modulating, *resonating* energy.

Remember the chair you smashed up until it became vibrating strings of light? That's what we all are when broken down into our smallest parts. That's one way in which we're all connected, through our make-up. You see, regardless of who you are, we are all made up of the same energy, which means we're all capable of achieving the same dreams in life. After all, we are *all* made up of the same energy governed by the same laws that maintain that energy, therefore, every time one of us achieves something incredible, it shifts the collective unconscious of what's possible and in so doing, opens up the door for the rest of us. So whenever you look around this world and see that house, car, trip, or job of your dreams, know that you can live in that dream... because someone *out there* did it. Someone *out there* had an idea and manifested it into reality and they are made up of the EXACT same stuff as you are. I'm being rather repetitive in this paragraph because this is vital—it's something you must not only understand, you must live by. In a few short minutes I'll share exactly what the "same stuff" is that we're all made of.

Chapter 59

Imagination:
Beyond the Ego-mind's Restrictions

I want to share another powerful and important quote by a man who, to most people, both scientist and laypersons alike have a lot of respect for. This one is far simpler, but just as challenging if you are stuck believing that all you are is walking meat.

> *"Imagination is more important than knowledge."*
> ~*Albert Einstein*

Imagination is, I believe, the catalyst for everything we call reality and to some degree take for granted as being an everyday part of life. Right now, take a moment and look around you. Unless you are standing in the middle of the desert or a forest right now, everything you see is a result of the one thing most of us were trained to ignore or at least have little respect for: Imagination. Actually, even if you are standing in a natural desert or a forest reading this, how you got there was by virtue of someone's imagination.

For something, anything to become part of our reality it had to first exist with the imagination of someone. Maybe you want to take that to its ultimate depth and say that there was a creative force in the universe, (call it God) who imagined the universe and here we are. In so doing we come back to something I mentioned much earlier in the book: *Let us create man in our image.* Genesis: 1:26

But what is imagination? Well, let's take a close look at the root of this powerful word, because I believe it contains within it some of the major keys we have been looking for with regards to manifesting our reality.

The word *imagination* can be separated into several pieces: I-magination. The *i* in this case means 'in', as in; in-ward, there-in, with-in. *Magi* (The Magi were said to be members of a priestly class, referred to in the new testament and other ancient texts). Magi is the root of the word *magic*, short for magic arts and what William Blake called the 'Divine Arts of Imagination'. And finally *nation* means 'to bring forth', 'to give birth to' derived from 'nature' and the Latin *natus* which means 'born'.

So what do we have? Well to reshuffle the root meaning of the word imagination we have: I; inward, Magi; divine arts and Nation; 'to bring forth', or 'to give birth to'. So what we have is: 'To give birth to – the inward – divine arts'. Pretty neat huh?

Simply put, in my language: The external expression of your inner being through divine arts.

Said even more simply, everything is an expression of what we imagine, consciously or unconsciously, good or bad.

"The imagination is a faculty of the soul, not the mind."
~ Dōv Baron

Know that anything *out there* that you see, or hear, was once only a dream in someone's imagination and through desire, determination, the willingness to *do something* and the confidence in themself to make it happen, regardless of what those around them say is possible, it's there right in front of you, clear as day and crisp as a bell. You can walk right up to whatever you see out there, touch it, taste it, lick it, feel it—because whatever you may have thought about yourself, that dream is there, in front of you, and it is achievable.

And with that in mind, I think you are ready to talk about the thing we've been leading up to. The big one. The mother of all ... you get the point. The **Equation for Manifestation™**. I know that most of you have been waiting for this. It's the cat's meow—one of the critical keys for manifesting. And it allows you to tap into that quantum field so that you can be open to the kind of guidance and knowledge that is beyond what it is that you know—beyond your own beliefs.

Chapter 60

The Equation for Manifestation™

At this point, I'm going to share with you the equation for conscious manifestation (note that I said conscious manifestation, you will understand precisely why over the next few pages). You are going to want to pay dynamic attention because what I'm going to give you here is an incredibly powerful tool that you can use immediately to create the life you want. I'm giving it to you at this point because you now have all the background needed to understand the reasons that this formula, this equation works and will now work for you.

Now, first and foremost, I want to make you aware that as I share each of the parts of the Equation for Manifestation™ with you, you may find your ego-mind saying "I know that." I want to once again warn you of the danger of those three words; they are a virus that will bring down the steel gate that will stop you from getting exactly what you need to begin creating the life of your dreams. Put simply, you can have all the ingredients for something, but without the recipe of how to bring those ingredients together, for how long and at what temperature you actually have nothing. The key is to know which technique to use in any given situation.

I don't know about you, but I like to know not just 'how' or even 'what' to do, I like to know 'why' things work. Are you the same? So when it comes to manifestation, I want to assist you in moving away from the oh so disappointing magical thinking that so many have had around the Law of Attraction. Does that make sense? I'm going to take you into a scientific approach that gives you the advanced understanding that so many others lack. As I go through this technique, I explain, not only what the technique is but also why it works and then precisely how to use it. I'll even explain how you've unconsciously been using it to bring you what you haven't wanted. Does that sound intriguing? Great! You will want to take in every morsel of this.

Too many people are all over the place trying one thing, then the next and never really getting focused on what it is that they want or where it is that they are going. You see when you have mastery over your ego-mind you are a great achiever and you know precisely what you are working towards all the time. Your foundations are solid and you are wealthy in every possible way, you are having incredible powers of concentration and focus. Most importantly, you are definitely not tied down to convention. You are in control of your manifesting mind, and therefore, your life. Now that's the life we want to lead isn't it?

Great achievers aren't afraid to experiment or make mistakes. However, they understand that there isn't time for them to make all the mistakes they need to make in order to find out precisely how to be the success they want to be. So what do they do? They learn from other people. People who have been there, know how to do 'it' and are doing it. Those who have the real knowledge of just what it takes to reach the successes you so deeply know you deserve.

You can remember when you first learned to ride a bike can't you? Did someone help you? Running alongside of you, holding the saddle, helping you keep your balance until that amazing moment when you finally realized what to do and then there you were off on your own, a wave of success and freedom washed over you, it was just great wasn't it? Think about it, you could have used a different strategy, you could have done it all on your own and some people do, but you know what would have happened? You would have fallen more than you needed to. You would have had more cuts and bruises than you needed to get, you wouldn't have succeeded as quickly. Now, why bleed unnecessarily? It's foolish isn't it? As I talked about in the chapter on the SH principle, life throws everyone curve balls. You and I can avoid so many of the problems that life throws at us if we become fast enough, smart enough, wise enough, to just learn from others. That my friend is one of the great key secrets of real success.

I know that there's a good chance that you've fiddled around, doing your best to understand the Law of Attraction and trying to get it to work for you. But what I'm going to share with you is both the art and the science of what actually make it work, and it will work for you just like it has worked for thousands of my students around the world.

Before we start let me make something crystal clear: Manifestation is NOT a magical process! Magic implies illusion. Manifestation is an active process. It enhances and facilitates getting what you want, but you must be involved at every turn. This means recognizing and applying the technology I'm going to share, technology that puts you closer to your dreams.

Simply said: Don't sit around waiting for miracles to show up in the outer world without being active in creating the miracles you have envisioned in your inner world.

As I explained earlier, efforts alone will never get you what you want, however, neither will no effort. Pay attention to the signs and take consistent action!

"Being spiritual or using spiritual technologies
is not an excuse to stop thinking."

~ *Dõv Baron*

The Structure of Conscious and Unconscious Manifestation

Here's a news flash: You are already a genius at manifesting, the challenge is that you've done most of it unconsciously and now you will be doing it consciously. Here's how it works...

Every thought we have creates words and or pictures. Every series of words and or pictures generates emotion because every series of words and pictures has a subjective meaning. (Remember back to "Nothing has any other meaning than the meaning we give it). The meaning generates the emotional response/re-action. When your thoughts become intently focused upon those emotions this goes deeper into the psyche and generates 'feeling'. Feeling references beliefs and or memories. Thoughts plus emotions generate feeling and when all three are held in focus this generates a quantum scalar wave of information that enters your QRF locally and non-locally broadcasts out into the universe, attracting to you whatever is in phase with whatever is being broadcast.

You now have a pretty solid grip on how you have been consciously and unconsciously creating your reality from the inside out, from within your own consciousness. Now, I want to briefly take you to the other side of the process and once again return to the quantum realm. Earlier in this book I introduced you to one of the forefathers of quantum theory, Werner Heisenberg. I shared with you how he had won the Nobel Prize in 1932 for a theory he created and is now known as 'Heisenberg Uncertainty Principle'.

You will remember we said that Heisenberg's Uncertainty Principle states that by simply observing something, just by looking at it, both you, and the thing you are observing are changed in some way. But what does that mean when it comes to manifesting our reality?

Quantum physics is both a fascinating subject and, at the same time, it can be an amazingly confusing one, particularly if we leave ourselves or rather our impact out of the equation. In quantum physics there is something known as 'the measurement problem'. The measurement problem is this: An atom only appears in a particular place if you are measuring it. In other words the atom only exists in what is called a 'state of potentiality' until a conscious being decides to look at it. It's kind of like one of your ex's who had no sign of style until you decided to find it for them and now they are all that and a bag of chips.

Anyway, back to how things go from being quantum potentiality to becoming physical reality: An atom only appears in a particular place if you are measuring it. The act of measuring it brings it into existence. On a grand scale the act of our observation brings about the entire universe. Contemporary scientific research tells us that the deeper we look into the nature of reality (matter), the less is there. Quantum physics reveals what every ancient philosophy has taught for millennia, matter does not exist; that is until we observe it. All information is merely patterns of energy, but what's fascinating about that is this matter (physical reality) is compressed energy. The more we understand, the more we can observe.

What that means is we may be experiencing ourselves as the result of what we are imagining. The fact is that we are only experiencing ourselves and our reality at the level of which we understand what we are observing. We cannot see that which we have no frame of reference for. There's a story of the Portuguese explorer Magellan sailing off the coast of what today would be Argentina and that the natives could not see his ships on the horizon because they had no concept, no frame of reference for a three sailed ship. Therefore to them these ships did not exist.

Everything that surrounds us is the result of a vibrating frequency, a resonating energy. Therefore, if we were to shift or amplify the frequency of a thing, then the structure of the matter changes. Everything that I'm sharing here is not some crazy concept I thought up over a couple of beers one Sunday afternoon. This is the material I've been sharing in one form or another for over twenty years. This quantum material is scientific fact.

We perceive reality through our five senses and therefore we tell ourselves and everyone else things like, 'I'll believe it when I see it'. The fact is; we are only seeing it because we believe it. As you learned earlier the most fundamental form of communication in the universe is resonance. Everything is resonating at its own frequency. In order to perceive an object we must be resonating with it, we must get in sync, in phase with it. To know and experience any part of our reality, our world is to literally be on its wavelength.

According to quantum physics two waves are said to be in phase when they are both having their peaks and troughs at the same time. One of the most important things for you to know about this is that these waves, these resonances are carriers of information. When two waves get in phase their combined amplitude is greater than the individual amplitude. All subatomic energy is constantly interacting with the quantum field, constantly communicating information. The Equation for Manifestation™ is the application of this knowledge into a practical form. As I was saying: To know and experience any part of our reality, our world, is to literally be on its wavelength. Using the Equation for Manifestation™ creates a deep signature wave of what you want and because everything exists in the universe in a state of potentiality before it becomes reality, by making your frequency, your resonant energy totally clear it looks for the corresponding frequency to get in phase with. When the frequencies come together the opportunity to manifest what you desire appears.

Now I know that part we've just been through can be a bit intense so if you have any confusion please go back and give it another read, because when you get it, it will knock your socks off.

Now, it has been my mission throughout this book to have you truly grasp that everything that has been showing up in your life has not been by some random accident, fate or through some cruel god. The equation I've just outlined above is the distilled reason for everything that you have encountered in your life, even if you have had many things you would not have (consciously) "chosen."

Okay, so now you've got all the background on how you have 'unconsciously' manifested everything in your life. Here's the way you can begin consciously manifesting what you want.

In its simplest application the Equation for Manifestation™ is actually only a three-step process.

> 1) Choose what it is you want in life.
> Simply choose what it is you really want.

You see, most of the time people are not specific in selecting what they want—they are very vague. (Remember what happened to Aladdin because he was not specific). So, be precise and pick exactly what you want. Focus intently on your desired outcome with an absolutely clear mind. You need to get very, very defined. In fact, the more detailed you can be, the better. The universe will give you absolutely anything you ask for; it really doesn't give a cat's fur ball about what you ask for, remember it's not judging, you are. It will give you anything, **so be very specific about what you want**.

> *There is, however, one proviso.* The universe will grant you absolutely anything **except for a 'specific' other human being**. One exceptional gift of being who we are is that we, human beings, have free will. As such, it's not possible for us to exert our free will over the free will of another.

So, with the exception of a 'specific' other human being, you can ask the universe for absolutely anything you want. However, at the risk of nagging, be very specific.

> 2) Hold that thought, and hold it until it gets you
> in touch with the feeling it arouses in you.

This is very important. (In my workshops I guide participants through the experience of this process so that they truly understand how and why this method works). Now, get really focused on the thought ... hold that thought until it generates an emotion. Begin feeling the emotions and let yourself go deeper into the emotion until it generates something even deeper ... feeling. Get in touch with the feeling until you begin to experience what it is you want in the 'now moment'... the right here right now moment ... begin experiencing it... becoming emotionally connected to it ... make it three dimensional ... see it ... see every detail of it ... see the colors ... see the texture of it ... see how big it is... how small it is ... exactly how it is ... smell it ... taste it ... feel it ... hear how it sounds. The more three-dimensional you make it, the better.

3) Go deep into your mind and focus on those feelings excluding all other thoughts or feelings.

And I mean *absolutely* at the expense of all other thoughts and feelings. Your ability to focus exclusively on the feeling will determine the degree to which you experience your desired outcome.

Here's what I want you to know. After trying this a few times people say, "Oh that's so hard, how do you get your mind to focus? How long do you have to maintain that focus?"

Listen carefully because when I share with you what I'm about to share you will realize you can do this and you can do it right now! **Sixteen seconds**; it takes sixteen seconds of **uninterrupted** thought and feeling. That's all it takes. Sixteen seconds and BANG it manifests. Astonishing, isn't it?

Look, you can do it and you can do it starting right now!

As I just said, your ability to focus exclusively on your feelings determines the degree to which you will experience the outcome. *And that's the Equation for Manifestation™* in action.

I know that we all have our own preferential way of learning, reading is great, but some of us need other mediums. For that reason if you would like to have me personally guide you through the Equation for Manifestation™ I've put together a multi-media home study that will support you getting more and more focused on whatever it is that you want. The Equation for Manifestation™ home study program is going to do it for you. When you go to www.equationformanifestation.com you will find just what you are looking for.

"Your life is absolutely, totally, and completely purposeful. However, its purpose is aligned with whatever you are resonating. Therefore, you must become aware of what resonance you are both surrounding yourself with and what resonance you are putting out into the quantum field."

~ *Dõv Baron*

Once you get in resonance with the outcomes you desire, anything is possible, and using the Equation for Manifestation™ does that for you. When you are in resonance with your deepest desires, you are continuously sending out that quantum wave of information to the universe. The universe, in turn, reflects that information back to you. And it doesn't just send you the warm fuzzies, either. It reflects back to you in two forms; one being opportunity (that's why awareness is so important in the manifesting process) and the other form is hard core reality.

Now that you understand how you have been unconsciously manifesting you realize that your life and everything going on in it is not by accident. Your life is absolutely, totally, and completely purposeful. But its purpose is aligned with whatever you are resonating. So it makes only logical sense that you need to be aware of resonating wealth in order to have wealth. You need to be resonating loving relationships in order to have loving relationships. You need to be resonating magnificent physical health in order to have magnificent physical health. However, again I want to drive home that manifestation is NOT a magical process. Do not sit around waiting for miracles to show up in the outer world without being active in creating the miracles you have envisioned in your inner world. Those who told you that no effort is required; lied! It's a different kind of effort, but, nonetheless it is effort, so pay attention to the signs and take consistent action in the direction of your desired outcome!

Angie the Skeptic

When Angie first applied the Equation for Manifestation™ it was at one of our live events about seven or eight years ago. A warm kind lady with a fiercely rationally trained mind anyone could see she was a trained skeptic. A financial planner by career, therefore if it didn't add up on paper for her it must be nonsense was her thinking. I had just walked everyone through the steps and the process and the entire room was vibrating with excitement. However, when I looked over at Angie it was clear she had something going on that she just didn't know how to deal with. It turned out she was in a full-blown screaming match with her own ego-mind. As I walked over to see what was going on I caught a glimpse of a tear in her eye and by the look on her face it appeared to be a tear of frustration.

Quietly taking her off to the side I asked her what was going on. She emphatically told me that 'this couldn't work'. I asked her if she had ever applied the Equation for Manifestation™ before, and of course she said, "No." "Then how can you be so certain?" I asked. "It just doesn't make sense." she replied. "Exactly, what doesn't make sense to you? Are you struggling with the science part of it?" "No, you explained that very well, it just doesn't make sense" she said. I was still baffled as to what 'it' was that didn't make sense, so I asked what it was she would like to manifest.

Angie told me that she was looking at buying a second home. However, she was looking at a particular place that was over her budget. The market was in the kind of boom where a property would go up for sale at a certain asking price and the person who would get it was the one who offered the most over that price. On top of all that the day before she had put in her offer on the property and had been told that she wouldn't qualify for a mortgage even at that price.

I gently walked her through the process again and asked her to tell me what came up. That was when I found out that she'd been in a screaming match with her ego-mind, and it had been winning. I asked her what the main objection her ego-mind would throw up was. To be honest her ego-mind threw up all kinds of half assed nonsense in order to keep her stuck. But I heard something that was running as an undercurrent of every answer. Finally I said: "Angie, it sounds a lot like there's a part of you that doesn't believe you deserve this house." The tears of frustration became the tears that flow when the truth is finally revealed. "Oh my God, you are right, that's exactly what it is."

I began taking Angie into another process that I won't go into right here. However, what I will tell you is she did come to very quickly realize that she did deserve to have what she wanted. This all took place on the second day of a three day event. Just two days later we received a call at the office from Angie, she sounded frantic and no one could work out what exactly she was saying except that she wanted to speak to me. I called her back later that day and by then she had calmed down, a little. Angie excitedly told me she had got the place. "But wait till you hear this," she said. Like an excited child she went on. "First of all I was given the mortgage that I had been told I didn't qualify for. Then there were five offers above mine yet mine was the one they accepted. And here's the big one; when I asked them why they had accepted my offer when there had been offers beyond mine they said: "We don't really know, we just had a good feeling that you were the right person to move into our home."

How's that for manifestation? And believe me that was just one of hundreds of other mind blowing results my students get from using the Equation for Manifestation™. So don't just read it, get it, use it!

Throughout this book I've stated that fear is a powerful manifester. This is because fear generates focus, and the more focused and unwavering you are, the more likely you are to manifest the object of your focus.

Think about it. How many of you have feared something and then BANG it shows up? Why? Well, fear is a great manifester because when you are afraid, you are absolutely focused.

Have you ever noticed that when fear is consuming you, it's very difficult to focus on anything other that what you are fearing? It's challenging to insert something else into your mind-set because fear can take up so much of your attention.

As you might guess, manifestation of what you don't want through fear happens all the time for many people because they invest so much energy into being afraid.

Fear of what you don't want doesn't have to consume every thought at every moment to manifest itself, either. It's that constant trickle of, "I sure hope that 'X' doesn't happen" that feeds into your QRF as emotional energy.

Understand that the universe doesn't listen to the content of what you are saying. It pays attention to what you are connecting to on the *emotional* level because that drives to the feelings, which connects to your old beliefs, most of which are buried in your unconscious.

Here's another way of putting it. Most people have only a vague idea of what they want in life. When you ask them what they want to achieve, they respond with objectives such as 'financial security', 'to be loved and accepted' or, even more vague, 'to be happy'. The problem is if you ask them to describe what that *means* to them—how it would *feel* to have the focus of their desire—they don't know. They can't clearly see those pictures. They are not feeling it with every fiber of their being.

However, if you were to ask them what they *don't* want, that's a different story. People can tell you what they don't want to happen in the most amazing detail, right down to the words the people around them would say. "Oh man, I'll never hear the end of it from my mother (or father, or friends)." Not only do they know what their friends will say, they know exactly how they'll feel, re-act, and in some cases how it'll keep happening over and over again until…

Do you now see what I mean when I talk about getting crystal clear? If you happen to be one of those people who only has a fuzzy idea of what you *do* want in comparison to what you don't, you better start using these techniques and cleaning out the garbage hidden in your unconscious. If you don't, then who you are today will be who you are tomorrow, because the ego-mind is always referencing history in order to predict the future.

I've said it more than once and I'll repeat it again because it's extremely important. Focus on what you want *in precise detail*. Make those pictures, sounds, smells, and tastes real, even more real than what you don't want. Because the articulation between sense and emotion is the language the universe responds to. Invest yourself emotionally in what you want even deeper than what you don't or else you will be walking into the restaurant of life and getting a plate full of, well, you get the idea.

I have personally used the Equation for Manifestation™ to attract the woman of my dreams. This wasn't some woman I'd had my eye on from afar – but a person who had the qualities that I wanted. I've used it to create this fabulous life that I live where I get up in the morning **excited** to go to work. I've created *my life*. I mean, you can do whatever you want to do. You can have whatever you want. You can create a life that's totally rewarding to you.

I'm betting that there are more than a few ego-minds reading this book right now screaming out, "No! It can't be that simple!"

Is it really that simple?

Before I answer that question there is something you will really want to sink in: You are already an expert in manifesting! You've just been doing it without knowing what you were doing and as a result you've had more than your fair share of what you didn't want.

I've coached people all around the world and watched their lives change right before my eyes. Even years after we've met, they call or write letters telling me all the wonderful ways this teaching has changed their lives.

You could be one of them too.

As you've probably already guessed, especially if you put this book down and tried the technique, this simple technique isn't always that easy. It seems very straight forward to tell yourself you are going to sit down and focus, but sometimes, it's just not easy. And you should be aware that there's a distinction between the two.

In order to get what you want to happen, you will have to be focused. This means that first and foremost you will have to make it important to you. Making something important is what makes it easy. When something becomes vital enough, you can do anything. · *You can absolutely, positively do anything.*

The fantastic news is even complex tasks can become easy if you practice them enough. You know, it's about repetition.

Take driving 'standard' (stick-shift) as an example.

If you drive or have tried to drive standard, you will appreciate this example. Think about the first time you ever drove standard. Well, that's a complicated job.

Not only do you have to watch the road, hold the steering wheel, and use your feet on all three of the pedals, you have to work out which pedal is the clutch, which pedal is the brake, which is the accelerator, and which one's that again? While you are doing all that you have to turn the wheel, put the indicator lights on if you are turning, decide whether you are turning left, turning right, or wandering down the middle of the road. I mean it is complex when you think about it, yet now, you've been doing it for ten or twenty or a hundred years. I'm even going to bet that you can eat your sandwich, talk on your cell phone, and drive your car without thinking about it.

That's how simple the Equation for Manifestation™ becomes with repetition. And guess what? It's not complex, especially when you compare it to driving standard! It's only three steps. Repetition and focus are the keys. This is a very manageable exercise.

Repetition and focus will get you there. Now, you might be wondering what the best form of practice is, and here's the answer: *Doing it.* Don't just pretend to practice. Don't try it once or twice and put it aside. We're not trying here, *we're doing.* Remember Mr. Miagi from The Karate Kid? He said, "There is no try, only do."

Let's say you want to learn how to hit a golf ball. You can go out on the golf course and learn how to hit a golf ball. You can decide that you are going to take a swing at that golf ball over and over again until you get it just right. You can stand there for weeks and weeks, and I'm willing to bet you are going to get better and maybe even quite good. Yet for some, there is a better way. They go out and get a coach; they get themselves somebody who knows *how* to do it and who can show them how to do it. They get themselves a mentor who's been through the process, someone who knows the game and who will walk them through it.

As you already know, it's a lot easier when you have a professional guide.

Hey, even Tiger Woods has a coach. Even Tiger Woods, who at the time of writing this book was ranked number one in the world at golf, has a coach who he works with constantly. You want to be at the top of the game. So find somebody who knows how to play at the top of the game.

The participants in my programs gain first-hand experience from someone who knows how. There is no guessing or wondering if they are doing it right. They reap the benefit of repetition from doing all the exercises we've covered here over and over again, including the Equation for Manifestation™. By working with someone who knows, you attain a higher level of confidence. Higher confidence increases competence. As you get better at it, you are more confident. It just keeps on getting easier and better .

Trust me, I know this works because apart from my vast personal experience, for the last twenty plus years, I've seen the people in my workshops get phenomenal results! That's how I can confidently make the promises I'm making in this book. *I know it works.* I've experienced it, seen it, and taught others. With me, you will directly experience everything that I teach here in this book and much more.

So we're clear on what 'experiencing it' means. Picture me, standing next to you, teaching you first-hand how, why, and when to do it. That's it. That's how simple it could be—just as simple as the steps themselves.

Challenges Along the Path
Now that you have a sense of how simple it can be, let me talk to you very briefly about the four obstacles that can get in the way of you manifesting the life that you really want.

1) As you probably remember this book's subtitle is 'your ego-mind won't like it'. It is the ego-mind that has been manifesting your reality in the form that it has been showing up. It has been using the Equation for Manifestation™ on a constant basis for one reason: Your ego-mind is attempting to tell you that things should stay the same. It uses excuses to keep you stuck.

As you may recall, that's what I was talking about throughout Part II. The ego-mind uses words like 'I know that'. The number one obstacle that is in the way of you manifesting the life of your dreams is your ego-mind trying to keep things the same. It does that by reminding you of past failures and the 'words of wisdom' (in case you hadn't guessed, I use that term sarcastically) handed down by the media, friends, and parents – albeit, in most cases with good intentions. But, then again, as the seventeenth century proverb goes, 'the road to hell is paved with good intentions'.

2) You are unconsciously maintaining the belief that you are less powerful than you are.

So many people have this crazy idea that only a few of us are capable of leading powerful and brilliant lives. Because of this, there aren't many of us living up to our full potentials. *You can live up to yours.*

Chapter 61

The 'X' Factor

By now you are probably wondering: What's the 'X' factor that makes manifestation work for some people and not for others? Well as I've clearly presented it's all about 'resonance'. However, I want it to be perfectly apparent about what it is that puts you in resonance with what you want. As I said, it's not the thoughts, although they are important. To some degree it's your emotions; however, as stated they are mostly transient. No the number one thing that puts you in resonance, the 'X' factor that determines whether something shows up in your life is: 'FEELINGS'!

More important than any other factor is the kind of feeling you are running. However, as I said stuffing your feelings doesn't work either, because those feelings become the very fuel that connects with the quantum field. Bear with me, because I'm going to show you a powerful piece of scientific evidence that will wipe away all doubt and give you absolute certainty that it's all about feelings.

You may not have been aware of the fact that for decades, scientific studies have actually demonstrated that the mind and more important-ly the feelings we have can affect our reality including physical matter. Leading scientists such as Dr. Roger Nelson out of Princeton University have developed what are known as Random Event Generators. These

REG's track and show the impact of human beings thoughts and feelings on a global level in relation to specific events.

The REG's have been shown to be directly affected by human consciousness. A body of scientists has come together to create: The Global Consciousness Project. The Global Consciousness Project has linked a series of these generators together around the world, creating an abundant supply of data which has revealed something totally fascinating. Put simply, these REG's are set up to be in what is known as a random state which means that they, of their own nature, are going to supply information that is 'random'. Think of flipping a coin over and over again. By and large the coin would average out quite evenly between heads and tails.

However, what the results have shown is that on a vast number of occasions there is an alteration in these REG's that is in direct response to major planetary events. These alterations occur in waves that manifest across the entire planet. According to Dr. Rodger Nelson, these fluctuations at the very least indicate interconnectedness between 'us' (all human beings) and our physical reality.

All of that is theoretically very interesting, right? Hold on to your chair, this will rock your world:

In September, 2001, Scientists began to see readings that were way outside the normal range of what they had seen in the past. Needless to say, the scientists were fascinated to discover what was creating such a huge fluctuation outside the 'norm'. They overlaid the data over a timetable-calendar and as I'm sure you are not surprised to learn the massive fluctuation was completely aligned with the happenings precisely during September 11, 2001. They got the data even more precisely honed to discover that the first major fluctuation took place exactly fifteen minutes after the first plane hit the first tower at the world trade center in New York City.

So, stop for a moment and think about whether your feelings are having a direct affect on your reality? If all the feelings brought up by those events shifted the results of a machine, (the random event generators) what are your feelings doing to your reality? Further research showed that the magnetic fields of the planet were also directly impacted during this exact same time.

Just to let you know that these mind blowing results led to a series of studies. The bottom line of those studies was this: It is human emotions and more specifically the magnetic fields produced by the heart during certain kinds of emotion that are now documented as extending far beyond our own bodies. To such a degree that satellites which measure the magnetic field of planet Earth, and are hundreds of miles above the surface of the earth, are able to pick up this shift in human emotion.

I know we've all been taught that it's what we 'think' that counts. However, I want to point out that that particular theory has its basis in a 'brain centered' reality. Meaning, we have all been taught that the brain is the be-all-and-end-all and that is quite simply outdated thinking. The human heart is now documented as having both the strongest electrical and magnetic field in the human body, in fact considerably stronger than that of the brain. Truth be told, the heart is about 100 times stronger electrically and about 5,000 times stronger magnetically than that of the brain. Now here's what you will want to let soak in: The physical world as we know it, is made up of those two fields, called the electro-magnetic field.

Now, think back to how I shared with you very early on in the book about how the Law of Attraction is a superficial understanding of how manifestation actually works. I know that many people who have been Law of Attraction fans may have been a bit insulted by that statement. However, you are now truly beginning to understand the depth of that statement. You can now see through this book I have done my best to assist you in understanding something of much great importance when it comes to manifestation, and that is the Law of Resonance.

What science is now beginning to show us is that when we begin to consciously create the feelings of what we choose to experience in our lives, whether that's consciously choosing to focus our feelings on love, gratitude, loving relationships, abundance or having a vibrantly healthy body, those feelings create the patterns of energy that effects the magnetic and electrical fields in our hearts. The scientific research shows us that those fields directly impact what the leading scientists call *the zero point field/the quantum field/the Divine matrix,* all names for the same thing. This is the field from which everything in our universe has its origin. So, despite what you may have been told by your friends who are into the whole Law of Attraction thing, at a scientific level it's not really about attracting something into your life, it's more about creating the feeling within ourselves so that the universe can mirror, match or get in phase with what it is that we are already holding the feeling of. In other words we must (at a feeling level) become 'it', before we can have 'it' show up in our lives. Just let all that sink in for a minute or two and you will see that for all the scientific reasons I just outlined; it's not about 'the Law of Attraction' it's about the feelings that you feed into the field and the best way to do that is through the Equation for Manifestation™.

Let me repeat; it's not about thinking the right thoughts, it's not about the Law of Attraction as such, what it all boils down to is this: 'As you feel, is as you attract'!

Now, I know that for many people this is a bit of a revelation, (to say the least), so let it rattle around in your head for a few minutes and you will see that it makes perfect logical sense. Once the implications of what you've just learned sink in think about whom you need to share that new knowledge with. By this point in time I'm sure that not only one person, but in all likelihood many people, sprang to mind. Remember that's good because sometimes we need to share something in order to really get it ourselves.

Chapter 62

Three Percent of Your Brain

I wonder how many of you have seen a fantastic movie called "Defending Your Life." In the film, protagonist played by Albert Brooks is in a sort of purgatory, (although the food and entertainment seem much better than the purgatory we were told about by certain religious teachings). Anyway, in this place between life and death, Albert Brooks' character is talking to somebody who assumes a role similar to that of his lawyer.

The lawyer tells jokes, most of which are at Albert's expense and begins explaining how he's going to defend Albert's life. He notes that Albert, as a human, only uses three percent of his brain. When you learn to use more than three percent of your brain, the lawyer says, you are no longer required to live down on earth.

This type of tale has been told for thousands of years in a hundred different ways. We as a people don't live up to our potential. In our culture, numerous films prominently echo this theme: The Matrix, Powder, Phenomenon, Star Wars, Revolver, What Dreams May Come, the list goes and on, (many of which are my favorite movies).

My favourite part in 'Defending Your Life' is when Albert asks, "Why am I only using so little of my brain?" To which he gets this fabulous reply, "Well, you use most of your brain to deal with fear. That's what people do on planet earth."

Sound familiar? We are so bloody focused on dealing with fear—so focused on the fear—that we don't even know how powerful we are. You will recall that because of our level of focus on it, fear is a powerful manifesting force.

Get this: *You are enormously powerful.*

This next one is one of the most common reasons people aren't living the life of their dreams.

1) Something has to happen before I...

There's this belief out there that says something must happen – that there's something you are waiting for, or that somebody or something needs to show up— in order for your life to get better.

If that has been you, then there's something I must tell you, something that will likely rock your world. Something you really need to understand... It's not coming!
By the way, if you are subject to this kind of thinking, even if something did show up, even if something dropped right into your hands, you'd still be waiting for something else.

The ego-mind has its excuses and it always will. So don't wait.

And finally...

2) All those conditioned, limited beliefs that we adopted in order to survive in our original environment stand in the way of manifesting the lives we really want.

Like we covered throughout Part II, the limited beliefs we needed to adopt to survive, to 'fit in', were fine and even terrific when you were five, six, seven, ten, or twelve years old. They are not so helpful anymore.

Listen, those four things combined have been blocking you, yet you can overcome them if you have enough desire and the willingness to learn. For the people who do have enough desire and willingness to learn, change can take place, as crazy or weird as it might seem, in as little as three days. That's it—three days.

Incredible as it sounds, focusing intently on what you want for 16 seconds, every day for three days, gets you what you want. Once again, for those of you who have an ego-mind that's still screaming, 'it's not that easy', put your doubts aside and take this in, *it is that easy*!

What's different about what I teach is that, as I said earlier, it's not some 'rah rah' and it's not about counting all the 'ah hahs' you would get. It's about *getting* it, *knowing* it, and most importantly, *living* it.

As you've probably noticed, I offer a logical, practical means to achieve your goals. The exercises in this book are a set of tools that teach you how to overcome any resistance and setbacks you may encounter in your life. They also provide you with the skills to break through limiting beliefs and ensure that the next challenge you face will be of a different caliber than the one you are currently negotiating – a calibre in keeping with a higher level of awareness.

As an example, if you are striving to overcome limiting beliefs which are keeping you from making your first fifty grand, when you achieve that goal, you will be ready for the higher challenge of making one million.

Whether you are fourteen, twenty-forty, or two hundred years old or young: It just works; it's that easy.

Make this knowledge a part of you because as I said to you, sh*% will happen. You better believe it's going to show up, and you better have an amazing set of skills to deal with it. If you want more help, and remember, it's okay to ask for help, then come to one of my programs. During the program, you will learn and utilize the skills, and after the program, you will use them every day of your life. Because life is going to throw curveballs, you better have what it takes to knock them out of the park.

Chapter 63

Live Your Life in Excellence!

Those who live their lives in excellence, those who live at the highest level—and those who have got the six foundations of success nailed down tight—those are the people who have the skill set and the knowledge to face their challenges head on. They are not running around seeking permission from other people about what they can and cannot do. They don't pass their plans and ambitions by everyone else, asking if it's 'okay', because they know that some of those people don't have their best interests at heart.

Stop asking other people how you should live your life. You don't want to be doing that. I know you don't want to be doing that anymore or else you wouldn't be reading this book.

The reality is that the people at the top of their games are masters of their ego-minds. They know to go within themselves when they are standing at a crossroads in life because they intuitively sense that they have the answers within. They've got the tools and skills to hit those curveballs out of the park. They don't look at life's S.H. as one devastating moment after another because they see challenges as opportunities to grow. To them, to 'thrivers', challenges in life become opportunities for advancement, for growth at a new level every time. This is a kind of excellence that's just not achieved through reading books alone. I'm sorry, it's not achieved through the reading of books alone or from sitting around and just thinking about it, quoting lines and phrases to your friends over coffee, tea or even a pint or two of your favorite beverage.

The capacity to hit life's curveballs out of the park—the ability to achieve one's dreams—comes as a result of taking informed, skillful action, action unhindered by limited beliefs and lies.

Just as I've been doing throughout this book, I teach people how to see the lies that they've been given. Once they've recognized and accepted those limited beliefs in their lives for what they really are, limitations, they begin changing them. If you are willing, you can begin seeing the truth about who you are and then you can realize what you are really capable of.

What if you actually have what it takes? What if you are not **broken**? What if you are just underutilized? What if you are a Masserati that's never gotten out of second gear?

I believe you are more than you think you are. I believe we're all magnificently powerful people, and I don't believe anyone is broken. We just have to grab hold of the steering wheel and take our feet off the brakes.

I know that some of you feel like you are trying very hard to move forward, and at times it seems like you've got one foot on the accelerator while the other's on the brake. The fact is, the foot that's on the brake represents the unconscious beliefs that run our programs. And like I said, anytime you are ready, you can get your foot off the brake.

Now, I invite you to really think about what you've always wanted.

What false beliefs do you have that keep you from living the life of your dreams? False beliefs come from fear, and fear is simply **False Evidence Appearing Real**.

Remember how in Part II I explained that you might keep getting what you don't want if you don't address your unconscious beliefs. The reason for this is that those false beliefs are setting up the resonance that's determining what you attract and what you repel.

The bottom line is that your old beliefs do not support your highest desires. They are not made for that. Your old beliefs were set up to protect you based on the situation that existed in your original environment. You are not living in that environment anymore and that is worth reminding yourself of on a regular basis.

Your old beliefs determine what you can and cannot attract and that includes the people you surround yourself with. You've heard it said time and time again, 'Misery loves company'. So…

> *"Don't expect those who have abandoned their dreams
> to sustain you in yours."*
>
> ~ *Dõv Baron*

People want to stay comfortable. They don't want to be around people who challenge them if they are committed to being stuck. This is because most people see challenges in life through the red lenses of fear.

The reality is, there are many people out there who respond to their life situations or yours by insisting , "Well you know, it's not so bad" or my personal favorite, 'It could be worse'.

Every time they say that, they demonstrate their beliefs about themselves and life through their behavior. This isn't much different than when someone warns, 'Don't get any big ideas'. If you believe them, you are letting them hold you back. Don't you want more? Don't you know that you can *be* more, *get* more, *give* more?

It seems there's always someone around saying, "Gee, it's not so bad, you've got a pension," or "What are you talking about? You have a roof over your head, you are in pretty good health. You should feel lucky!" You know what my response would be? 'Lucky? I should feel lucky that I'm *J*ust *O*ver *B*roke with my J.O.B.? There's so much more to life out there and I know it, I can see it! I hear about it everywhere, and I'm going out getting it—*for me*'.

With that in mind, when you think about what it is you want in life, you have to ask yourself: **Are you asking failures for advice on how to be successful?**

Are you asking those who have given up on their dreams to support you in yours? Think about it. If you are, it's a recipe for making sure that you don't get what you want and that you keep getting more of what you don't want.

Do yourself a huge favour. When you ask for support, you, like me, should ask the right people. Be sure to be willing to ask for help even when your own ego-mind says, "No! No, I'm fine." Ask for help when your ego-mind says, "I don't need help, I already know this stuff."

Hey, give yourself a break, get the answers from those who have them. If you know that there's more to life than this, if you've always sensed that there's more to life than this and you are sure that you want more, ask those who are living their dreams how to get there. After all, when you are carrying the right map, getting where you want to go is a lot easier than plotting it out through trial and error.

Remember how I said, 'Behavior demonstrates belief'? Well, don't ask for advice from people who are demonstrating beliefs that scream out limitation, hesitation, and fear. I'm not saying that there's anything wrong with them. They are choosing to live life a certain way and that's fine. You yourself don't have to live that way. *You don't have to live that way.*

Don't rely on the knowledge of this alone; it's not the knowing that counts. Wisdom is the key. And wisdom is in the doing, so you need to get some direction and get some help. You also need the desire and the willingness to learn how to get from stuck to unstuck, and you get that from being around people who are not afraid to live life at the highest possible level. Many people are afraid to ask for help. They are afraid. And those are the people who will continue to live 'hum drum' lives. Many people believe that those who are super successful have big egos, what I want you to truly understand is that it takes a massive ego-mind to stay stuck where you don't want to be!

You are probably familiar with the typical scenario of a guy driving around lost while his wife says, "Let's stop and ask for directions, honey."

The guy tenses up, chokes. Sometimes even says or thinks, "Oh no!"

Right there, that's the ego-mind. That's the ego saying "Oh no."

It's pride. And pride gets in the way of growing and becoming more, because pride is fear-based.

There's a false message out there that says, if you admit that *you don't know*, the world thinks less of you—the world might even find you weak. Or worse yet, you might think less of yourself, you may think of yourself as weak. Because of this, it takes a certain courage – a certain sense of self – to admit you don't know. It also takes a strong desire and willingness to learn.

As you ask for help when you need it, you are doing three things.

1) You are admitting there's more to know. In essence, you are emptying some of the water from your cup to let more in. That is one of the first steps into genius.

2) By realizing there's more to learn, you begin regaining mastery over the ego-mind. This occurs because you are challenging yourself to be more, to accept that you don't know everything.

3) Foremost, you are challenging a limited belief that says that asking for help is a sign of weakness.

Throughout this book, you've seen how you've been running your unconscious beliefs as 'truth'. If you want more, I'll personally teach you how to get to the real truth: The truth clouded behind all the smoke and mirrors created by limited beliefs and weak foundations.

As a result, you will get the kind of changes that you want. In most cases, sometimes during the breaks we take in my live events, people come back and they've just *got it*. Breakthroughs come that take them by surprise, just like that. POW!

I have to tell you, I've heard some very persuasive stories from participants in my programs.

This one lady I worked with a while back came to me and told me that she had taken one of Anthony Robbins' programs (and I personally think Tony's great). Anyway, she had taken EST back in the seventies and had done the forum called 'The Millionaire Mind'. She tried psychotherapy, hypnotherapy, hell, she'd tried almost everything out there. At the end of one of our weekends, she came up to me and said that she had gotten more out of that program than all the others combined.

People break through fears and illusions in my courses all the time.

I remember one gentleman who attended felt that he had been forced to come to the program by his boss. Before the program even started he told me he thought it would be a complete waste of his time.

That same guy went through the program and discovered the unconscious beliefs he had and how they had been impacting the way that he parented. By using what he learned, he was able to undo thirty years of damage. Three months later when we connected again, he told me he was still flying on high-octane fuel. Breaking through those unconscious beliefs had changed him as a parent, and according to rumors this almost seventy year old man had become a much better husband, too.

Now, give yourself a moment to think about this. Do you think that collapsing your unconscious, limited beliefs might change the way you see the world?

I'm sure if you've begun practicing the exercises, you are already discovering that removing those filters can change everything. Because unconscious beliefs are just that—filters.

Do you think that removing those filters that are in place—those old beliefs—might change your level of fear about anything?

If you were able to get in there—and you can—and change those beliefs and in some cases even remove the fear, do you think that would change the quality of your life, your relationships?

How would it change your income? How would that change if you removed those unconscious beliefs? When you regain mastery over the ego-mind, everything changes, and it changes for the better.

Let's talk about relationships again for a moment. One thing I want to stress here is that your greatest source of joy and for that matter, your source of income, is a direct result of the relationships that you nurture. I know you've heard the saying, 'It's not what you know, it's who you know'. That's a relationship.

Let me ask you: What unconscious beliefs are keeping you out of the kinds of loving, healthy relationships that you want? Trust me here, it's all about relationships, particularly the one with yourself.

In my experience, one huge area that people tend to overlook is the relationship they have with themselves, and this is the fundamental relationship in our lives. We need to treat ourselves well before we can achieve our dreams, and sometimes that translates into spending money on ourselves.

Something I hear all the time is people telling me how much they spent on seminars and self-help books. I know how that can add up. I myself spend approximately $20,000 a year on improving my education.

I do it without any hesitation, and not because I'm sleeping in a bed of hundred dollar bills. No, I do it because I understand that I have a relationship with myself that must be nurtured. In order to do that one of the things that is extraordinarily important is to go out and get knowledge from wherever and whoever has it.

If your ego-mind is using the excuse of money as a reason not to tend to your personal growth, for instance attending a program where you feel you will improve somehow, then cast it aside; despite what 'they' might be telling you. It's never been less about money than it is right now. You have to do what it takes to get where you want and you have to go to the right people. I know this could sound like a giant sales pitch, and I'm not going to lie to you—it is. But I'm not saying, "Come to my program! It's the only way!"

I am telling you that sometimes, self-help books aren't enough. I would be excited to see you at my seminar, I really would. I would also be just as excited to hear that these words motivated you to go to anyone's program that you felt benefited you. The giant sales pitch is for you to invest in you because that's not only how you will become the person you are capable of becoming, but you will also make the kind of difference in the world that you are capable of making.

Price versus Value
It is not unusual, although it's always a gift, for an amazing breakthrough to strike an individual at one of our programs. Sometimes, that 'Ah ha moment', is shared and emotionally felt by a large number of those in attendance. and they all get impacted in a way that I could not have planned. Call it the unique chemistry of a particular audience if you like, but in fact, it's the massive wave of energy felt and resonated out into the audience.

Part of this program included a module where I was demonstration the difference between 'price' and 'value'. This section of the program included a story from my past about the difference of purchasing an item for $2 and having to replace it every week compared to spending $100 for a superior version of the same item and having it come with a life-time guarantee. The question was and is, which actually cost less when you consider the long term.

In this program, there was an older lady that we will call Jennifer. She was not working at the time and was able to attend by taking advantage of a tuition gift that was made available to her for that particular session. During this section regarding the comparison of price and value I got a surprise. All of a sudden, without warning, Jennifer approached the stage waving a ten dollar bill. She exclaimed, "I got it! I understand what you are teaching us!" She went on to say that all she had was this $10 and she wanted me to take it, because she realized that with all she had received at the training it would get her lots more later. The exercise had given her the breakthrough she needed!

Tears of joy rolled down her face as she handed me her only $10. Again, without prediction, the audience was incredible charged by emotion, and before Jennifer was able to return to her seat, three or more people handed her $20 each because they too understood the power of price vs. value. She gave all she had and all of a sudden it multiplied at least six times.

If that wasn't enough, while she was at the front of the room giving me the $10 bill, she gained the courage to also say she wanted to get a job so she could afford to visit her grandchildren on the east coast. Guess what? Two people offered her a job on the spot. Today, Jennifer is doing well and in fact, later that year she was written about in a local business monthly featuring her on the cover. Again, it's never about the price, but it is always about the value.

If what I've said motivated any part of you to *be more*—to become more than you were when you started this book—then I've done a part of my job. If your eyes have been opened to a new world, if you can once again smell the roses and hear the crowd cheering at your feet, "GO GO GO," then I've begun to fulfill my promise. If there are those of you who want more, go out and get it. Don't let anything hold you back, take action! Because when you take action with what I've shared then and only then I have done my job. If you are one of those who want more from me, then I have the desire and the willingness to teach you.

If you've been paying attention up until now, you will know that your ego-mind has been running your life and the best kept secret of life is that you can take control back and you can run your own manifesting mind.

You will also recognize *how* your ego-mind has been running your life and the steps you need to take to reclaim mastery of your ego-mind.

The result of mastering your ego-mind is that you create a laser like focus that can actually double, triple, or even quadruple your performance, your income, and your effectiveness in any area of life. That will of course free you to reach for dreams and outcomes that you may have considered to be only that, dreams.

Chapter 64

At Book's End, and Journey's Beginning

Before you turn the last pages, I want you to realize how much you've learned throughout this book. I'm sure you will be absolutely stunned by how much we've covered in this short, short time. I know you want to begin turning the knowledge contained in these pages into wisdom by living it, so I'm going to keep this part brief. I encourage you to go back and re-read any of the three parts and any of the chapters that don't spark a bright and clear remembrance.

Here's a Concise Review:
First, we covered the *Six Foundations of Success* and how those foundations allow you to live a life of what I call *Full Spectrum Success*.

We discussed *Suzanne*, and how the limited beliefs she adopted through her mother prevented her from being in a healthy, loving, and satisfying relationship.

You discovered how luck, or fate, or karma are NOT the reasons your life is the way it is. Rather, *You Are the Manifester of Your Own Life*.

You had the opportunity to decide *how you want to learn – through joy or pain*? For the record, I'm hoping you chose joy!

In the section *Unconscious Beliefs and the Illusions They Create*, you were shown how you are an evolving individual who has the power to do what it takes to affect your own training—to choose your own path and your own truths.

They Don't Lie, Do They? You know who I'm talking about: Older people from the generations before you, the media, the government. Well... do they?

You were taught about *Protective Lies* and how even though they have been told with the utmost care in mind, they don't really protect you.

In *Perception is Personal Reality, and Your Perception is Trained*, I discussed how our perceptions are trained to see what the world around us wants us to see, and whether this is good or bad, useful or not, they are still trained.

You realized that you have your own personal *genie*; ready, willing, and able to grant your wishes.

We took a huge leap into the world of physics in *What's a Quantum? and Subatomic, huh?*

You learned about Resonance in general and what Quantum Resonance is. And because Quantum Resonance is so fundamental to everything you are learning in this book, I would even suggest going over that section again. The more you understand Quantum Resonance the more you can achieve with the Equation for Manifestation™.

There were some valuable *Lessons from Aladdin*. You learned how if you are not crystal clear and specific about what you are ordering from the universe, you are not going to get quite what you are asking for.

How do *Fate, Luck, and Other Myths* affect my QRF? If you don't remember, you can now flip back and find out!

I explained how *Thoughts and Beliefs Create Reality.*

You learned the label I gave to beliefs you hold without question: *Unconscious Deserving.* We discussed how this draws and repels people and events throughout your life.

Under the heading *Exercises for mastering your ego-mind and getting what you want,* you learned how *Resonance is the only logical explanation, That (you) deserve something better, and how Little changes (cause) big effects.* You also had the opportunity (and you STILL have the opportunity to do it right now if you haven't yet!) to write down five beliefs, discover where you adopted them, and consider, "Why do I believe that?" You then asked yourself: *Why do the people who love me, love me?* Finally, you wrote down your greatest achievements.

We did a little math. We found out that the only common denominator in your life is *you.* What does that mean? You are the one common factor in all the events that have occurred throughout your entire life. This means that if anything in this world has to change so that you can start living life the way YOU want to, it needs to be you.

We looked at *Why Would Anyone Adopt Beliefs?* I provided some explanations for this puzzling phenomenon.

You met Suzanne, who as I introduced as an example of the *ego-mind in action.* I explained that the universe delivers whatever is in your QRF.

There was a distinction made between *What you know versus what you do.* I said if you are not doing it, you don't know it.

I asked you to imagine yourself *Living the Life of Your Dreams*. In doing so, I'm hoping you received extra motivation to begin using the techniques you've been given.

Remember, *it is your divine right to have the life you want.*

And if you choose not to take up your divine right to have the life you want, you can be assured that you will have plenty of company, as you read in *Misery Loves Company*.

Under the title, *Thoughts, Beliefs, Perceptions, and Addictions*, you were shown how your mind does in fact have a mind of its own, it's called 'ego'. You also learned that we all have addictions but some are more socially acceptable than others. Using Little Bobby as an example, I demonstrated how we were all trained from childhood to lie. Then, I took you by the hand and showed you *How Lies Affect Us* in our everyday lives. If we allow ourselves to tell little lies—which do eventually add up—we lose touch with our *Intuition*, our "gut" feelings.

You were cordially introduced to your ego-mind, whom I playfully referred to as the grumpy old man. This guy is in charge of filing away and defending the beliefs that you carry in your life. As a reminder, the exercises I've given you (the ones where you wrote down a belief and your reasons for believing it) are a way of communicating with that old man, seeing for yourself what he's stored away in your unconscious, and allowing yourself to decide if that belief helps you thrive in your life today.

On a scientific level, you learned some *Neurochemistry* including some information about *Neuropeptides* and how they contain the blueprints of your thoughts and beliefs. When 'eaten' by the cell receptors located throughout your body, you can see how your thoughts and beliefs literally feed your body.

In *Events and the Meanings We Attach to Them* we took the concept of the common denominator (which is you) and beliefs one step further. I made the statement, **"Beliefs determine your reality because they become the *filters and lenses that distort information.*"** The reason beliefs distort information is because one of the jobs the ego-mind has is to defend those beliefs. In doing so, it sometimes cheats by distorting information that's coming in from the world.

We spoke about four people who have certainly inspired my life, as well as the lives of countless others: *Nelson, Roger, MLK, and Rosa.* These are four people who fought against all odds and whose beliefs changed the world demonstrating that average people can live monumental lives.

The analogy of *Roller Coasters: Friends or Foes?* demonstrated that no events in life have any meaning other than the meanings we attach to them. One of the most compelling proofs I provided was that chemists have demonstrated that neuropeptides released in fear and excitement are almost identical.

In case the roller coaster analogy wasn't clear enough, I supplied another two analogies under the headings, *Life through a Lens and Maps: Another Way to Look at Filters.*

We then dove right back into *The Physics of It*, where I used quotations from Anais Nin and Werner Heisenberg who both wrote (though each expressed this differently) that what we observe in this world is not nature itself, but nature as we choose to see it. And by that I'm referring to the ego-mind's use of filters and distortion of information to prove itself true.

In: *How Lenses, Filters, Maps, Physics, and Chemistry come Together* I tied in many of the concepts I had introduced. I explained how, in my experience, the greatest fear that most people have is not death, but life. Climbing the highest peaks and swimming the deepest oceans, living the life your dreams are made of – these concepts frighten people to death! I noted that people are bloody scared of having to draw a new map to live wide open in a world abundantly full of opportunity and adventure because it involves change, which, as you now know, has that grumpy old man (the ego-mind) pacing around in an uproar waving his cane around.

That's why shining a flashlight on your unconscious beliefs is so vital if you want to turn this knowledge into wisdom. After all, *Mastery is When You Do It.*

You were given a *Bonus Exercise* where I asked you to take a look at your habits to see your own autopilot in action.

Tattoo onto your brain: Mastery is when you go from knowing it to doing it.

I have to take a moment myself for a quick breather because believe it or not, that was only a summary of Part II! Can you believe how much you'd learned only up until then?

In Part III we put a lot more of this together because you had the groundwork in place to really absorb what I had to say.

We spoke about how *Visualization and Affirmation* when used alone don't work because they never truly address what lies beneath in the unconscious.

You read my explanation for why I hyphenated the words re-act and re-action in *Action versus Re-action*. I explained that re-act literally means to act again, to do or experience it as an automatic response to an initial event. When you act—regardless of how many times something happens to you—you choose the re-action you are going to have. It's the fact that it's not automatic that keeps it from being a re-action.

I took you deep inside the illusion of building self-esteem and I elaborated on the concepts of *Self-worth, Self-esteem and What's In-between*. Understanding the difference between them allows you the chance to look at your own ways of valuing yourself to truly see where you are now and where you want to be—living the life of your dreams.

In a particularly important heading titled *You Are Not Your Beliefs*, you learned just that: You are not your beliefs. For some, that may not have seemed empowering at first, but if you think about it you can see that not being your beliefs means **you can change the beliefs** that hold you back from living the life of your dreams and mastering your ego-mind.

We are all friends here ... Right? I'm referring here to personality tests and people who tell you what you can and cannot achieve in your life based on your past. I reminded you that your past does not predict your future unless you let it.

You were introduced to three more people: *James, Walt and Albert*. Those three all experienced disadvantages in life far beyond what most do—and look what they did with their lives. When you believe nothing can hold you back... nothing can.

We highlighted two **critical** factors to you achieving the life of your dreams: *Desire and Willingness and the Dangers of Comparison.* With those two, and with the right knowledge at your fingertips, regaining mastery of your ego-mind can happen in a heartbeat.

I shared the S.H. Principle with you. Stated simply, sh*% does happen in life, but it's within your capacity to maintain belief in yourself and realize that it's not just sh*%, it's a challenge. We also shared that challenges in life are opportunities for growth for those with the desire to achieve.

Through example and metaphor, I expanded on what I call *Resonance.* Resonance is what I believe is one of the most important missing keys in most theories of manifestation. Resonance is your QRF in action. On the level of the mind, it's your conscious and unconscious beliefs combined. On the level of physics, it's your vibratory quality. It is **the** answer. As you resonate, you attract and repel everything in your life.

After you understood that, I presented you with the *Equation for Manifestation*™. This is the three-step process in which you choose what you want, hold the thought until you get in touch with a feeling, and then focus on those feelings at the expense of all other thoughts.

You were warned about the *Challenges Along* (your) *Path* that can get in the way of you manifesting the life of your dreams:

1) Your ego-mind is attempting to tell you that things should stay the same.

2) You maintain the belief that you are less powerful than you are.

3) You are waiting for something or somebody to make your life better.

4) The conditioned, limited beliefs you adopted in order to survive are standing in the way of you manifesting the life you really want.

Under the heading *Three Percent of Your Brain*, I made reference to a movie that depicts something I find to be very accurate about people today—they live in fear! If you didn't quite fully understand why that holds true for you, I want you to take a quick moment to think back to Neuropeptides.

If you tend to worry a fair amount (and generally, we worry about things we DON'T want), you are releasing a lot of emotionally charged neuropeptides into your body carrying the blueprints of whatever you are worrying about. Those feed into your QRF, which affects your *Resonance*—generally attracting what you were worrying about in the first place.

I asked you to begin to *Live Your Life in Excellence!* The people who achieve their dreams don't ask for permission from the world—they go out and do something to fulfill them. Whether it's going to school to get an education, working long hours to gain experience, or finding a coach, they do what they have to do. So if you are asking permission from friends or family to live your life the way you want to, **stop**.

Why?

You were reminded of the saying: *Misery Loves Company!* It's your life, and it's yours to live your way. The only people you should be asking advice for on how to live your life are those who believe you are capable of being anything you dream. These are people who are already living their dreams and you can be sure they've demonstrated *Desire and Willingness* in their lives which proves they not only have knowledge, but wisdom.

That's what we covered. That's what you've learned. Looking back on these paragraphs, I'm sure you are astonished at how much information has been packed into one book. I know I am—my fingers hurt just typing all this out!

You are on your way; you now have a proven method that lets you know precisely what you have to do to get what you want in any and every area of your life. **You can see just how well that will work for you, can't you?**

Now, you have a complete list of the actions that you know for a fact will get you to achieve your outcomes. And you can use this method for anything; making money, finding a soul mate, getting in shape, lowering your golf handicap, being a better partner or parent, getting a promotion and getting a raise... Anything and everything where you need to manifest what you want and the clarity to take action to achieve your desired outcome. And isn't that every desired goal?

Here's my suggestion; try the Equation for Manifestation™ technology on one of the goals you want to achieve for twenty eight days. Do it consistently, try to do it at the same time everyday and pay attention as you see all the amazing opportunities that start showing up in the direction of your goal.

Also, may I suggest that you share this method with a trusted family member, friend or colleague and you talk them through it. Don't just tell them what to do, walk them through the entire process while you are there with them. Just wait until you see the look on their faces when they suddenly realize that they have the correct and fully applicable technique to achieve any goal, any dream, or any desire.

Earlier I shared with you that we all have a deep desire to be a winner and the reason so many people end up feeling like a loser is not because they set a goal, went for it and failed. No, the reason they failed is because they set their sights to low. As I said, we have to examine how willing we are to be bold in the face of what 'they" say.

As you now know if we do not examine the automatic adopted limiting beliefs that have been running our lives we will most certainly end up living limited lives. Those limiting beliefs will end up being a self-fulfilling prophecy!

With everything I've given you within these pages you now have some powerful tools to flip some of those old ideas about what you can't do on their ass. Let's make sure that we get to be, do, have and give our heart's desires. I know after going through this book you are not willing to be run by your ego-mind's crappy ideas of going nowhere in life.

Let yourself be warned by those around you who have given in to the ego-mind and set their sights on mediocrity. Let me give you some examples: The couples whose lives just crawl along, they do the same old things, in the same old way, day after day. Comfortable, sure, in an old pair of slippers kind of way. There is no exhilaration and there is no passion. The business person whose business provides them just enough to get by but lives in fear of a call from the bank because they don't make enough to give themselves or their family the life they really want. Then there's the sales person who is always just under target on their sales and has that constant nagging fear that in the cut-backs they might be the next one to be laid off. Don't forget the student who barely scrapes by after pulling an 'all-nighter' to cram for the morning exams. All of these people are avoiding the reality that is before them, avoiding responsibility and in turn avoiding what could so easily be theirs, if only.

Yes, if only they'd take a couple of minutes and lift their sights. Grab a pad and a pen and really think about what they want out of life, get really clear. How do they want their relationship to be, what more could they do to truly show the person they love that they really do deeply care for and respect them? In what way could they do what it takes to make that relationship one that makes them breathless with excitement and one that others would look at with envy, wish that theirs was so loving, fun and equal? The business person, again early morning with a journal opened, favorite pen rolling between their fingers in anticipation, could so easily design a business or life that truly gave them the satisfying results they dreamed of when they first went into business. The sales person who again in writing resolves to go the extra mile. No longer willing to just get by, willing to do anything and everything it takes to provide the best service, products and relationship to every client and customer. Taking the time to develop themselves, to study, to improve, taking full and complete responsibility for their thoughts, their actions, their results, their lives as a whole. The student who truly sits down and writes out why they are studying their subject. Outlining every reason they are on this path and them giving it everything they've got. Proud of what they accomplish as they move the world capitalizing on all those hours of mental dedication.

Here is something fascinating: When we set our goals higher than we are used to it doesn't matter if we reach them. I know I can hear you saying "What the heck are you talking about Dōv?" You see that's the mistake that is so common; most people think that setting goals is done in order for you to reach the goal and have a party to celebrate. Although there's nothing wrong with that there is something considerably more important. You see there's a good chance that achieving your goals will make more money for you, but that is nowhere near as important as what working towards that will make of you. You see when you set your sights higher it demands that you show up in your life at a higher level of commitment and that is the stuff that makes for a champion in life.

> *"The privilege of a lifetime*
> *is being who you are."*
>
> ~ *Joseph Campbell*

Here are some suggestions of the action you can take. Having gone through all the great material within these pages, take some thinking time and think!

Ask yourself: What could I do to make my relationship the best it could be? What would make my business the highly profitable adventure I'd love it to be? How can I provide an even higher level of service to my clients and be rewarded more than I've ever been before?

I know your ego-mind would like to keep everything the same, but you know that's no longer possible. You now have skills tools and knowledge that make mediocrity no longer an option.

So before I sign off let me ask you: Will you step off the edge? Are you willing to fly on the wings of knowledge I've given you? Will you commit right now to be the best you can be in every single area of your life? If you will, if you dare, if you will become determined to do so, then like the other great ones who have gone before you, you will always have the wind beneath your wings to assist you to fly to higher and higher views.

"Every leader, every genius, every star must face the pull toward mediocrity. The pull that will keep you from your own brilliance is the need to be accepted. Remember no greatness was ever achieved without opposition."

~ Dōv Baron

Now, I don't know just how much more successful you are going to be, I don't know how much more money you will make, or how much better you will feel about yourself and the life you will be living. All I do know is what my students have told me who have taken this knowledge and put it into their lives. They say "Dōv, it is no wonder that people have so much success with what you teach them, the Equation for Manifestation™ is so easy to put into practice."

So, as we come to the end of our time together in these pages let me make a serious point: I believe there are three things you can do with the knowledge I've shared with you here.

One—you can nod and say: "Yes, Dōv, this was great" and then do nothing. In which case I'm sure you know the results...

Two—you could do what some non achievers do and say: "Yes Dōv, I'm going to attend one of your live events" and then they do nothing, they put it off and keep doing so with a never ending list of reasons the ego-mind can always come up with.

Or three—you can do what the truly successful do; you and I know that formula for success. Do what the truly successful do and you will get what the truly successful get. It's not rocket science is it? Yes, because you are one of the elite few, who I believe want to grab life by the horns and make it happen. After I sign off, I'm going to tell you how you can attend one of my live events and truly take your life to places you have only dreamed of.

Now I really do look forward to meeting you soon, maybe in person and looking you in the eye and shaking your hand as you share your success stories with me.

Until then my friend and fellow traveler of the path, I remind you that no matter what appears to be going on in the world please remember the greatest investment you can ever make is the one no one can ever take from you. That is the investment you make in the development of your heart, your soul and your mind.

Will you come with me and fly to the highs you are truly capable of, yes? If you will that's great, thank you.

This is Dōv Baron signing off and saying that it has been a pleasure to carry out all these years of study and research and an honor to share this knowledge with you and I know it will be a pleasure to hear from you.

Or perhaps we can indeed meet in person in the near future.

Until then I wish you every success in all your life's adventures and your quest to live the life you were born to live. This is your life, live it with courage.

Dōv...

Information for those who want to take in the exhilarating experience of a live Baron Mastery Institute event.

For Those Who Want More

This section of the book is reserved for those of you are interested in the specifics of what you are going to learn in the Quantum Mind Mastery™ Program. www.QuantumMindMastery.com/bookbonus

This program is not about making major changes to every area of your life all at once. It's about having the skills and unique tools to be able to make subtle adjustments on the internal level which will in turn greatly affect your outer life. The result is that you are able to dramatically shift your life into high gear so that you are at peak performance. As you go through the Quantum Mind Mastery™ Program I'll never ask you to do something that I can't personally recommend, because I never ask my students to do what I have not been willing to do myself. I don't expect you to put any faith in these proven techniques that I teach without you testing them in your life.

Somebody asked me recently, "So, how do you change your QRF?" It's kind of like dominoes. You know that game where you stack all the dominoes up in an elaborate shape, you knock one over and it starts knocking over all the rest?

That said, allow me to describe the program . In the Quantum Mind Mastery Program, you will learn:

• How to apply practical quantum physics into your everyday life.

• You will learn how to make affirmations and visualizations work the way they can work, but not the way you've been taught.

• How to be more powerful in any situation. I teach about something called Power Moments which is a concept that as far as I know has never been taught before and is an immensely powerful principle.

• How to be twenty-seven percent more intelligent in stressful situations. You will learn how to tell the universe exactly what you want so that it responds the way you expect. There's also a section on how to recognize and overcome emotional addictions.

• There is large emphasis on belief addictions.

• How to change your thinking in order for your body to absorb the nutrients it needs.

• Oh, and one of my favorites. I teach you how to access your genius using a technique that was used by both Albert Einstein and Thomas Edison. Personally, I think both of those guys were pretty smart.

• How to build a powerful magnet that naturally attracts to you the things that you want, including health, happiness, and the full spectrum of abundance that I have covered so extensively in this book.

• What your intuition is telling you. A big part of the program is dedicated to this. I know that most people get intuitive, but they are not fully aware of how and why it works. You will learn both how, and why.

• How you are exactly as old as you feel, and how your ego-mind has been blocking you from having the success, money, and abundance in your life that you desire.

• Where your fears about abundance, success, and committed relationships come from and how these are the biggest obstacles that keep you from having the level of success you desire.

• The mysterious power of letting go and walking away.

• How your ego-mind's obsession with the status quo is preventing you from experiencing the full spectrum of success.

• What you can do when all things seem lost.

• The secret that transforms people from being just employees into being millionaires. And so you know, we've had many people go through the program who have done just that.

• And, of course, way, way more than I could possibly fit into this summary.

As you've heard me say, "Life is filled with people who are waiting, people who are waiting for something to change their lives, waiting for something to come in and make everything better".

My experience, as I've said to you, is that this is just not going to happen. My experience is that there will always be some other excuse the ego-mind will create to prevent you from seizing opportunities. Though with the right tools, the right knowledge, and the wisdom to act, the excuses will dissolve like honey in tea.

If you are in this program, you are in this program because you are not willing to wait any longer. This book has given you an immense amount of life-changing knowledge. You've read what I've put into this. Now it's up to you to decide what *you are* going to put into this. What are you going to step up and do for yourself? Stop waiting for some outside miracle. It's not coming, and now you know why. The wait is over because you are the miracle. Your authentic self is the miracle. You are the one you've been waiting for. You just need to get committed to revealing that authentic self.

You can do that, and you can do it now by going to the website www.QuantumMindMastery.com/bookbonus and registering there. No matter what they say, it's your life. Remember that. Now you have to do what it takes to claim it.

You know how much you've learned through this book. I'm confident you've received lots from it and I'm very excited to hear about it. I'm sure you can imagine what you would get out of a multi-day program and how enormously shifting it would be to peel back the filters. Come do the program, give up your excuses and reclaim your life.

Resources for You

Free e-book explaining the Movie: What the Bleep do we know?! For you to share with friends: www.WhatTheBleepDoesItMean.com

Want to further explore the subject of resonance and overcoming fear. As a reward for investing in this book you can receive more than $1,000 discount on the tuition for you and a friend. Find out more about attending at www.AttractingForce.com/bookbonus

Find out more about the **Quantum Mind Mastery** Program by now going to a special page my team has set up as a reward for readers of this book: www.QuantumMindMastery.com/bookbonus
There, you will not only find out about this outstanding five-day live event, you will also discover how you can save more than $1,000 on the tuition for you and a friend.

If you would like to have Dōv personally guide you through the Equation for Manifestation™ you can find out about the multi-media home study program that will support you getting more and more focused on whatever it is that you want. When you go to www.equationformanifestation.com you will find just what you are looking for.

Tell Us What You Think

If you've enjoyed reading this book, write down this number.
(214) 615-6505 ext 3162

I've given you this number because I want to celebrate the successes you gained by applying the things you learned from this book.

Just call 214-615-6505, extension 3162 and leave me your personal message.

Tell me what you got out of this book and what you are doing with what you learned.

What results you achieved by applying what you learned.

The answer to these questions are very important to me.
I look forward to hearing from you!

A Word of Thanks

As always, my first thank you is to my beloved wife and business partner **Renuka**: You are my muse, my greatest inspiration. Renuka works so diligently with me to bring our message to the world. Renuka, you are the light of my life, my 'guru of kind'. You continue to inspire me, even through the many nights when you have lost your partner to as you call it 'my girl friend', (my computer).

My thanks also go out to the many members of my spiritual family, team, friends, and associates who believe in the teachings we share and as a result have committed to getting the word out there. Extra special thanks to Lady Lisa Haeck, you have been, our in the background force of nature. Lisa your support is so very, very appreciated, you think I don't know, but believe me, I know! Special thanks to Vally Haeck, Alan Lary, Damian Loth, Lee Edward Födi, Barbara Madani, Scott Schilling, Michael Mills, Eitan Sharir, Carol Aitken, Grant & Natalie Gibson, Maeve Reynolds, Steve Kiges, Scott Paton, Shane Jeremy James, John Rowley, John Drennan, Harris Abro and Arthur Samuel Joseph your support and friendship are deeply felt and appreciated. Last but not least, the hysterically funny Kathy Buckley. I'm sorry that I can't write in everyone of you who have been so wonderful kind and supportive, I know I have only named a few of the so many, I am filled with deep and sincere gratitude.

There are three people I want to separately thank with all my heart, not just for what they do, but for who they are. A special thank you to **Lee Edward Födi:** *Lee, you are my 'go-to guy' Your editing, design and all-round freakin' amazing skills have saved my rear end way too many times. Above all, you are one of the most courageous men I know—a true friend and a brother. Thank you!*

Alan Lary: *Al, your tireless conviction to be a conduit for the work that we do, the knowledge that we bring and the lives that we touch is beyond anything I could have asked for. You are a blessing in our lives. You have put yourself on the line for us so many times, and in so many ways. It has been an honour to watch the transformation from who you were to the outstanding example of an ever growing, ever developing spectacular human being. Thank you is clearly inadequate; I have no words that can convey my sincere gratitude, except to say, "I love you."*

Vally Haeck: *Vally, you are f*#kin amazing! You came to us like a gift from heaven, (well S.A.). Day-after-day you have been the carrier of our mission. You are the one who has committed to doing what it takes to make sure everyone who can possibly get on-line finds out about who we are and what we do. So many lives have been touched and changed by who 'you are' and 'what you do'. I know you like to stay off center stage; however, you are center stage in my respect and love. You have always gone above and beyond the call of duty and in so doing you have brought me back to 'the' focus, by planting my feet in the ground and pointing my head into the wind. We always knew we needed a 'Fred' However, we never knew 'Fred' would become someone we deeply love and care about, a dear friend. You too are a blessing in our lives. Never a day goes by where we are not filled with gratitude for Vallderie 'Fred' Haeck.*

Even though some of these people were mentioned earlier, I would like to say a big thank you for being members of the Baron Mastery Institute Team: Vally Haeck, Al Lary, Augustian 'Gus' Hermanto, Marilyn Anderson and Maeve Reynolds. Your commitment to the mission is an inspiration to me. There are of course many more members of the Baron Mastery Institute team and I want you to all know how grateful I am to you all. A special thank you to all the BMI Ambassadors, you guys rock.

Thanks would be incomplete without acknowledging my editorial team including the editorial assistants who found all the mistakes I'd missed, (and there were lots): Chief eagle eyes; Nicki Eve and Maeve Reynolds, Kim Baker, George Greenwood, Nicole Steeves and Brad Mesaros. You did an amazing job of a mammoth task in a record time. Special thanks to my NLP languaging editor extraordinaire, Paul Zimeras, whose enthusiasm for this project beat out many with more experience but less fire.

My thanks also goes out to our editorial consultant Marni Norwich, Marni kept my writing on track and the project moving forward.
Finally, I would like to thank my students around the world – past, present and future—for your inquiring minds, warm hearts, and bright souls. Each one of you lifts my life to progressively higher levels.

Let's keep raising the consciousness of our world until we all master our own ego-minds, and in so doing, truly know that we can create the world and reality we want, a world that honors the greatness inherent in all of mankind.

About the Author

Dóv Baron now serves as an advisor to corporate, creative and personal leaders around the world. He is a relationship expert, specialist in the psychology of leadership, peak performance, communication and the power of the mind. He is also recognized as the world's leading authority in the area of "Quantum Resonance Fields™" (QRF). QRF is the science of how our beliefs, emotions and thinking effect and sculpt every aspect of our lives. Another way to think of it is as the science of 'karma'.

As a renowned professional speaker, author, and television personality, Dóv is a man who lives with passion every day of his life.

He has risen to international prominence by delivering high energy, passionate, and often profoundly funny messages that guide his students away from mediocrity and push them to live up to their innate greatness, to become who they were born to be. This is a message Dóv has learned from overcoming the challenges of his own life, and one he is helping others apply to theirs.

Having traveled the world to study with Eastern and Western thinkers, Dóv brings the wisdom of the East and powerfully applies it to the practicalities of the West. He is a featured expert for television, radio and newspapers.

Today Dóv conducts seminars, keynote speeches, and live training for the public and leading companies and organizations. In 2002 Dóv wrote a dissertation on Personal Emotional Resonance Fields, the fields that determine and sculpt every aspect of our lives.

Quantum Resonance Fields set the unconscious ceilings for our health, wealth, success and even love.

Dōv's specialized knowledge is a highly in demand commodity as through this work Dōv is able to create the kind of shift that has taken companies to a place that has more than doubled productivity and revenue. Shifting an individual's Resonance Field changes not only one's income potential but also the quality of their relationships and joy in every area of life.

Dōv is an authority in understanding and stimulating human potential. Utilizing a powerful delivery and his ever-emerging insight, Dōv's customized presentations teach and inspire his listeners to innovative levels of accomplishment.

To find out more about Dōv Baron and Baron Mastery Institute go to www.BaronMasteryInstitute.com

Or visit Dōv's blog: www.DovBaron.com